By Arthur C. Clarke

Fiction
REACH FOR TOMORROW
THE OTHER SIDE OF THE SKY
A FALL OF MOONDUST
TALES OF TEN WORLDS
DOLPHIN ISLAND
THE DEEP RANGE
THE CITY AND THE STARS
THE LION OF COMARRE
THE WIND FROM THE SUN
OF TIME AND STARS
RENDEZVOUS WITH RAMA
IMPERIAL EARTH
THE FOUNTAINS OF PARADISE
THE GHOST FROM THE GRAND BANKS

Non-Fiction
PROFILES OF THE FUTURE
VOICES FROM THE SKY
REPORT ON PLANET THREE
THE VIEW FROM SERENDIP
ASTOUNDING DAYS

By Arthur C. Clarke and Gentry Lee

CRADLE
RAMA II
THE GARDEN OF RAMA

By Arthur C. Clarke and Gregory Benford

AGAINST THE FALL OF NIGHT
BEYOND THE FALL OF NIGHT

HOW THE WORLD WAS O

BEYOND THE GLOBAL VILLA

HOW THE WORLD WAS ONE
BEYOND THE GLOBAL VILLAGE

Arthur C. Clarke

LONDON
VICTOR GOLLANCZ LTD
1992

First published in Great Britain 1992
by Victor Gollancz Ltd
14 Henrietta Street, London, WC2E 8QJ

A catalogue record for this book is available
from the British Library

ISBN 0 575 05226 0

.

Index compiled by Indexing Specialists,
202 Church Road, Hove, East Sussex BN3 2DJ, UK
Typeset at The Spartan Press Ltd, Lymington, Hants
Text printed in Great Britain by St Edmundsbury Press Ltd,
Bury St Edmunds, Suffolk
Illustrations printed in Great Britain by
WBC Print Ltd, Bridgend

Dedicated to the Real Fathers of the Communications Satellite,
John Pierce and Harold Rosen,
by the Godfather

FOREWORD

Much of Europe and Japan was still in ruins when, two years after the end of World War II, the famous historian Arnold Toynbee gave a lecture at London University's Senate House entitled 'The Unification of the World'. I cannot recall what prompted me to attend, and all I remember of the talk is its basic thesis: that developments in transport and communications had created – or would create – a single planetary society. In November 1947, that was an unusually far-sighted view; the phrase 'global village' still lay a decade in the future, and Marshall McLuhan had yet to herald the dawn of electronic culture.

Thanks to the transistor and the microchip, that dawn has certainly arrived – if one uses a somewhat generous definition of the word 'culture'. The world, however, is still far from being unified; in some regions, indeed, it appears to be rapidly coming apart at the seams.

Nevertheless, Toynbee was essentially correct. Except for a few dwindling tribes in (alas) equally dwindling forests, the human race has now become almost a single entity, divided by time zones rather than the natural frontiers of geography. The same TV news networks cover the globe; the world's markets are linked by the most complex machine ever devised by mankind – the international telephone/telex/fax/data transfer system. The same newspapers, magazines, fashions, consumer goods, automobiles, soft drinks may be found anywhere between the North and South Poles; and at a World Cup Final, at least 50 per cent of the males of the species will be found sitting in front of a TV set, probably made in Japan.

Despite all the linguistic, religious and cultural barriers that still sunder nations and divide them into yet smaller tribes, the unification of the world has passed the point of no return, even if it is sometimes a shot-gun marriage between reluctant partners. The greater problem now is to preserve our planet's diversity, and to save what is best of the past before it is obliterated. One World is better than its all-too-probable alternative – No World; but who would wish it to be a world of featureless uniformity?

The present global society has been largely created by the two technologies of transportation and communication, and it could be argued that the second is the more important. One can imagine a planet (I generously present the idea to my fellow science-fiction writers) where long-distance travel was extremely difficult, or indeed impossible. But if the inhabitants of such a world had developed efficient communications, they might still consider themselves members of a single society.

I have been involved with communications for most of my life, usually as a customer, but sometimes as an active agent. And it was not always telecommunications; I was a part-time postman for some years, delivering the mail by bicycle over a dozen or so miles of Somerset countryside for a modest stipend from my aunt Hepzibah Grimstone, the village postmistress. We were, in fact, an old Post Office family; my father Charles Wright Clarke was a GPO engineer, and my mother Nora Mary Clarke (née Willis) was a telegraph operator. Charlie courted her in Morse Code, which she could still send and read at high speed even in her old age.

The telephone came to our rather isolated farm in the early twenties, in circumstances which I always thought were somewhat suspicious. A large number of poles had to be dragged across fields and duly erected, since we were at least a kilometre from the nearest connection. This must have been a fairly expensive operation; and guess which farmer got the contract . . . As far as the local telephone exchange was concerned, it must have been years before Bishop's Lydeard 228 showed a profit.

After I had delivered the morning mail and done my day's studies at Huish's Grammar School, Taunton – which involved another ten kilometres on my one-speed bicycle – I would return to the post office and spend the night sleeping beside the telephone switchboard. This was a massive wood-and-brass affair festooned with plugs and cables, and covered with little mechanical eyelids which blinked when there was an incoming call. Fortunately, these were infrequent during the night, and I soon learned to safeguard my sleep by immobilising the more annoying eyelids with a well-placed pencil.

One night, when for a change I was doing my job conscientiously, something extraordinary happened. *There was a call from the United States.* Fascinated, I started to eavesdrop – only to be reprimanded on another circuit by the supervisor at the international exchange. My illicit monitoring had overloaded the system, and I was brusquely ordered to get off the line. I have often wondered who was making that expensive call to our remote village. It was already almost lost in the hiss of cosmic noise, even before I started to siphon away its few remaining microwatts.

For in those days (*circa* 1933) the only way to make an intercontinental telephone call was by short-wave radio, with the limitations well known to a couple of generations of 'ham' operators. Establishing a voice circuit was a gamble on the state of the ionosphere, which in turn depended upon the weather in the sun (yes, the sun has storms, and occasional rain – of incandescent carbon particles). This was a terrible way to run a business, but no one could think of anything better. The only *reliable* way of communicating across the oceans was through submarine cables; and, owing to apparently fundamental engineering constraints, these could not handle signals more complex than the dots and dashes of telegraph messages.

This situation changed dramatically as a result of the great advances in electronics stimulated by World War II, and a transatlantic telephone cable was planned, as a joint Anglo-American effort, in 1953. A few years later, knowing my interest in all forms of communication, my friend Dr John Pierce (then Director of Research at Bell Labs) persuaded me to write a non-technical account of this history-making enterprise. The book would be timed to celebrate the approaching centennial of the first Atlantic *telegraph* cable, 1858 – a piece of which is hanging on my office wall at this very moment (courtesy of FCC Commissioner and Ambassador Abbott Washburn, who represented the United States in the complex negotiations setting up INTELSAT – see Chapter 32).

Voice across the Sea (dedicated 'To John Pierce, who bullied me into writing it') was duly published by Harper in 1958 – just in time to record the launch of Sputnik 1, which opened the Space Age. I had already written another book, *The Making of a Moon* (1957), about the planned US artificial satellite, and had devoted a chapter to the immense potential of what are now known as 'comsats'. So even as TAT-1, the first Atlantic telephone cable, was being laid, the technology that would rival – and perhaps supersede it – was undergoing its painful birth, with spectacular explosions at Cape Canaveral and Baikonur. The final chapter of *Voice across the Sea* concluded: 'It may well be that the submarine cable, even in the moment of its greatest technical triumph for a hundred years, is already doomed . . . Even if this is so, there can be no doubt that it still has many decades of service ahead of it. It may not celebrate its second century, but nevertheless its old age will be even more vigorous and active than its youth.'

Those words, written in 1957, indicate that though I believed cables would be around for quite a while yet, I did not really believe that they had a long-term future. Satellites would eventually replace them, especially as there appeared to be no way in which submarine cables could provide the enormous band-width required for the most exciting form of communication – intercontinental television. The pioneering TAT-1 could handle only thirty-six speech circuits; it would have required at least twenty similar cables, working in parallel, to carry a single TV channel. Not a technical impossibility – but economic madness. For this type of service, at least, there was no way that cable could compete with the satellites I expected to be launched during the next few decades.

I should have recalled Clarke's First Law (see *Profiles of the Future*): 'When a distinguished but elderly scientist says that something is possible, he is almost certainly right. When he says it is impossible, he is very probably wrong.'

During the seventies and eighties, communications satellites did indeed perform even beyond my most optimistic expectations, as recorded later in this book. But the submarine cable systems fought back, providing a textbook example of Toynbee's 'challenge and response' thesis. The transistor arrived just in time to replace the power-hungry vacuum tubes used in TAT-1, and within twenty years the transatlantic capability of a mere thirty-six voice circuit had been increased to several thousand. Cable TV between Europe and America was theoretically possible, and if the satellites had not existed it might have been attempted for major news or sports items important enough to pre-empt a hundred revenue-earning telephone circuits.

Then, in one of the most dramatic – and unexpected – breakthroughs in any technology, the potential of cable systems was abruptly transformed. The two-centuries-old monopoly of the electric current was suddenly ended; light waves could give an orders-of-magnitude better performance. Massive copper cables were replaced by slim bundles of glass fibres – and, for the third time since the 1850s, the sea-beds of the world began to be draped with the newest and most sophisticated artefacts of human engineering.

From the nature of the subject, this book (whose title, alas, cannot be properly translated from English into any other language) falls into two distinct sections. The first is the more romantic, for it covers the brave pioneering days when fortunes were made and lost in bold gambles against the forces of Nature, and the fabulous *Great Eastern* dominated the seas as no ship will ever do again. By contrast, today's story is one of scientific, not physical, adventure; yet it will, I hope, appeal to those who have no technical background or interests whatsoever.

The first section is contained in Part I, 'Wiring the Abyss', which describes the laying of the first Atlantic telegraph cables – the Victorian Age's equivalent of the Apollo Project. Now largely forgotten, it still has many lessons for our time. Part II, 'Voice across the Sea', jumps forward a century to the time in the late 1950s when the submarine cables started to talk, and true intercontinental telephony was born. Most of Parts I and II originally appeared in my 1958 book, but I have added three chapters to cover the early days of radio. Part III, 'A Brief Prehistory of Comsats', concerns my personal involvement in the communications satellite story; some readers may be surprised to encounter fiction in a book of this nature – but that fiction is, in the circumstances, part of the history. Part IV, 'Starry Messengers', describes how science fiction became science fact. Because this is a continuing story, well documented in hundreds of books and technical journals – not to mention public media – I have not gone into anything like as much detail as in the first two parts. To do that is not only unnecessary, but would require a book many times the size of this one. However, as I have known many of the characters involved in this continuing saga, I have not hesitated to include a good deal of personal material. And, in the chapter entitled 'CNN Live', I touch on the dramatic events which took place while this book was being written. Though I wish that such a demonstration could have been avoided, the world's first – and hopefully last – 'satellite war' proved beyond any doubt the power of the new technology. Part V, 'Let There Be Light!', touches briefly on the cable renaissance brought about by fibre optics; which, although it has barely begun, already has the satellite builders and launchers looking anxiously over their shoulders.

Many readers may regard the final chapter, 'As Far As Eye Can See' as another exercise in science fiction. However, as Part III demonstrated, almost all of this book was SF less than a lifetime ago, and it is folly to imagine that our present technology represents the last word in telecommunications – or anything else.

Still, I wouldn't bet too much money on any of the possibilities (or impossibilities) discussed in this final chapter. I suspect that the truth, as always, will be far stranger.

Colombo, Sri Lanka
20 April 1991

CONTENTS

1

WIRING THE ABYSS

2

VOICE ACROSS THE SEA

3

A Brief Prehistory of Comsats

4

Starry Messengers

5

Let There Be Light!

1

WIRING THE ABYSS

1

INTRODUCTION

This is the story of Man's newest victory in an age-old conflict – his war against the sea. It is a story of great moral courage, of scientific skill, of million-dollar gambles; and though it affects every one of us directly or indirectly, it is almost entirely unknown to the general public.

Our civilisation could not exist without efficient communications; we find it impossible to imagine a time when it took a month to get a message across the Atlantic and another month (if the winds were favourable) to receive the reply. It is hard to see how international trade or cultural exchanges could flourish or even exist in such circumstances. News from far parts of the world must have been rather like the information that astronomers glean about distant stars – something that happened a long time ago, and about which there is nothing that can be done.

This state of affairs has existed for the greater part of human history. During all that time, the only methods of signalling to distant points depended upon sound or light. The human voice – even aided by the very ingenious modulation techniques employed by Swiss yodellers and Basque mountaineers – carries only one or two kilometres at the most. Jungle drums have a much greater range, which can be extended indefinitely by relaying. However, this reduces the rate of transmission and, even worse, vastly increases the possibility of error.

The simplest, and perhaps oldest, ways of sending information over long distances were smoke signals during the daytime and beacon fires at night. Both methods were vulnerable to weather and limited in content, being restricted to prearranged messages of the type 'The Armada has/has not been sighted' or 'The British are coming by day/night'.

Much more sophisticated was signalling by flags (used by ships even today), semaphores (see your local railway, if you have one) and heliographs – the walkie-talkies of Kipling's India, whose delicately-balanced mirrors used sunlight to flash Morse code along the Khyber Pass.

The world's first regular telegraph network was established in France by Claude Chappe in 1793; the word itself, meaning 'writing from afar' had been invented from the Greek just two years earlier, so is due for its Bicentennial.

Chappe's system used movable arms on towers in line-of-sight of each other, and the operators read the messages by means of telescopes. It was clumsy but effective, and as there was no practical alternative it was soon copied everywhere. Though it lasted only a few decades, it left its mark. There are still many 'Telegraph Hills' on the map.

But when Queen Victoria came to the throne in 1837, she had no swifter means of sending messages to the far parts of her empire than had Julius Caesar – or, for that matter, Moses. The galloping horse and the wind-driven sailing-ship remained the swiftest means of transport, as they had been for 5000 years. *Real* telecommunication, with virtually no limitations on range, speed or contents, was not possible until the scientists of the early nineteenth century started to investigate the curious properties of electricity.

Here was a servant which within little more than two lifetimes would transform the world almost beyond recognition and sweep away the ancient barriers of time and distance. It was soon found that the 'electric fluid' travelled through conducting wires at a velocity so great that there was no way of measuring it, and at once ingenious experimenters in many countries attempted to use this fact for the transmission of messages. By 1840 the electric telegraph had left the laboratory and become a commercial instrument of vast possibilities. Within ten years it had covered most of Europe and the settled portions of North America – but it still stopped at the edge of the sea.

How the ocean was at last defeated is the main theme of this book. In 1858 a handful of far-sighted men succeeded in laying a telegraph cable across the North Atlantic, and at the closing of a switch the gap between Europe and America dwindled abruptly from a month to a second.

But this first triumph was short-lived; the ocean was too strong to be bound by so slender a thread, and in a few days the continents were as far apart as ever. The way in which, after an eight-year saga of almost unbelievable courage and persistence, a successful Atlantic telegraph was finally laid is one of the great engineering epics of all time, and has many lessons for us even today.

The Victorians built well; some of the cables laid down in the last century were still in use by the 1950s, after having carried incomputable millions of words for mankind. There is a section of cable in mid-Atlantic which began work in 1873 and has been quietly doing its job while the theologians agonised over Darwin, the Curies discovered radium, a couple of bicycle mechanics in North Carolina fitted an engine to an oversized kite, Einstein gave up his job at the patent office, Fermi piled up uranium blocks in a Chicago squash court, and the first rocket climbed into space. It would be hard to find any other technical device which has given continuous service while the world around it has changed to such an extent.

The first submarine cables, however, had one fundamental limitation. They could transmit telegraph signals but could not – except over relatively short distances – carry the far more complex pattern of vibrations which constitutes speech. Alexander Graham Bell's invention of the telephone in 1876 opened up a new era in communications, but had no effect on the world-wide submarine cable system. The requirements of speech transmission were so severe that there seemed no hope at all of ever sending the human voice across the Atlantic.

The discovery of radio changed the situation radically, and also presented the submarine cables with a major challenge. To the great surprise of science, and the great good fortune of the communications industry, it turned out that the earth is surrounded by an invisible mirror which reflects radio waves which would otherwise escape into space. When this mirror – the ionosphere – is co-operating, it is possible to send speech around the curve of the globe after one or more reflections. Unfortunately the ionosphere is not a smooth, stable layer; it is continually changing under the influence of the sun, and during times of solar disturbance it may be so convulsed that long-distance radio is impossible. Even when conditions are good, radio links which depend on the ionosphere are liable to pick up all sorts of curious cracklings and bangings, for the universe is a very noisy place in the radio spectrum. Pascal, who complained that the silence of infinite space terrified him, was a little wide of the mark. He would have been astonished to learn that it is full of the sound of solar eruptions, exploding stars, and even colliding galaxies. These electromagnetic noises add a background, and all too often a foreground, to the radio messages transmitted from one continent to another.

Nevertheless, a radio-telephone service was established across the Atlantic in February 1927; until 1956, this was the only means whereby the human voice could pass from Europe to America. Yet it is probably true to say that most people who ever thought of the matter assumed that the transatlantic telephone depended on cables, not on radio. One German spy even claimed to have listened in to conversations between Roosevelt and Churchill by tapping submarine cables; unfortunately for the truth of this story, Roosevelt had been dead for a dozen years before men spoke to each other across the bed of the Atlantic.

In 1956, the impossible was achieved and the first submarine telephone cable was laid between Europe and America. The inflexible laws which state that one cannot send speech for more than a few score miles through an underwater cable had not been repealed; they had been bypassed by a new and daring approach to the problem – one that involved sinking a chain of more than a hundred amplifiers, each more complex than the average radio set, along the bed of the ocean.

Any great engineering achievement, especially if it has long been considered impossible, can provide both an emotional and an intellectual stimulus. It is true that a submarine cable is not something that everyone can see, like a giant bridge, a skyscraper or an ocean liner. It does its work in the darkness of the abyss, in an unimaginable world of eternal night and cold and pressure, peopled by creatures which no man could have conceived in the wildest delirium. Yet it serves a function as vital as that of the nerves in the human body; it is an essential part of the world's communication system – which, if it ever failed, would throw us back instantly to the isolation of our ancestors.

I should like to emphasise that this is not a history of submarine communications. As far as it goes it is, I believe, accurate, but it makes no attempt to be complete. My object has been, frankly, to entertain as much as to instruct, and as a result I have wandered down some odd byways whenever the scenery has intrigued me. It will contribute little to anyone's understanding of telegraphy to know how Oliver Heaviside made tea, why Lord Kelvin's monocle revolutionised electrical measurements, what a Kentucky colonel was doing in Whitehall, how Western Union lost $3,000,000 in Alaska, and what unlikely articles the Victorians made from gutta-percha. Yet it is precisely such trivia that make history three-dimensional, and I do not apologise for including them.

THE COMING OF THE TELEGRAPH

Like most great inventions, the electric telegraph has a complex and disputed ancestry. America, Russia, Germany and England have approximately equal claims to its origin, and although today Samuel Morse is remembered above most of his rivals, he was very far from being the first man to transmit information by electricity.

Morse sent his famous message 'What hath God wrought?' (a question which, incidentally, still lacks a suitable reply) on 24 May 1844. But one standard history of the subject lists no less than forty-seven telegraph systems between the years 1753 and 1839, and although most of these were only paper proposals, some of them actually worked.

Perhaps the first really determined attempt at the electrical communication of intelligence was Sommering's 'chemical telegraph', constructed in Munich in 1809. In this system, every letter was represented by a separate wire which terminated at the bottom of a water-filled container. When current was passed through a given wire, bubbles formed at its end, and by watching where the bubbles appeared an observer could tell which letter was being transmitted. Although the method was only barely workable, it was a notable achievement and attracted much attention at the time.

A still more elaborate system, depending on static electricity, was set up in 1816 by Sir Francis Ronald in his garden at Hammersmith, London. Ronald erected no less than eight miles of overhead wire, and read messages passed through the line by the movement of light pithballs at the end of it. As they were electrified, their mutual repulsion swung them aside to expose the letter it was desired to transmit.

Sir Francis deserves credit as the first man to realise the possible business, social and international possibilities of this new method of communication. A brochure he published in 1823 was the first work on telegraphy ever printed; it even contained proposals for locating the position of faults on a telegraph line. Unfortunately, Sir Francis was about a generation too early. When he offered his system to the British Admiralty, he was told that their Lordships were perfectly satisfied with the telegraph they already had, and there was no question of its being replaced by anything else. The Navy's 'telegraph' at that time consisted of a string of semaphore towers by which, in clear weather, messages could be transmitted from Portsmouth to London slightly faster than a pony express could have done the job.

By one of the minor ironies of technology, the Secretary of the Admiralty who signed the letter of rejection lived to write the article on telegraphy in the *Encyclopaedia Britannica*; by another, Sir Francis's house was later occupied by William Morris, leader of the romantic back-to-the-Middle-Ages revival, who could hardly have felt a great deal of sympathy for an invention which was to do so much to sweep mankind into a strange and tumultuous future.

The systems devised by Ronald, Sommering and other inventors were inefficacious because they lacked a simple and sensitive means of detecting the flow of electricity. In 1820, however, came the great discovery which was to make the world we know. The Danish scientist Oersted found that an electric current could produce a deflection of a magnet placed near it. For the first time, electricity had exerted force. From that simple observation stemmed in due course the myriads of generators, motors, relays, telephones, meters, loudspeakers and other electromagnetic devices which are now civilisation's most ubiquitous slaves.

Around 1825, this new knowledge was applied to telegraphy by Baron Schilling, attaché to the Russian Embassy in Munich, who had been much impressed by Sommering's earlier work. Amongst other arrangements, Schilling devised a magnetic telegraph in which letters were indicated by movements of a needle over the white or black segments of a card. He employed a code based on the same principle as that later made famous by Morse; in Schilling's alphabet, A was 'black, white', B was 'black, black, black', C was 'black, white, white' and so on. (Such bi-signal alphabets, incidentally, go back at least to Greek and Roman times.)

Here at last was the basis of a really effective telegraph, and the time was ripe for its exploitation, which occurred almost simultaneously in America and England. In 1836, W. F. Cooke, an English medical student at Heidelberg, heard of Schilling's work, realised its importance, and immediately abandoned his intended profession. He knew a good thing when he saw one, and hurried back to England to find an electrical expert who could help him to put his ideas into practice, since his own knowledge of science was rudimentary.

The man he contacted was Charles Wheatstone, Professor of Physics at King's College, London. Wheatstone's name is remembered through a whole series of basic electrical inventions, the most famous being the Wheatstone bridge, a method of measuring resistances by balancing an unknown against a known one. I have some affection for his shade as a result of spending two years in the Wheatstone Laboratory at King's College, a period during which, at least according to the experiments recorded in my Practical Physics notebooks, the constants of nature were remarkably variable.

Cooke and Wheatstone produced their first telegraph patent in June 1837, and carried out their first practical trials in the same year over a mile-and-a-quarter-long line between two London railway stations. The receivers they used were the so-called needle instruments, in which letters were indicated by the deflection to right or left of vertical pointers. The system was slow and somewhat elaborate, but messages could be sent and read by unskilled staff. Instruments of this general type were still in use in out-of-the-way British railway stations well into the twentieth century.

For a long time railways and telegraphs went hand in hand; the new means of transport could not have operated without some such rapid form of communication. Within a very few years the steel rails and the copper wires had spread their networks over much of Europe, and Cooke and Wheatstone netted fortunes in royalties. Success promptly ruined their relationship, which broke up into a squalid argument as to which of them really invented the telegraph. The answer, of course, was neither.

While this was going on in England, a mildly talented portrait-painter named Samuel Finley Breese Morse was trying, without much success, to get support for his ideas on the other side of the Atlantic. He had heard about the possibilities of electrical communication during a casual conversation with a fellow passenger while sailing back to the United States from Europe in 1832, and the concept had immediately fired his mind. Owing to the problem of making a living, however, he did not produce his first working telegraph instrument until 1836.

There is a striking parallel between the histories of Morse in America and Cooke in England. Each was an amateur scientist and each had to consult a professional in order to make any progress. Morse was helped by Joseph Henry, the great pioneer of electromagnetism, who has now given his name to the unit of induction; and in due time Morse and Henry became involved in quarrels over priority, exactly as Cooke and Wheatstone had done.

The beauty of Morse's system was its simplicity. It is so simple, indeed, that we tend to take it for granted and forget that *someone* had to invent it. Earlier telegraph systems had involved many wires and cumbersome sending and receiving apparatus. Morse produced a telegraph that needed only one wire (the earth providing a return circuit) and whose transmitter was nothing more than a key to make and break the connection. By means of the dot–dash code, this single key could send any letter or combination of letters.

The first receiver Morse built consisted of a magnet-operated pen which automatically wrote the incoming dots and dashes as jiggles on a moving tape, thus providing a permanent record. Very soon, however, it was discovered that the ear could interpret the long and short buzzes, and the

Morse sounder or buzzer came into general use. It survives, virtually unchanged, to this day. Morse was also responsible for introducing the relay, which, in theory at least, made it possible to transmit messages over indefinite distances. In this simple but basic device the feeble current at the end of a telegraph line was used to close a contact which was, in effect, a second Morse key, starting a new current from another set of batteries along the next section of line. The relay was the earliest form of 'repeater', a device which we shall meet later in a much more sophisticated form.

After years of effort and a fruitless journey to Europe to sell his invention, Morse finally obtained $30,000 from Congress in 1842 for the construction of a line between Washington and Baltimore. The debate over the allocation does not reflect much credit on the elected representatives of the American people; several of them were quite unable to appreciate the difference between magnetism and mesmerism. But Morse got his money, and two years later America got the telegraph. Without it, the immense continent could never have become a united country.

The manner in which the telegraph spread from Atlantic to Pacific, the wars between the desperately competing companies, the eventual triumph of Western Union over its rivals – this is now part of American history and, indeed, folklore. For half a century, until he was displaced by automatic instruments such as the teleprinter, the telegraph operator was one of the picturesque, and essential, figures of the American scene. In this brief span of time he perfected and practised a skill which had lain dormant and unsuspected in mankind since the beginning of history: the ability to read and transmit up to forty words a minute by an almost continuous series of broken buzzes, hour after hour.

Some of the feats of these men – of whom the young Edison was the most famous though certainly not the most characteristic – were quite incredible and could probably not be repeated today. There is one well-authenticated account of a telegraph operator who, to show off, deliberately ignored his racing Morse sounder while it went full speed for a couple of minutes, and then sat down to catch up on the messages that had already come through. After fifteen minutes of writing, he eventually absorbed the backlog and was taking down the words at the moment they arrived. Such a feat of memory can perhaps be compared to playing a dozen games of blindfold chess simultaneously – and against the clock.

These skills have now vanished from the earth, because they are no longer needed. The Morse code has been superseded by the digital language of bits and bytes – which can be understood and spoken only by machines, not by men.

3

CHANNEL CROSSING

By 1850 the tentacles of the electric telegraph had spread all over England, as well as over much of Europe and the more settled areas of North America. But the wires still stopped at the edge of the sea, and it was obvious where the first submarine cable should be laid – across the Strait of Dover.

The first serious scheme for a cross-Channel telegraph had been put forward by Professor Wheatstone in 1840 to a House of Commons committee. A few years later he carried out experiments in Swansea Bay, Wales, sending signals between a boat and a lighthouse. These were not, however, the first underwater signals ever transmitted; priority for this seems to go to a Dr O'Shaughnessy, Director of the East India Company's Telegraphs, who laid a primitive submarine cable across the River Hooghly in 1839. A little later – in 1842 – Morse carried out experiments in New York Harbour, sending signals through a length of rubber insulated wire enclosed in a lead pipe. Although this is going ahead of our story, these tests had led Morse to conclude, as early as 1843, that 'telegraph communication may with certainty be established across the Atlantic Ocean. Startling as this may now seem, I am confident the time will come when the project will be realised.'

By an unlikely turn of events, the man who first linked England and France together was a retired antique dealer. John Watkins Brett had made a fortune in this peculiar trade, and at the age of forty-five was still full of energy and prepared to try something new. His younger brother Jacob, who was an engineer, first interested him in the possibilities of submarine telegraphy, and between them the Bretts formed a grandiloquently titled 'General Oceanic and Subterranean Electric Printing Telegraph Company'. Perhaps it should be explained that it was the telegraphy, not the 'Electric Printing', which was intended to be subterranean.

After negotiating with the French Government, the Bretts secured a ten-year concession for the laying of a cross-Channel cable and contracted with the Gutta Percha Company for its manufacture. As was all too often the case with such pioneering projects, the whole scheme was rushed through far too quickly, without a proper understanding of the problems involved. The Bretts were working against a deadline; if they could not establish communication between France and England by 1 September 1850, their concession would lapse.

The cable was so primitive that it seems incredible that anyone could have expected it to work. It was nothing more than a single copper wire, surrounded by a quarter of an inch of gutta-percha for insulation. It was assumed that once the cable had been safely laid on the sea-bed nothing could happen to it and so it would need no armouring. Only the shore ends were given protection by being encased in lead tubes.

Very few people took the scheme seriously, and as usual those who knew least about it were the most critical. One gentleman, seeing the cable being paid out, declared roundly that the promoters must be fools; anyone should know that it was impossible to drag a wire that long over the rough bed of the Channel. He was under the impression that signals would be transmitted by jerking the cable, as in the system of wires, pulleys and bells which the wealthier Victorians employed to summon their numerous domestics from kitchen to drawing-room.

The Bretts had a scant three days to spare when they loaded their twenty-five miles of cable aboard the small steam tug *Goliath* and set out from Dover on the morning of 28 August 1850. The cable had been coiled on a large drum seven feet in diameter and fifteen feet long, which was placed on the after-deck with its axis horizontal, so that it spanned the entire width of the tiny boat. The drum, looking like an enormous cotton-reel, revolved as the cable was paid out, so that as the *Goliath* proceeded she was rather like an angler letting his line run out by walking backwards away from a point where the hook had been fixed. This system was only practicable with very small and light cables; all later ones were coiled in circular wells and paid out layer by layer.

Since the Bretts' cable was much too light to sink properly, it was necessary to attach lead weights to it every hundred yards or so. Despite the general chaos caused by this operation, and the strain on the cable when the *Goliath* stopped to fix the weights, the end of the cable was safely landed at Cap Gris-Nez on the evening of the 28th after an uneventful crossing.

There was great excitement as the automatic printer was connected up and the party on the French coast waited for the first message to come through – a flowery greeting from John Brett to Prince Louis Napoleon Bonaparte. Alas, all that emerged from the printer was a mass of jumbled characters which made no sense whatsoever; it almost appeared as if the English operators had been celebrating a little too soon. The automatic printer was disconnected and a needle instrument put in circuit; this time some words got through without mutilation, so at least the Bretts were able to claim that they had fulfilled the terms of their contract. But whether any complete and intelligible messages were exchanged seems highly doubtful, for the signals in both directions were equally jumbled.

They did not know it yet, but the telegraph engineers had now come face to face with an enemy that was to cause them endless trouble in the years ahead. At first sight, it would appear that if a properly insulated cable worked on land, it would work just as well in the sea. But this is not the case; when it is submerged in water, and thus surrounded by a conducting medium, the transmitting properties of a cable are completely altered. As we shall see later, it becomes much more sluggish owing to its greatly increased electrical capacity. Signals no longer pass through it at speeds comparable to that of light, but may move so slowly that before a 'dash' has emerged from the far end, a 'dot' may already be treading on its heels. It was this retardation that had foiled the Bretts. If their operators had slowed down their normal rate of sending to match the characteristics of the cable, the messages would have got through.

Unfortunately, there was no chance of continuing the experiments. When the tired and rather dispirited telegraphists sat down at their instruments the next morning, the line was completely dead. Electrical tests showed that it had broken somewhere near the French coast, and it was subsequently discovered that a fisherman had fouled the line with his anchor. As the line was so light he was able to haul it aboard, and he was immensely puzzled by this new kind of seaweed with a metal core. Thinking that it might be gold, he cut out a section to show his friends, and thus started the long war between the cable companies and the other users of the sea that has lasted to this day. More damage has been done to submarine cables by dragged anchors or trawls than by any other cause, and the annoyance is often mutual. A small boat that hooks its anchor around a modern armoured cable is as likely to lose its anchor as to damage the cable.

Despite its failure, the 1850 cable had shown that signals could be sent across the Channel. Nevertheless, the Bretts had the utmost difficulty in raising money for a second attempt, and it was not until a year later that the enterprise went ahead once more. This time the prime mover was Thomas Crampton, a railway engineer, who not only subscribed half the £15,000 needed for the project, but designed the new cable himself. And this time it was a real cable, not a single insulated wire. The four insulated conductors produced by the Gutta Percha Company were protected with hemp, and a layer of galvanised iron was spun on top of that to act as armouring. No fisherman would be able to haul up *this* cable; it looked like a large hawser and weighed more than thirty times as much as its predecessor.

This very weight almost defeated the project when the cable was laid on 25 September 1851. The year before, it had been necessary to attach lead weights to the line to make it sink – but this cable was only too eager to reach the sea-bed. It paid out so fast that the inadequate brake could not prevent excessive wastage, and as the ship was also carried off course by wind and tide the French coast was still a mile away when the end of the cable was reached. Luckily there was a spare length aboard for just such an emergency and a temporary splice was made to complete the connection. After a few weeks of testing, the cable was opened to the public, and no point in Europe was more than a few seconds away from England.

After the initial failure and the complete scepticism of all but a few enthusiasts, the establishment of this cross-Channel link – the world's first efficient submarine cable – created a great impression. With typically Victorian optimism, this new miracle of communications was hailed as a triumph for peace, which would undoubtedly improve understanding and co-operation between nations. Today we are sadly aware that though civilisation cannot function without such links, it by no means follows that they automatically bring peace. As the mathematicians would say, they are necessary – but not sufficient.

Punch, that ubiquitous commentator upon the times, celebrated the event with a cartoon showing what appears to be a two-headed angel with an olive branch tripping lightly along the bed of the Channel, delicately balancing on the cable with one toe like a ballet dancer walking the tightrope. According to the artist, the bottom of the English Channel is a much more interesting place than I have ever found it to be; it is liberally strewn with cutlasses, guns, broken spars and the skulls of unfortunate seamen.

The submarine cable boom was now under way; within the next two years the Gutta Percha Company, which had a virtual monopoly of core-insulation, supplied no less than 1500 miles of covered wire to the manufacturers who provided the protective armouring. If one could have watched a map of Europe which showed, like an animated cartoon, the progress of the cables, the period 1851 to 1856 would have shown remarkable, and all too often fruitless, activity. Thin black lines would have extended out in all directions from England, only to fade away again after a short period of existence. There were two attempts to span the Irish Sea before a permanent cable was laid; then Dover and Ostend were successfully linked, and after that no less than four sound cables were laid between England and Holland.

In 1855, a famous cable was laid across the Black Sea for the British Government to speed communications in the Crimean War. (So much for peace and understanding between nations!) This cable was needed in such a hurry that there was no time to get it armoured; like the first cross-Channel cable, it was simply an insulated wire. Yet it gave good service for nearly a year, and helped to shorten a war which the incompetence of the general staff had done so much to prolong.

The Mediterranean was first tackled in 1854, when a short cable was successfully laid between Corsica and Sardinia. Then a longer link was established between Corsica and the Italian coast, but the telegraph engineers were now running into – literally – deep waters, and disastrous failures resulted from attempts to connect Sardinia and Algeria so that Europe and Africa could speak to one another. These failures must have been tragically disheartening to all concerned, but their causes (as we shall see in Chapter 8) now appear extremely comic.

The general principles of submarine telegraphy were being learned by trial and error; though they did not appreciate the privilege, the shareholders were paying for the education of their engineers. And as soon as a few submarine cables had been successfully laid, it was inevitable that men's thoughts would turn to spanning the most important ocean of all: the Atlantic.

With her overseas possessions, maritime interests and technical 'know-how' – primitive though that appears to us today – it was also inevitable that Great Britain should be the pioneer in the field of submarine cables, and not surprising that she held this lead for a hundred years. Indeed, by 1950 more than 90 per cent of the cables in the world had been made by a single British firm, the Telegraph Construction and Maintenance Company. Yet the initiative and drive which finally resulted in the laying of a successful Atlantic cable, after years of setbacks and disasters, came from an American.

It is time to meet Cyrus W. Field.

4

A GREAT AMERICAN

Cyrus West Field was one of the greatest Americans of the nineteenth century, but today there can be few of his countrymen who remember him. He opened up no frontiers, killed no Indians, founded no industrial empires, won no battles; the work he did has been buried deep in the Atlantic ooze for more than a hundred years. Yet he helped to change history, and now that his dream of a telegraph to Europe has been surpassed by yet more wonderful achievements, it is only right that we should pay tribute to the almost superhuman courage which enabled him to triumph over repeated disasters.

His face is looking at me now, across the century that lies between us. It is not at all the face of the international financier or the company promoter, though Field was both these things. The thin, sensitive nose, the regular features, the deep-set, brooding eyes – these add up to a poet or musician, not to the stereotyped sad success, indistinguishable from all his ulcer-ridden colleagues, that we see today in the business section of *Time* magazine. 'Visionary and chivalrous' were the words applied to Field many years later, and no one without vision would have set off on the long and arduous quest that dominated his life for almost twelve years. But the vision would not have been enough without the practical shrewdness which had made him what would be a millionaire by our standards while he was still in his early thirties.

Cyrus Field was born on 30 November 1819, from New England stock, being a descendant of one Zechariah Field who had emigrated from England around 1629. His father was a Congregational minister at Stockbridge, Mass., and perhaps because he was the youngest of seven sons Cyrus matured unusually early. When he was only fifteen he asked permission to leave home and seek his fortune; with $8 in his pocket he drove fifty miles to the Hudson and sailed downstream to New York.

Like many boys before and since, he discovered that the streets of Manhattan were not as well paved with gold as he had hoped. During his first year as an errand boy in a Broadway dry-goods store he earned a dollar a week; though this was doubled in the second year, Cyrus came to the conclusion that his talents were not appreciated in New York and returned to Massachusetts. At the age of eighteen he became an assistant to his brother Matthew, a paper-maker, and only two years later went into business himself in the same trade.

Soon he was all set to make his fortune; he became a partner in a large New York firm of wholesale paper-dealers, and – still only twenty-one – married Mary Bryan Stone, of Guilford, Connecticut. Six months later, the roof fell in on him. The firm with which he had associated himself failed, and though he was the junior partner he was left holding the debts. Out of the wreckage he built Cyrus W. Field & Co., and worked with such intensity that his family saw him only on Sundays. By the time he was thirty-three he had paid off all his obligations, and was able to retire with $250,000 in the bank – all of which he had made in nine exhausting years.

Now he could relax; indeed, his doctor ordered him to do so. Like every other wealthy American, he 'did' Europe with his wife; then, rather more adventurously, he explored South America with his friend Frederick E. Church, a famous landscape-painter of the time, whose study of that totally impossible subject, Niagara Falls, is still considered one of the best ever put on canvas. Field and Church crossed the Andes – no mean feat in those days – and brought back as souvenirs a live jaguar and an Indian boy. It would be interesting to know which gave them more trouble.

Field might have remained in obscure retirement for the rest of his days if chance had not brought him into contact with F. N. Gisborne, an English engineer engaged on building a telegraph line across Newfoundland. This project was much more important than it may seem at first sight, for if it could be achieved it would reduce by several days the length of time it took for news to cross the Atlantic. Steamers from Europe would call at St John's and any urgent messages could be flashed ahead of them along the telegraph to New York. Unfortunately, building a line across Newfoundland is practically as difficult, because of the climate and the wild nature of the country, as laying a cable across the Atlantic. Even the original survey was bad enough; Gisborne reported, 'My original party, consisting of six white men, were exchanged for four Indians; of the latter party, two deserted, one died a few days after my return, and the other has ever since proclaimed himself an ailing man.'

In the face of such hardships, it was not surprising that the Newfoundland Electric Telegraph Company went bankrupt in 1853 before more than forty miles of line had been erected. Gisborne, who had been left holding the company's debts, went to New York the next year in an attempt to raise more money for the scheme. By good fortune he met Cyrus Field, who was then relaxing after his South American trip and was not at first at all keen on becoming involved in any further business undertakings. He listened politely to Gisborne, but did not commit himself to any promise of help. Only the uncompleted line across Newfoundland was discussed, but when the meeting was over and he was alone in his library Field started to play with the globe and suddenly realised that the Newfoundland telegraph was merely one link in a far more important project. Why wait for steamers to bring news from Europe? Let the telegraph do the whole job . . .

From that moment, Field became obsessed with the Atlantic telegraph. True, he was not the first man to conceive of a submarine cable linking Europe and America – we have already noted Morse's prediction – but he was the first to do anything practical. The next morning he wrote letters to Morse and to Lieutenant Maury, founder of the modern science of oceanography.

Matthew Fontaine Maury's classic book *The Physical Geography of the Sea* had not yet been published, but he was already famous – more famous, in the view of many of his superior officers, than a mere lieutenant should be. Though he had spent some years at sea, he had been accidentally lamed at the age of thirty-three and had then become head of the Depot of Charts and Instruments (the Hydrographic Office, as it is today). This had given him a unique opportunity of using his scientific talents, and by collating information from hundreds of ships' logs he had compiled the first detailed charts showing ocean currents and wind directions. These soon proved of immense value to navigators; by using Maury's charts, for example, ships rounding Cape Horn were able to cut their sailing time between New York and San Francisco from 180 days to a mere 133. Maury would have been astonished could he have known that, a century later, airline pilots were to profit in a similar way from a study of the winds, riding the jet-streams of the stratosphere to span the continent in almost as many minutes as the old windjammers took days.

Unfortunately, the lieutenant's services to his country and the world were not fully appreciated at higher levels; perhaps a series of scathing articles he had written about naval red tape had not helped his popularity. In 1855 a secret board, set up to conduct an efficiency and economy drive, put Maury on the permanent leave list. One would have thought that since his charts were now estimated to save several million dollars a year in reduced voyage times, the Navy could have afforded to keep him on its payroll. A good many of Maury's contemporaries thought so too, and there was so much newspaper agitation that three years later the Navy was forced to reinstate him with the rank of commander. There is an uncanny resemblance between the case of Lieutenant Maury and that of Admiral Rickhover, who dragged the United States Navy kicking and struggling into the Atomic Age – and was duly passed over for promotion. But unfortunately for his future prospects, Maury – a Virginian – joined the losing side in the Civil War, and that was the end of his naval career.

By one of those coincidences which is inevitable when many people are thinking along the same lines, Maury received Field's letter at a moment when he had written to the Secretary of the Navy on the same subject. He had been forwarding a report of a recent survey of the North Atlantic, carried out by Lieutenant Berryman, which had disclosed the existence of a plateau between Newfoundland and Ireland. Maury had commented to the Secretary on 22 February 1854 that this plateau 'seems to have been placed there especially for the purpose of holding the wires of a submarine telegraph and of keeping them out of harm's way'.

Field could hardly have hoped for better news, and a few days later Morse called to see him with equally encouraging advice. With the world's greatest names in oceanography and telegraphy to back him up, Field now had only to convince the financiers.

This was not as difficult as it was to prove a few years later. Field's next-door neighbour in Gramercy Square, the influential millionaire Peter Cooper, gave him his support and this encouraged other capitalists to join in. The names of these far-sighted men are worth recording: besides Peter Cooper they were Moses Taylor, Marshall O. Roberts and Chandler White. With their backing and the legal advice of his elder brother Dudley, Cyrus went to Newfoundland early in 1854 and took over the affairs of the moribund telegraph company. Its debts were paid, much local goodwill was thereby established, and Field obtained an exclusive charter for all cables touching Newfoundland and Labrador for the next fifty years. With this in his pocket, he returned triumphantly to New York, where it was the work of literally a few minutes (at six o'clock in the morning, which is not usually a good time to discuss business) for the subscribers to pledge $1,250,000 and float the 'New York, Newfoundland and London Telegraph Company'.

It took two and a half years of toil to substantiate the 'New York, Newfoundland' part of the company's title. Work was delayed for a whole year by the loss of the submarine cable that was to have spanned the St Lawrence, but in 1856 the line was opened and the first part of Field's dream had come true. It was only a stepping-stone to his main objective, which had never been far from his mind.

One of his first acts had been to promote new surveys of the North Atlantic by both the British and American navies, which confirmed the existence of the so-called 'Telegraph Plateau'. It was not quite as smooth and flat as had been first supposed, but its changes of slope were no worse than those met with on many city streets. Submarine charts tend to be misleading in this respect, owing to the great exaggeration of the vertical scale. When one tries to show on one piece of paper a strip two thousand miles wide and five miles high, even the gentlest hills look like precipices. The encouraging thing about Telegraph Plateau, however, was not its relative flatness but the fact that its greatest distance from the surface was less than 15,000 feet – and submarine cables had already been laid in water as deep as this.

Field needed such encouragement; his troubles – financial and personal – were just beginning. While he was trying to raise money for the projected cable, his only son died and at about the same time he lost his brother-in-law and business partner. It proved impossible to get the support he needed in the United States, which was now heading for one of its periodic depressions. So in 1856 Field sailed for England, in the hope that money would be less hard to find there.

At this point I cannot resist quoting from two modern books on telecommunications, leaving the reader to guess their countries of origin: 'The British capitalists were at first a bit timid about investing in what they considered an extravagant undertaking . . .' 'American big business had great difficulty in screwing up its courage to subscribe £27,000 and it was the merchants of Liverpool, Manchester, Glasgow, London and other British cities who only too willingly provided the rest . . .'

What actually happened was as follows. As soon as he arrived in England, Field arranged to meet the British telegraphic pioneers – notably John Brett, who was looking for fresh waters to conquer after his victory over the Channel. He also met the famous engineer Isambard Kingdom Brunel, then building the *Great Eastern*, which for half a century was to remain the mightiest ship that had ever moved upon the sea. In a prophetic moment, Brunel remarked to Field: 'There is the ship to lay your cable.' Killed by his labours over the leviathan, the great engineer did not live to see his words come true ten years later, after both Field and the *Great Eastern* had survived endless disasters and defeats.

Fortunately for the project, Professor Morse was also in London at the time, and carried out a series of experiments which proved beyond doubt that signals could be sent through 2000 miles of cable. By connecting together ten circuits each of 200 miles in length (the London to Manchester line was used) Morse constructed a replica of the proposed Atlantic cable and succeeded in passing up to 200 signals a minute through it.

This encouraging result convinced the British scientific world that the scheme was practicable. Luckily, no one realised that the result was quite misleading; the line on which Morse conducted his tests was electrically much superior to the cable that was actually built and laid. It is not the first time that an over-optimistic report has launched a project and sustained its originators in the face of difficulties that they might never have faced had they known the facts.

Armed with the evidence provided by his scientific experts, Field was now ready to tackle the British Government as represented by the Navy and the Foreign Office. It is pleasant to record that he met neither scepticism nor, what is even more deadly, the 'all aid short of actual help' type of treatment. The Foreign Secretary, Lord Clarendon, was particularly interested in the project, but asked Field: 'Suppose you don't succeed? Suppose you make the attempt and fail – your cable is lost in the sea – then what will you do?' 'Charge it to profit and loss, and go to work to make another,' Field answered at once. It was an all-too-prophetic reply.

In the face of this optimism and perseverance, even the Treasury, that graveyard of lost hopes, gave its support. Within only a few days of explaining his scheme to its Secretary, Field received official promise of a Government subsidy of £14,000 a year, i.e. 4 per cent on the £350,000 capital which the project was expected to cost. The only condition was that the still-to-be-formed Atlantic Telegraph Company would carry any messages the British Government desired to send, giving them priority over all other traffic except that of the United States Government. The British Navy would also provide facilities for surveying the route and laying the cable.

The cast of characters for the forthcoming production was now assembled. The most important was a brilliant young telegraph engineer named Charles Tilston Bright, who at twenty-four now became chief engineer for one of the most ambitious projects of the century. Charles Bright was another of those phenomenal Victorians who sometimes make one wonder if the human race has since deteriorated. When only nineteen, he had laid a complete system of telegraph wires under the streets of Manchester in a single night, without causing any disturbance to traffic. A year later, he had taken out twenty-four patents for basic inventions, some of which – such as the porcelain insulator for overhead wires – are still in use. A man of action as well as a brilliant engineer, Bright became a Member of Parliament at thirty-three and died at the early age of fifty-five, burned out by his exertions. His monument is a network of telegraph cables stretching more than half-way round the globe and linking together all the countries of the world.

Bright had become interested in the Atlantic telegraph even earlier than Field. Between 1853 and 1855 he had conducted experiments to study the propagation of signals through 2000 miles of line, using for this purpose the ten circuits of 200 miles each between London and Manchester, connected in series. In the summer of 1855 he had carried out a survey of the Irish coast and had decided that Valentia Bay, near the south-western tip of Ireland, was the best place to land a transatlantic cable. This decision was endorsed by every company which took a cable to Ireland for the next 100 years.

A much less fortunate appointment was that of Dr Edward Orange Wildman Whitehouse as the company's electrician. Dr Whitehouse was a Brighton surgeon who had interested himself in telegraphy and had acquired a considerable knowledge of the subject by practical experimenting. He was a man of strong personality and fixed ideas, and although his enthusiasm did much to get the company started in its early days, his refusal to recognise his limitations was later to bring disaster.

The first meeting of the Atlantic Telegraph Company took place at Liverpool on 12 November 1856, and Field, Brett and Bright outlined the

commercial prospects of the enterprise with such effect that the entire
£350,000 was subscribed in a few days. Field took up £75,000 of this, not for
his own benefit but on behalf – as he fondly imagined – of his fellow
Americans. When he got back to his own country, however, he had the utmost
difficulty in unloading even £27,000 of this amount, and was left holding the
remainder himself. Most of the capital was taken up by British business
houses, though among the private subscribers it is interesting to note the
names of Lady Byron and William Makepeace Thackeray. These literary
figures were obviously keener on progress than their contemporary Thoreau,
who had written in *Walden* two years before:

> We are in great haste to construct a magnetic telegraph from Maine to Texas; but
> Maine and Texas, it may be, have nothing important to communicate. We are eager
> to tunnel under the Atlantic and bring the Old World some weeks nearer to the
> New; but perchance the first news that will leak through into the broad, flapping
> American ear will be that Princess Adelaide has the whooping-cough . . .

With the Atlantic Telegraph Company now organised, £350,000 in the bank
and the financial and material support of the British Government secured,
Field returned to the United States at the end of 1856 fully confident that
he would obtain equal support in his own country. However, when he
approached President Buchanan to obtain the same terms that Britain had
granted, he at once met violent opposition from Congress. As his brother
Henry later remarked:

> He now found that it was much easier to deal with the English than with the
> American Government . . . Those few weeks in Washington were worse than any
> icebergs off the coast of Newfoundland. The Atlantic cable has had many a kink
> since, but never did it seem to be entangled in such a hopeless twist as when it got
> among the politicians.

The arguments raised against what one would have thought to be a proposal
of obvious and vital importance to the country now seem completely fantastic.
(But let us not forget how later Congresses fought tooth and nail against the St
Lawrence Seaway for more than a quarter of a century.) Some senators
objected to the enormous fee of $70,000 a year which the Government would
have to pay for the privilege of swift and efficient transatlantic communication.
Others thought that the State had no right to dabble in private business, and
some objected to the proposed line because both ends were on British
territory and the cable might therefore be put out of action in the event of war
between the two countries. One Senator Jones of Tennessee opposed the
scheme for the frank and forthright reason that 'he did not want anything to do
with England or Englishmen'. There seemed a general fear (not yet wholly
extinct in the United States) that if the British were keen on something there

must be a catch in it, and any poor innocent Americans who became involved were liable to lose their shirts.

However, largely thanks to the support of Senator Thomas Rusk of Texas, the bill was passed by a single vote on 3 March 1856. The United States Government granted the subsidy which would give the company a guaranteed source of income, and also made arrangements to provide ships to help with the cable-laying. A thankful but somewhat exhausted Cyrus Field hurried back to England to see how his British colleagues were faring.

They were making fine progress, spinning out cable at a rate which has seldom been matched since, and ought not to have been attempted then. Largely because Field had promised his backers that the telegraph would start working in 1857, specifications had been sent out to the manufacturers even before the board of management had been set up, and the production of the cable in the short time of six months was a remarkable performance. It involved drawing and spinning 335,000 miles of iron and copper wire and covering that with 300,000 miles of tarred hemp to form a cable 2500 miles long. (The actual distance from Ireland to Newfoundland is about 500 miles less than this, but the extra length was needed for slack in paying out, and to allow for possible losses.)

Progress, though swift, was far from smooth. Quite apart from the making of the cable, the expedition's ships had to be fitted out and a multitude of details supervised. Chief Engineer Bright, who was still twenty-four but ageing rapidly, commented in terms which will find an echo in the heart of anyone who has ever been engaged in what is so often rightly called a 'crash programme': 'At first one goes nearly mad with vexation at the delays; but one soon finds that they are the rule, and then it becomes necessary to feign a rage one does not feel . . . I look upon it as the natural order of things that if I give an order it will not be carried out; or if by accident it is carried out, it will be carried out wrongly.'

The company's engineers were not helped by streams of advice and criticism from outside experts, such as the Astronomer Royal, Sir George Airy, who stated dogmatically that 'it was a mathematical impossibility to submerge the cable successfully at so great a depth, and if it were possible, no signals could be transmitted through so great a length . . .' When distinguished scientists made such fools of themselves, it is easy to excuse the numerous inventors who wrote to Bright with proposals based on the ancient fallacy that heavy objects did not sink to the sea-bed, but eventually came to rest at a level where their density was matched by that of the surrounding water. There is, of course, no truth in this idea, for water is so nearly incompressible that even at the greatest depths encountered in the ocean its density is only very slightly greater than at sea-level.*

*At the bottom of the Atlantic, the increase in density due to pressure alone is less than 2 per cent.

Some of the hopeful inventors wished to suspend the cable in mid-ocean by underwater parachutes or balloons; others even more optimistically wanted to connect it to a string of floating call-boxes across the Atlantic, so that ships could keep in touch with land as they crossed from continent to continent. Whether they were crazy or not, Charles Bright replied politely to all these proposals, few of which were inhibited by the slightest practical knowledge of the oceanographic and telegraphic facts of life.

The Atlantic Telegraph Company, in any event, had little need for outside help. On its own board of directors was a scientific genius (and for once the word is not misapplied) who was later to do more than any man to save the lost cause of submarine telegraphy and to retrieve the company's fortunes. Professor William Thomson had already come into collision with that opinionated amateur Dr Whitehouse, and unluckily for all concerned his views had not prevailed over those of the project's official electrician.

5

LORD OF SCIENCE

William Thomson, Lord Kelvin, was not the greatest scientist of the nineteenth century; on any reasonable list, he must come below Darwin and Maxwell. But it is probably true to say that he was the most famous man of science of his age, and the one whom the general public chiefly identified with the astonishing inventions and technical advances of the era.

In this, public opinion was correct, for Thomson was a unique bridge between the laboratory and the world of industry. He was an 'applied scientist' *par excellence*, using his wonderful insight to solve urgent practical problems. Yet he was very much more than this, being also one of the greatest of mathematical physicists. The range of his interests and activities was enormous; the multiplication of knowledge that has taken place since his time makes it impossible that we should see his like again. It would not be unfair to say that if one took half the talents of Einstein, and half the talents of Edison, and succeeded in fusing such incompatible gifts into a single person, the result would be rather like William Thomson. What his contemporaries thought of him is shown by the fact that he was the first scientist ever to be raised to the peerage. Although we are really concerned with Thomson only as he affects the story of submarine telegraphy, he is such a fascinating and dynamic character that it is difficult to pass him by with no more than a glance. Moreover, it is impossible to understand his share of the story unless one has some appreciation of his extraordinary gifts and the use he made of them.

Heredity and environment between them left young William Thomson no chance of escaping from his destiny, even had he wished to do so. His father was Professor of Mathematics at Glasgow University, and from the tenderest age William was trained intensively for the academic life. He never went to school, all his teaching coming from his father, and as his mother died when he was only six years old the infant prodigy was clearly doomed to a life of interesting neuroses. In actual fact, about the only sign of Thomson's unorthodox upbringing was a certain lack of social graces and an inability to stop his brilliant mind from galloping off in all directions. No one can be certain that even these small defects can be blamed on his devoted father's training; moreover, as J. G. Crowther points out in his biography of

Thomson, 'the indiscipline that hampered his scientific genius did not extend to his financial affairs'. It makes a most refreshing change to read of a scientist who accumulated a 128-ton yacht and a fortune of £162,000 by his own efforts. But, of course, Thomson was a Scot as well as a scientist.

Having matriculated at the age of ten, the young genius soon proved that his gifts were not limited to science. Two years later he won a prize for translating a dialogue of the Greek satirist Lucian – the author, incidentally, of the first interplanetary romance (*True History*, AD 160). And at the ripe age of sixteen, he produced a brilliant eighty-five-page essay, *On the Figure of the Earth*. For the benefit of any mathematically minded teenagers who feel like pursuing the matter further, this essay contained 'a discussion of the perturbation of the Moon's motion in longitude, and a deduction of the ellipticity from the constant of precession combined with Laplace's hypothetical law of density in the interior of the Earth'.

After such a start, it was not surprising that Thomson became Professor of Natural Philosophy at Glasgow University at the age of twenty-two. One of his earliest acts was to establish a physics laboratory in which the students could do practical work; this was the first such laboratory in Britain, if not in the world, and Thomson was granted the vast sum of £100 for the purchase of instruments.

As a lecturer, Thomson was not an unqualified success; indeed, when he had become Sir William, one of his students made the unkind comment: 'Behold the knight cometh, when no man can work.' However, by his personality and his genius he had an overwhelming effect upon two generations of physicists and engineers. Apart from his interest in telegraphy, he helped to lay the foundations of thermodynamics – the mathematical science of heat – and also conquered vast areas of magnetism, electricity and optics. His researches into astronomy and geophysics were also notable; some of his most famous calculations concerned the ages of the sun and Earth, and he produced consternation among the geologists by claiming that the Earth could not possibly be as old as they maintained; indeed, he set an upper limit of a miserable twenty million years to its age as a solid body. This was one occasion when Thomson was completely wrong; he lived to witness the discovery of the energy source – radioactivity – which meant that the universe was much older than he had supposed. But by this time he was in his seventies and unable to appreciate the breakthrough into new fields of knowledge, so he never conceded his mistake.

Thomson became involved in the telegraph story as a result of his investigations into what are known as transient electric currents. What happens, he asked himself in 1853, when a battery is connected up to a circuit, in the minute interval of time before the current settles down to its steady value? At one moment nothing is happening; a fraction of a second later, a current of some definite amount is flowing. The problem was to discover what took place during the transition period, which is seldom as much as a hundredth of a second in duration, and is usually very much shorter. Nothing could have seemed more academic and of less practical importance. Yet these studies led directly to the understanding of all electrical communication, and, some thirty years later, to the discovery of radio waves. If Thomson could have obtained a 5 per cent royalty on the use of the equations he derived, he would not have left a mere £162,000. He would have been the richest man on earth.*

Thomson showed that there were two possible ways in which a current could rise from zero to its steady value, depending upon the electrical characteristics of the circuit. A pendulum set swinging in a resisting medium – immersed in water, for example – gives a very exact analogy. If the friction is too great, the pendulum will drop slowly down to its point of rest without overshooting, but if the friction – the 'damping' – is sufficiently small, a whole series of oscillations of diminishing amplitude will take place. Precisely the same thing happens with the electric current, though this fact was not easy to demonstrate experimentally in the 1850s. Now we prove it in our homes a dozen times a day; when somebody switches on an electrical appliance and we hear a crackle on the radio, that is one of Thomson's oscillatory currents advertising its ephemeral presence.

A year later, using the same mathematical tools, Thomson began to investigate the behaviour of telegraph cables. It is possible to understand his main results, and to appreciate their importance, without any knowledge of the mathematics he used to obtain them. Putting it briefly, the problem involved was this: how long does it take for a signal to reach the far end of a telegraph cable?

It is a common error to imagine that electricity travels along a wire at the speed of light – 186,000 miles a second. This is never true, although in some circumstances this velocity can be approached. In most cases, the speed of a current is very much less than that of light – sometimes, indeed, only a tenth or a hundredth of its value. This slowing-down is due to the electrical capacity of the line. There is no need to be alarmed by this phrase; it means exactly what it says. A telegraph cable behaves very much like a hosepipe; it takes a certain amount of electricity to 'fill it up' before there is any appreciable result at the other end.

Fortunately for the progress of the telegraphic art, this effect was of no practical importance in the early days of land lines. Their capacity was so low that messages passed through them without any appreciable delay, and it was not until the first submarine cables were laid across the English Channel and the North Sea that signal-retardation became a source of trouble. Its prime

*A title which was later applied, with some justice, to his protégé Calouste Gulbenkian – who cornered half the world's oil after he gave up physics.

cause is the presence of the conducting sea-water which surrounds a cable and thus greatly increases its capacity. Because of this effect, a cable may need twenty times as much electricity to charge it up when it is submerged as it would require if suspended in air.

Thomson's analysis led him to his famous 'Law of Squares', which states that the speed with which messages can be sent through a given cable decreases with the square of its length. In other words, if one multiplies the length of a cable ten times, the rate of signalling will be reduced a hundredfold. This law is obviously of fundamental importance in long-distance submarine tele-graphy; the only way of circumventing it is to increase the size of the conducting core.

This was not appreciated by all telegraph engineers, and was even denied by some – including, unfortunately, Dr Whitehouse. He had carried out experiments purporting to refute the law of squares; these had also led him to conclude that a *small* conducting wire might be better than a large one, which was the exact reverse of the truth. When such confusion prevailed among the 'experts', it is hardly surprising that the first Atlantic cable was badly designed. It had about as much chance of success as a bridge built by engineers who did not understand the laws governing the strength of materials.

Thomson was only one of the company's directors, and had no authority – beyond his scientific prestige – over the men who were in charge of its technical affairs. He was thus in the difficult position, during the first act of the drama that was now beginning, of standing off-stage and making criticisms which the producer could ignore or accept as he saw fit.

Because of their determination to lay the cable during the summer of 1857, the promoters of the scheme had left no time for the experiments and tests which were essential for its success. The dynamic energy of Cyrus Field was partly responsible for this; when Thomson arrived on the scene, he discovered that the specifications for the cable had already been sent out to the manufacturers, and that it was now too late to alter them. What was more, when he had an opportunity of testing the completed article, he was shocked to discover that the quality of the copper varied so much that some sections conducted twice as well as others. There was nothing that could be done, except to insist that future lengths be made of the purest possible copper, and to hope that the existing cable would be good enough for the job.

The conductor itself consisted of seven strands of copper wire twisted together and insulated by three separate layers of gutta-percha (see Chapter 14). If there was a hole or imperfection in one layer, the other two would still provide adequate protection. Only in the extremely improbable event of three flaws occurring in exactly the same place would there be a danger of an electrical failure. The insulated core was then covered with a layer of hemp, which in turn was armoured with eighteen strands of twisted iron wire. The resulting cable was about five-eighths of an inch in thickness, and weighed one ton per mile. This at once raised a serious problem, for the length needed to span the Atlantic weighed 2500 tons – far too great a load to be carried in any single ship of the time.

The total cost of the cable was £224,000 – many millions by today's standards, though it is about as difficult to relate our present currency to the Victorian pound's real purchasing power as to that of the Russian rouble. The core was supplied by the Gutta Percha Company of Greenwich, London, but because of the time factor the armouring was divided between two firms: Glass, Elliott & Co., also of Greenwich, and Newall & Co., of Birkenhead. Owing to one of those slight oversights which can so easily wreck an enterprise of this kind, the wire armouring on the two halves of the cable was laid or twisted in opposite directions. This is a matter of great practical importance when it comes to joining together two cable-ends in mid-Atlantic; it is a little too late then to reverse one of the 1250-mile-long sections so that all the heavy armouring corkscrews in the same direction at the point where you wish to make your splice.

The cable was completed within the remarkably short time of six months, and by July 1857 it was ready to go to sea. By rights, Whitehouse should have sailed with it, but at the last moment he pleaded ill health and Thomson was asked to fill the breach. It says much for the scientist's greatness of character that he agreed to do this, without any payment. The misshapen infant dumped on his doorstep was certainly not his baby, but he would give it the best start in life he could.

6

FALSE START

To share the enormous weight of the cable between them, the warships *Niagara* and *Agamemnon* had been provided by the United States and British governments respectively. The ninety-one-gun *Niagara* was the finest ship in the American Navy; the largest steam frigate in the world, she had lines like a yacht and her single screw could drive her with ease at twelve miles an hour. The *Agamemnon*, on the other hand, would not have looked out of place at Trafalgar; she was one of the last of the wooden walls of England, and though she had steam power as well as sail one would not have guessed it by looking at her. Both ships had been extensively modified to allow them to carry and pay out their 1250 tons of cable. Their holds had been enlarged into circular wells or tanks in which the cable could be coiled; even so, the *Agamemnon* was forced to carry several hundred tons of it on deck – a fact which later brought her to the edge of disaster.

The *Niagara* was carrying two Russian officers as observers, which could not have been too pleasing to the British, since the Crimean War had finished only a year before. There were no journalists on board, this being against service regulations. Perhaps the American Navy was still smarting under the impact of a recent devastating exposé in a book named *White-Jacket*, though it could take some consolation from the knowledge that the author's latest work, a tedious novel called *Moby Dick*, had been a complete flop.

The British had no such inhibitions, and their share of the enterprise was fully covered by the Press. It is from an issue of the London *Times* dated 24 July 1857 that we have salvaged this account of a banquet given to the workmen of the cable company and the crew of the *Agamemnon* just before she was due to sail; its subtle nuances say more about the manners of the time than many volumes of social history:

> The manufacturers provided a magnificent banquet for the guests, and a substantial one for the sailors . . . by an admirable arrangement, the guests were accommodated at a vast semicircular table, while the sailors and workmen sat at a number of long tables arranged at right-angles with the chord, so that the general effect was that all dined together, while at the same time sufficient distinction was preserved to satisfy the most fastidious . . .

After loading their respective halves of the cable the two warships (with their escorts the *Susquehanna* and *Leopard*) sailed to their rendezvous at Valentia Bay, County Kerry. The plan that had been adopted, at the insistence of the directors, was for the *Niagara* to lay the whole of her cable westward from Ireland, and for the *Agamemnon* to splice on in mid-Atlantic and then complete the job. This would have the advantage that the expedition would be in continuous contact with land and could report progress through the unwinding cable all the way across the Atlantic. On the other hand, if the ships arrived in mid-ocean during bad weather, and it was impossible to make the splice, half the cable would be lost.

The arrival of the telegraph fleet in this remote corner of Ireland attracted crowds of sightseers, and the local nobility rose to the occasion with inspiring speeches. Everyone realised the importance of the event, and when the shore end of the cable was landed on 5 August 1857 Henry Field reports:

Valentia Bay was studded with innumerable small craft, decked with the gayest bunting – small boats flitted hither and thither, their occupants cheering enthusiastically as the work successfully progressed. The cable boats were managed by the sailors of the *Niagara* and *Susquehanna*, and it was a well-designed compliment, and indicative of the future fraternisation of nations, that the shore-rope was arranged to be presented at this side of the Atlantic to the representative of the Queen, by the officers and men of the United States Navy, and at the other side British officers and sailors would make a similar presentation to the President of the great Republic.

For several hours the Lord Lieutenant of Ireland stood on the beach, surrounded by his staff and the directors of the cable company, watching the arrival of the cable, and when at length the American sailors jumped through the surge with the hawser to which it was attached, his Excellency was among the first to lay hold of it and pull it lustily to shore . . .

It was too late to set sail that day, so the cable-laying began the next morning – Thursday, 6 August 1857. Almost at once there was a minor but annoying setback; five miles out, the cable caught in the primitive paying-out mechanism and broke. It was necessary to go back to the beginning, lift the section that had already been laid, and run along it until the break was reached.

At length (continues Henry Field),

the end was lifted out of the water and spliced to the gigantic coil [i.e. the 1250 miles in the *Niagara's* hold], and as it dipped safely to the bottom of the sea, the mighty ship began to stir. At first she moved very slowly, not more than two miles an hour, to avoid the danger of accident; but the feeling that they are away at last is itself a relief. The ships are all in sight, and so near that they can hear each other's bells. The *Niagara*, as if knowing that she is bound for the land out of whose forests she came, bends her head to the waves, as her prow is turned towards her native shores.

Slow passed the hours of that day. But all went well, and the ships were moving out into the broad Atlantic. At length the sun went down in the west and stars came out on the face of the deep. But no man slept. A thousand eyes were watching a great experiment as those who have a personal interest in the issue . . . There was a strange, unnatural silence in the ship. Men paced the deck with soft and muffled tread, speaking only in whispers, as if a loud voice or a heavy footfall might snap the vital chord. So much have they grown to feel for the enterprise, that the cable seemed to them like a human creature, on whose fate they hung, as if it were to decide their own destiny . . .

So it went for the next three days. Let us, without any perceptible change of style, switch narrators in mid-ocean from the American Henry Field to the quintessentially British London *Times*:

The cable was paid out at a speed a little faster than the ship, to allow for any inequalities on the bottom of the sea. While it was thus going overboard, communication was kept up constantly with the land. Every moment the current was passing between ship and shore . . . On Monday they were over 200 miles to sea. They had got far beyond the shallow waters of the coast. They had passed over the submarine mountain . . . where Mr Bright's log gives a descent from 550 to 1750 fathoms within eight miles. Then they came to the deeper waters of the Atlantic, where the cable sank to the awful depth of two thousand fathoms. Still the iron cord buried itself in the wave, and every instant the flash of light in the darkened telegraph room told of the passage of the electric current . . .

But not for much longer – for at 9 a.m. that morning the line suddenly went dead. There was a gloomy consultation among the engineers, and all hope had been abandoned when, quite unexpectedly, signals started coming through again. This two-and-a-half-hour break in continuity was never satisfactorily explained; it might have been due to a faulty connection in the equipment at either end, or to a flaw in the cable itself.

This was a disturbing setback, but the next day brought catastrophe. The cable had been running out so rapidly (at six miles an hour against the ship's four) that it was necessary to tighten the brake on the paying-out mechanism. By an unfortunate error, the tension was applied too suddenly, and the cable snapped under the strain. There was nothing to do but to postpone the attempt until the next year, since the amount of cable in the tanks was not sufficient to risk another try. But Field and his colleagues, though disappointed, were not despondent. They had successfully laid 335 miles of cable, a third of it in water more than two miles deep, and had been in telegraphic communication with land until the moment the line had parted. This proved, it seemed to them, that there was nothing impossible in the job they were attempting.

The ships returned to England and unloaded the 2200 miles of cable they had brought back. It was coiled up on a wharf at Plymouth to await the next expedition, while the *Niagara* and *Agamemnon* reverted to their naval duties – somewhat handicapped by the gaping holes that had been torn in their entrails.

Meanwhile, the mistakes revealed by the first attempt were studied by the engineers to prevent them occurring again. The paying-out mechanism, which had been the prime cause of the failure, was completely redesigned. A new type of friction brake was used which would automatically release if too much tension was applied; we read with morbid fascination that 'this clever appliance had been introduced in connection with the crank apparatus in gaols, so as to regulate the amount of labour in proportion to the strength of the prisoner'.

The indefatigable Field had returned to America to raise more money, only to find a depression sweeping the country and much of his fortune lost. The failure of the first expedition had also shaken confidence in the project and it was hard to obtain support on either side of the Atlantic; nevertheless the new capital was secured and 700 miles of fresh cable was ordered.

While the preparations were going ahead for the next expedition, Professor Thomson was far from idle. In addition to his normal work at the university, he continued to study the problem of the Atlantic telegraph. One important fact that had emerged from his mathematical analysis was that if a sufficiently sensitive detector could be used at the receiving end of the cable, the rate of signalling would be much increased. This results from the fact that when a sudden electrical impulse (say a dot or a dash) is applied to one end of a cable, it does not appear at the other end as an equally abrupt rise of voltage. The first intimation at the receiver is a gently rising wave of electricity which takes an appreciable time to reach its maximum value. If the first onset of this wave could be sensed by a sufficiently delicate instrument, there would be no need to wait for the crest of the wave to arrive. The signal would have been detected, and the next one would now be sent.

The way in which the clearly defined pulse of electricity from, say, a Morse key is 'smeared out' as it progresses along a submarine cable can be appreciated from the following analogy. Think of the water behind a dam; it forms a vertical wall, which we can liken to the original sharp-edged pulse sent into the cable. The moment of transmission corresponds to the sudden breaking of the dam; at once the water starts to collapse – to flatten out. At a point a considerable distance away, the first intimation that anything has happened is an almost inconspicuous wave that may take a considerable time to build up to its maximum value. And once you have noticed this little wave, there is no point in waiting any longer. You know what's coming.

Thomson's objective, therefore, was extreme detector sensitivity. But Whitehouse, with his remarkable talent for doing the wrong thing, took just the opposite approach. He proposed to use brute force at the transmitting end of the cable, pushing so much current into it that even insensitive instruments – such as his own patent automatic printer – could read the messages sent. The result of this policy we shall see in due course.

The solution to the receiving problem was given by Thomson's monocle; he was twirling it one day, and noticed how swiftly the reflected light danced around the room. This led him to his famous mirror galvanometer, in which the minute deflection of a coil carrying an electric current was greatly magnified by a spot of light reflected from a tiny mirror attached to it. Thomson had, in effect, invented an instrument with a weightless pointer.

In passing, it might be mentioned that the story of Thomson's monocle appears more authentic than that of Newton and the apple (though there are grounds for believing that that also may be true). And discoveries prompted by such chance observations are never accidents; they only happen to those who have been thinking long and earnestly about a problem, and whose minds are therefore in a sensitive, receptive mood. How many philosophers before Newton had seen apples falling? How many bacteriologists before Fleming had noticed inexplicable moulds on their cultures?

The mirror galvanometer, because of its delicacy, simplicity and elegance made a great impression on Thomson's contemporaries. Clerk Maxwell, one of whose relaxations was writing light verse, produced a Tennysonian parody in celebration which opens:

> The lamplight falls on blackened walls
> And streams through narrow perforations
> The long beam trail o'er pasteboard scales
> With slow, decaying oscillations.
> Flow, current, flow! Set the quick light-spot flying!
> Flow, current, answer light-spot, flashing, quivering, dying . . .

In the spring of 1858, the great enterprise got under way again. Once more the *Agamemnon* and the *Niagara* were commissioned as cable-layers, and the Admiralty provided the sloop *Gorgon* as an escort. The United States Navy had promised that the *Susquehanna* would also be available as in the previous year, but she was quarantined in the West Indies with yellow fever aboard. As soon as he heard this news – which threatened the success of the whole project – Field promptly buttonholed the First Lord of the Admiralty, and apologetically asked if the British Navy could add a third vessel to the two it was already providing. The First Lord explained that the Navy was so short of ships that it was hiring them, but promised to do his best. Within a few hours the *Valorous* had been made available; the Victorians could move quickly when they wanted to, even without benefit of telephones.

This time, at the insistence of the engineers, it was decided to start from

Ronald's Telegraph of 1816: an early experiment in electrical telegraphy, requiring eight miles of overhead wire (*BT Museum*)

Sir William Thompson (Lord Kelvin), Cyrus Field and Oliver Heaviside: three great pioneers in the development of telecommunications (*Telefocus, BT Museum*)

The Agamemnon battling in stormy seas during the first cable-laying expedition of 1858 (*BT Museum*)

Cable being paid out from one of the storage tanks on board the Great Eastern (*Science Museum*)

The Atlantic Telegraph: all the details, from a contemporary poster (*BT Museum*)

A WORD TO THE MERMAIDS.

NEPTUNE. 'Aho-o-o-oy, there! Get off o'that 'ere cable, can't yer – that's the way t'other one was wrecked!!!' Poking fun in an 1865 *Punch* (*Science Museum*)

With the loss of the 1865 cable, the skill of grappling for a thread 2½ miles beneath the ocean required excellent navigation and equipment. Unfortunately the sectioned rope was found to be inadequate (*BT Museum*)

Testing the recovered cable, 1865 (*BT Museum*)

mid-Atlantic and let the ships lay the cable in opposite directions. Not only would this be more economical in time, but it would mean that the all-important splice could be made at leisure, when weather conditions were most suitable.

After some initial tests in the Bay of Biscay (where, almost a hundred years later, the components of the Atlantic telephone cable also had their baptism of deep water) the little fleet sailed from Plymouth under fair skies on 10 June 1858. Once again Whitehouse had asked to be excused on medical grounds, and once again Thomson took his place (unpaid). It was lucky for Whitehouse that he stayed on land, for only two days after they had left harbour beneath clear skies, the four ships ran into one of the worst Atlantic storms ever recorded.

They were scattered over the face of the sea, each ship fighting desperately for its life. The *Agamemnon* was in particular danger, being made almost unmanageable owing to the 1300 tons of cable in her hold and, a still more serious hazard, the 250 tons coiled on deck. Thanks to Nicholas Woods, correspondent of the London *Times*, we have an account of the storm which must be among the most vivid in the literature of the sea. Listen to his description of the *Agamemnon* in her hour of peril:

> The massive beams under her upper deck coil cracked and snapped with a noise resembling that of small artillery, almost drowning the hideous roar of the wind as it moaned and howled through the rigging . . . At 4 a.m. sail was shortened – a long and tedious job, for the wind so roared and howled, and the hiss of the boiling sea was so deafening, that words of command were useless, and the men aloft, holding on with all their might to the yards as the ship rolled over and over almost to the water, were quite incapable of struggling with the masses of wet canvas, that flapped and plunged as if men and yards and everything were going away together . . . At about half-past ten o'clock three or four gigantic waves were seen approaching the ship, coming slowly on through the mist nearer and nearer, rolling on like hills of green water, with a crown of foam that seemed to double their height. The *Agamemnon* rose heavily to the first, and then went lower quickly into the deep trough of the sea, falling over as she did so, so as almost to capsize completely. There was a fearful crashing as she lay over this way, for everything broke adrift . . . a confused mass of sailors, boys, marines, with deck-buckets, ropes, ladders and everything that could get loose, were being hurled in a mass across the ship . . . The lurch of the ship was calculated at forty-five degrees each way for five times in rapid succession . . . The coil in the main hold . . . had begun to get adrift, and the top kept working and shifting as the ship lurched, until some forty or fifty miles were in a hopeless state of tangle, resembling nothing so much as a cargo of live eels . . .
>
> The sun set upon as wild and wicked a night as ever taxed the courage and coolness of a sailor . . . The night was thick and very dark, the low black clouds almost hemming the vessel in; now and then a fiercer blast than usual drove the

great masses slowly aside, and showed the moon, a dim, greasy blotch upon the sky, with the ocean, white as driven snow, boiling and seething like a cauldron. But these were only glimpses, which were soon lost, and again it was all darkness, through which the waves, suddenly upheaving, rushed upon the ship as though they must overwhelm it . . . The grandeur of the scene was almost lost in its dangers and terrors, for of all the many forms in which death approaches man there is none so easy in fact, so terrific in appearance, as death by shipwreck . . .

But all things have an end, and this long gale – of over a week's duration – at last blew itself out, and the weary ocean rocked itself to rest . . . As we approached the place of meeting the angry sea went down. The *Valorous* hove in sight at noon; in the afternoon the *Niagara* came in from the north; and at even, the *Gorgon* from the south; and then, almost for the first time since starting, the squadron was reunited near the spot where the great work was to have commenced fifteen days previously – as tranquil in the middle of the Atlantic as if in Plymouth Sound.

After this ordeal, one would have thought that the expedition had earned the right to success. The battered vessels were made shipshape, the cable-ends were spliced together, and on 26 June the *Niagara* sailed west for Newfoundland and the *Agamemnon* headed east towards Ireland.

They had gone only three miles when the cable fouled the paying-out machinery on board the *Niagara* and snapped. This was anticlimax number one, but nobody was too upset as little time and cable had been lost.

On the second attempt, the ships got eighty miles apart before anything went wrong. Then they suddenly lost telegraphic contact, and each assumed that the cable had broken aboard the other. They hurried back to the rendezvous and hailed each other simultaneously with the words: 'How did the cable part?' It was very disconcerting to find no explanation for what had happened; for some unknown reason, the cable had broken on the sea-bed.

A third time the splice was made, and, no doubt with all aboard wondering when they would meet again, the ships sailed apart once more. Unfortunately, it was not a case of third time lucky. After 200 miles had been paid out, the cable parted on the *Agamemnon*. The ships were now short of provisions, and according to prearranged plans they headed back independently to Ireland for a council of war.

It was an unhappy board of directors which met to consider the next move. Some, in despair, wished to sell the remaining cable and abandon the whole enterprise. But Field and Thomson argued for a fresh attempt, and in the end their counsel prevailed. The faint-hearted directors resigned in disgust at such stubborn foolishness, and by 29 July the ships were back in mid-Atlantic, ready for the fourth try.

There was no ceremony or enthusiasm this time when the splice went overboard and the ships parted. Many felt that they were on a fool's errand; as Field's brother remarked in his memoirs: 'All hoped for success, no one dared to expect it.'

And certainly no one could have guessed that they were about to achieve, in the highest degree, both success and failure.

7

TRIUMPH AND DISASTER

It was just as well for the American Press that it had no representative on board the *Niagara*, for the westward voyage was a monotonously peaceful one with the cable paying out uneventfully hour after hour. The only excitement was in the electricians' cabin, for twice during the week the signals from the *Agamemnon* failed but came back again in full strength after a few hours' anxiety. Apart from this, the *Niagara*'s log records 'light breeze and moderate sea' almost all the way, until the moment she arrived in Trinity Bay, Newfoundland, with her 1300 miles of cable safely strung across the bed of the Atlantic.

The eastward-sailing *Agamemnon*, on the other hand, had once again experienced an adventurous voyage, and several times had skirted mechanical or electrical disaster. Considering the conditions under which Thomson and his assistants worked, it is astonishing that they were able to keep their instruments operating at all. Listen to this description of the telegraph room as given by the *Sydney Morning Herald*:

> The electrical room is on the starboard side of the main deck forward. The arrangements have been altered several times in order to avoid the water which showers down from the upper deck. At one end of the little place the batteries are ranged on shelves and railed in . . . The most valuable observation is taken in sending on the marine galvanometer. Three seconds before it is taken, the clerk who times all the observations by a watch regulated by a chronometer too valuable to be brought into so wet a place says 'Look out'. The other clerk at once fixes his eye on the spot of light, and immediately the word is given 'Now' records the indication. This testing is made from minute to minute, so that a flaw is detected the moment it occurs.

The ships had spliced the cable on 29 July 1858, midway between Europe and America, in water 1500 fathoms deep. To let *The Times* continue the story:

> For the first three hours the ships proceeded very slowly, paying out a great quantity of slack, but after the expiration of this time, the speed of the *Agamemnon* was increased to about five knots, the cable going at about six . . . Shortly after six o'clock a very large whale was seen approaching the starboard bow at a great speed, rolling and tossing the sea into foam all around . . . it appeared as if it were making

direct for the cable, and great was the relief of all when the ponderous living mass was seen slowly to pass astern, just grazing the cable where it entered the water . . .

A few hours later, there was a real crisis, vividly depicted by the *Sydney Morning Herald*'s reporter:

We had signalled the *Niagara* '40 miles submerged' and she was just beginning her acknowledgement when suddenly, at 10 p.m., communication ceased. According to orders, those on duty sent at once for Dr Thomson. He came in a fearful state of excitement. The very thought of disaster seemed to overpower him. His hand shook so much that he could scarcely adjust his eyeglass. The veins on his forehead were swollen. His face was deathly pale. After consulting his marine galvanometer, he said the conducting wire was broken, but still insulated from the water . . . There did not seem to be any room for hope; but still it was determined to keep the cable going out, that all opportunity might be given for resuscitation. The scene in and about the electrical room was such as I shall never forget. The two clerks on duty, watching, with the common anxiety depicted on their faces, for a propitious signal; Dr Thomson, in a perfect fever of nervous excitement, shaking like an aspen leaf, yet in mind keen and collected, testing and waiting . . . Mr Bright, standing like a boy caught in a fault, his lips and cheeks smeared with tar, biting his nails and looking to the Professor for advice . . . The eyes of all were directed on the instruments, watching for the slightest quiver indicative of life. Such a scene was never witnessed save by the bedside of the dying . . . Dr Thomson and the others left the room, convinced that they were once more doomed to disappointment . . .

But they were not. No one ever knew exactly what had happened; perhaps the cable's conducting core had broken under the strain of laying, but reunited on the sea-bed when the tension was relaxed, and the elasticity of the coverings brought the wires together again. In any event, the signals returned at last, and the cable spoke again.

Our joy was so deep and earnest that it did not suffer us to speak for some seconds. But when the first stun of surprise and pleasure passed, each one began trying to express his feelings in some way more or less energetic. Dr Thomson laughed right loud and heartily. Never was more anxiety compressed into such a space. It lasted exactly one hour and a half, but it did not seem to us a third of that time . . .

The ship now began to run into heavy seas, and started to pitch and roll in a manner that put a great strain on the cable.

During Sunday the sea and wind increased, and before the evening it blew a smart gale. Now indeed were the energy and activity of all engaged in the operation tasked to the utmost . . . the engineers durst not let their attention be removed from their occupation for one moment, for on their releasing the brake on the paying-out gear every time the stern of the ship fell into the trough of the sea entirely depended the safety of the cable . . . . Throughout the night, there were few who had the least expectation of the cable holding on till morning, and many remained awake, listening for the sound that all most dreaded to hear – namely, the gun which should announce the failure of all our hopes. But still the cable, which, in comparison with the ship from which it was paid out, and the gigantic waves among which it was delivered, was but a mere thread, continued to hold on, only leaving a silvery phosphorus line upon the stupendous seas as they rolled on towards the ship . . .

Quite apart from the extreme danger to the cable, the need to maintain speed caused the supply of coal to dwindle at an alarming rate. At one time it looked as if it would be necessary to start burning up the spars and planking in a grand finale like the last lap of *Around the World in Eighty Days*. But luckily the gale slowly abated; both the *Agamemnon* and her cable had weathered the storm.

There was a brief flurry of excitement towards the end of the voyage when an inquisitive American barque bore down upon the telegraph fleet as it ploughed along on its predetermined and unalterable course. The escorting *Valorous* had to fire her guns to scare away the interloper, who was doubtless surprised by such a rude reception. Luckily, no international incident resulted from this display of arms, though as *The Times* put it: 'Whether those on board her considered that we were engaged in some filibustering expedition, or regarded our proceedings as another British outrage against the American flag, it was impossible to say; but in great trepidation she remained hove-to until we lost sight of her.' But at last, on the morning of Tuesday, 5 August:

. . . the bold and rocky mountains which entirely surround the wild and pictur-esque neighbourhood of Valentia, rose right before us at a few miles distance. Never, probably, was the sight of land more welcome, as it brought to a success-ful termination one of the greatest, but at the same time, most difficult, schemes which was ever undertaken. Had it been the dullest and most melancholy swamp on the face of the earth that lay before us, we would have found it a pleasant prospect; but as the sun rose from the estuary of Dingle Bay, tingeing with a deep soft purple the lofty summits of the steep mountains which surround its shores, and illuminating the masses of morning vapour which hung upon them, it was a scene which might vie in beauty with anything that could be produced by the most florid imagination of an artist.

No one on shore was apparently conscious of our approach, so the *Valorous* steamed ahead to the mouth of the harbour and fired a gun . . . As soon as the inhabitants became aware of our approach, there was a general desertion of the place, and hundreds of boats crowded around us, their passengers in the greatest state of excitement to hear all about our voyage . . . Soon after our arrival, a signal was received from the *Niagara* that they were preparing to land, having paid out one thousand and thirty nautical miles of cable, while the *Agamemnon* had accomp-lished her portion of the distance with an expenditure of one thousand and twenty miles, making the total length of the wire submerged two thousand and fifty geographical miles . . .

Dr Thomson came into the electrical cabin, evidently in a state of enjoyment so intense as almost to absorb the whole soul and create absence of mind. His countenance beamed with placid satisfaction. He did not speak for a little, but enjoyed himself stretching scraps of sheet gutta-percha over the hot globe of our lamp, watching them with an absent eye as they curled and shrank . . . When we got close inshore we threw off the cable boat. Before her prow grated on the strand her impetus had taken her ashore. The *Valorous*, in the distance, fired her guns. The end was seized by the jolly tars and run off with; a good-humoured scuffle ensued between them and the gentlemen of the island for the honour of pulling the cable up into the office. The Knight of Kerry was upset in the water . . .

Europe and America had at last been linked together. The news of this completely unexpected success, when everyone except a few enthusiasts had been convinced that the enterprise was hopeless, created a sensation. To read the papers of the time, one would think that the millennium had arrived. Even the staid *Times*, not prone to hyperbole, informed its readers: 'The Atlantic is dried up, and we become in reality as well as in wish one country . . . The Atlantic Telegraph has half undone the Declaration of 1776, and has gone far to make us once again, in spite of ourselves, one people . . .'

There were, of course, celebrations all over the United States; countless sermons were preached, many of them based on the Psalmist's verse, 'Their line is gone out through all the earth, and their words to the end of the world.' Inspiring poetry, almost as good as that which can now be produced by any self-respecting electronic computer, was churned out by the yard to fit the occasion. Enthusiasm was sustained despite the long delay in opening the service to the eagerly waiting public; this delay, it was explained, was due to the delicacy of the instruments and the careful adjustment they required.

When a message from Queen Victoria to President Buchanan was received on 16 August further rejoicings and demonstrations broke out, to such effect that the roof of the New York City Hall was ignited by the fireworks and the whole structure was barely saved from the flames. In England, Charles Bright received a knighthood at the early age of twenty-six for his work as chief engineer of the project; in New York, on 1 September, Cyrus Field was given a vast public ovation – at the very moment, ironically enough, when the Atlantic Telegraph had given up the ghost.

For the cable which had been laid with such expense and difficulty, and after so many failures, was slowly dying. Indeed, when one considers the

imperfections in its manufacture, and the various ordeals it had gone
through, it is astonishing that it had ever worked at all.

In his effort to prove that no direct Atlantic line could be an economic
proposition, Colonel Tal Shaffner was later to produce a full transcript of
the 1858 cable's working. It is a record of defeat and frustration – a four-
week history of fading hopes. Even after five days had been allowed for
setting up the receiving and transmitting equipment, this log of all the
messages sent from Newfoundland to Ireland on the whole of the sixth day
speaks for itself:

> 'Repeat, please.'
> 'Please send slower for the present.' 'How?'
> 'How do you receive?'
> 'Send slower.'
> 'Please send slower.'
> 'How do you receive?'
> 'Please say if you can read this.' 'Can you read this?'
> 'Yes.'
> 'How are signals?'
> 'Do you receive?'
> 'Please send something.' 'Please send V's and B's.'
> 'How are signals?'

This, remember, is an entire day's working. It was not until more than a
week after the laying of the cable-ends that the first complete message got
through. Part of the delay was due to the fact that as soon as intelligible
signals were received from Newfoundland on Thomson's mirror galvanometer, Whitehouse at the Valentia end immediately had his patent automatic
recorder switched into the circuit. This instrument functioned adequately
on short lines, but was quite incapable of interpreting the minute and
distorted signals which were trickling through the injured cable.

There was similar confusion over the sending of the signals. Whereas
Thomson wished to use low-voltage batteries to provide power for signalling,
Whitehouse insisted on employing the huge induction or spark coils he had
built, which were five feet long and developed at least 2000 volts. The
use of these coils was to result in a great deal of public controversy when
the cable finally failed, and there can be little doubt that they helped to
break down the faulty insulation.

It was nine days before a single word got through the cable from east to
west, but on the twelfth day (16 August) the line was working well enough
to start transmitting a ninety-nine-word message of greetings from Queen
Victoria to President Buchanan. It took sixteen and a half hours before the
message was completed; it would arrive in America today more quickly by

air mail. The first commercial message ever telegraphed across the Atlantic was sent the next day (17 August) from Newfoundland to Ireland. It is one which we can still fully appreciate: 'Mr Cunard wishes telegraph McIver *Europa* collision *Arabia*. Put into St John's. No lives lost.'

More days went by while the operators struggled to keep in contact and to transmit the messages which were piling up at either end. Sometimes a personal note intruded, as when Newfoundland remarked plaintively to Ireland, 'Mosquitoes keep biting. This is a funny place to live in – fearfully swampy' or when Thomson, no doubt after turning the Valentia office upside-down, was forced to ask Newfoundland: 'Where are the keys of the glass cases and drawers in the apparatus room?' (The helpful answer: 'Don't recollect.')

Finally, after Newfoundland had signalled, 'Pray give some news for New York, they are mad for news,' the first Press dispatch was successfully sent on the twenty-third day (27 August). It is interesting to compare the headlines of 1858 with those of a hundred years later: 'Emperor of France returned to Paris Saturday. King of Prussia too ill to visit Queen Victoria. Her Majesty returns to England 31 August. Settlement of Chinese question. Chinese empire open to trade; Christian religion allowed; foreign diplomatic agents admitted; indemnity to England and France. Gwalior insurgent army broken up. All India becoming tranquil.'

Yes, a lot has happened since that far-off summer. Where are the Emperor of France and the King of Prussia today? And if there had been a United Nations back in 1858, it would have been an indemnity *from* England and France. The final reference in the message is to the Indian Mutiny, which was then nearing its end. It was in connection with the Mutiny that the cable gave a dramatic proof of its value; only a day before it broke down completely it carried orders countermanding the sailing of the 62nd Regiment from Nova Scotia to India, where it was no longer needed. This single message was estimated to have saved the War Office no less than £50,000 – one-seventh of the entire cost of the cable.

The last message passed through the cable at 1.30 p.m. on 1 September; it was, ironically enough, a message to Cyrus Field at the banquet in his honour in New York, asking him to inform the American Government that the company was now in a position to forward its messages to England . . .

Thereafter, all was silence. After their brief union, the continents were once more as far apart as ever. The Atlantic had swallowed up the months of toil, the 2500 tons of cable, the £350,000 of hard-raised capital.

The public reaction was violent, and those who had been most fervent in their praise now seemed ashamed of their earlier enthusiasm. Indeed, it was even suggested that the whole affair had been a fraud of some kind – perhaps a stock manipulation on the part of Cyrus Field. One Boston newspaper asked in a trenchant headline, 'Was it a hoax?' and an English writer proved that the cable had never been laid at all.

What had been hailed as the greatest achievement of the century had collapsed in ruins; it was to be eight long years before Europe and America would speak to each other again across the bed of the ocean.

8

POST-MORTEM

With the failure of the 1858 cable, a third of a million pounds of private capital had been irretrievably sunk into the Atlantic. Within a year, the submarine telegraph engineers had achieved an even more resounding catastrophe. A cable through the Red Sea to India, laid at a cost of £800,000, had also failed completely – and this time it was Government money that was lost. It is not surprising that there was a general public outcry, much correspondence in the London *Times*, and a demand for a commission of inquiry.

The report of this commission, which sat from December 1859 to September 1860, must be one of the more monumental publications of Her Majesty's Stationery Office. Running to over 500 foolscap pages of small print, it is longer than the Bible. Its title is correspondingly impressive: *Report of the Joint Committee appointed by the Lords of the Committee of Privy Council for Trade and the Atlantic Telegraph Company to inquire into the Construction of Submarine Telegraph Cables: together with the Minutes of Evidence and Appendix.*

There is a strange resemblance, across almost a century of time, between the inquiry into the failure of the Atlantic cable and that which took place in 1954 to discover the causes of the disasters to the Comet jet airliners. In each case British engineering prestige was at stake, immense sums had been lost, great hopes had been raised and then dashed to the ground. And it would not be unfair to say that the final verdicts were similar: the daring of the engineers had outrun their knowledge of a new technology.*

The report of the Privy Council, which was issued in April 1861, is not only a summary of the electrical art a hundred years ago; it provides fascinating glimpses of the personalities involved, from the mighty Professor Thomson to the unfortunate Dr Whitehouse, who was widely blamed as chief architect of the disaster. It also contains many proposals for designing or laying submarine cables which are entertainingly absurd, and not a few which were more prophetic than their authors could ever guess.

*The loss of the world's first commercial jet was still very much in the news when *Voice across the Sea* was written. Its impact at the time was similar to that of the *Challenger* disaster, thirty years later.

For example, one Captain Selwyn, RN, wanted to avoid paying out cable from tanks inside the ship (with the attendant risk of kinks and breakages) by having it wound on a large floating drum which would be towed behind a steamer. The drum would revolve in the water as the cable uncoiled, but the committee remarked, 'We have great doubts as to the practicability of this plan.' As far as the open Atlantic was concerned, the committee was quite correct. However, in 1944 just such floating drums were used to lay the underwater pipeline PLUTO (Pipe Line Under The Ocean) through which fuel was pumped across the English Channel to power the invasion of Europe in 1944.

The committee consisted of eight members, four appointed by the Board of Trade and four appointed by the Atlantic Telegraph Company, which thus had one foot in the dock and the other on the judges' bench. But though there was occasional acrimony in the evidence given, there seems to have been no whitewashing; the 1861 report arrived at the facts, and its masses of technical information marked the transition of submarine telegraphy from guesswork to science.

Of the eight men who spent almost a year listening to half a million words of evidence, only one is remembered today. He is Professor Charles Wheatstone, whose contributions to telegraph engineering have already been mentioned. Another of the Board of Trade representatives was George Parker Bidder, famous in his day as a mathematical prodigy. So astonishing were his gifts, indeed, that it is worth reminding ourselves – in this age of electronic computers – that the human brain is still the most remarkable calculating machine in the known universe. Here are a few of Bidder's fully authenticated feats, in case anyone feels like trying to match them.

At the age of nine, he was asked how long it would take to travel 123,256 miles at four miles a minute. He answered 21 days, 9 hours, 34 minutes – taking one minute to do the sum in his head. A year later he graduated to tougher problems; when asked how many times a coach-wheel 5 feet 10 inches in circumference would revolve in running 800,000,000 miles it took him less than a minute to answer: '724,114,285,704 times with twenty inches left over.' The square root of 119,550,669,121 (345,761) took him only thirty seconds.

The interesting thing about Bidder was that, unlike many other lightning calculators, he was an able and intelligent man who became a very distinguished engineer, and was able to give an analysis of the methods he used. He also retained his powers throughout his life; when he was over seventy a friend happened to comment on the enormous number of light vibrations that must hit the eye every second, if there were 36,918 waves of red light in every inch and light travelled at 190,000 miles a second. 'You needn't work that out,' Bidder replied. 'The number is 444,443,651,200,000.'

When the committee presented its report in 1861, no less than 11,364 miles of submarine cable had been laid in various parts of the world – and only 3000 miles were operating. Most of the failures were due to bad design, workmanship or materials, the gutta-percha insulation being the chief cause of trouble. But the people who built the cables were not always to blame, as the farcical misadventures of the line from Sardinia to Algeria amply proved.

This cable was laid in the deepest water yet attempted, and the operation was in the charge of John Brett, the pioneer of the English Channel cable. The French Government provided ships and navigation, and the net result was a superb example (not the last, one is tempted to add) of combined Anglo-French ineptitude.

On the first try, the cable was paid out so rapidly that the length provided was not sufficient for the job; Brett put the blame upon unexpected precipices on the Mediterranean sea-bed, whose presence had not been revealed by the French charts. His skipper remarked outright at the hearings, with a fine display of the Nelson spirit: 'It has been sounded by Frenchmen, and I have no reliance on their soundings.' But the Frenchmen were perfectly correct. The cable had not vanished into unknown abysses – it had merely run off the ship too quickly. Some years later another contractor hauled it up and, as he told the committee: 'We found huge masses of cable all tied together in a sort of Gordian knot, and that must have been one of Mr Brett's precipices.'

On the second attempt, however, French seamanship was undoubtedly to blame for the disaster. Listen to the indignant Mr Brett's own account of the way in which success was missed by the small margin which in such a case meant total failure:

We passed all the great depths with perfect safety in the night, and arrived within ten miles of the land. At daylight in the early break of the morning, I saw the French vessel decorated with flags . . . according to the reckoning of the French captain, we are safe, and should land our cable with some miles to spare. They decorated their vessel as a triumph, and they were drinking champagne . . . Our captain had given us warning in the night that he thought we were drifting very much out of our course. This I communicated to Monsieur de la Marche, the officer appointed by the French Government, and he replied: 'We know what we are doing.' I thought very probably they did. By the next morning our captain said: 'Ask the French captain what his bearings are, to give us the latitude and longitude.' He did so, and it was found to be wrong, and to agree rather with the opinion of our captain . . . I then begged our captain to give his figures, and I told him to get me a large board, and I chalked them up, I think about two feet long, so that there might be no mistake about it. I saw, on the part of the French officers, something like consternation; they retired to the cabin, and went through the calculation. When they returned they said: 'We find that we are wrong and you are right.'

And so Mr Brett was left holding the end of his cable almost within sight of the

African coast, while the chastened Monsieur de la Marche departed to Algiers in search of help:

> I said: 'How long shall you be gone?' He said, 'Five or six days.' The question then, of course, became hopeless; we did the best we could to hold on for five or six days; we took the end of the cable, passed it round the vessel and stopped it so that no strain could come upon it. We sent, among many other messages by the cable, one to London to immediately put in hand from thirty to fifty miles of cable, and send it out to us as rapidly as possible . . . We held on for five days and nights; the last two days there was a very violent strain, and a very heavy sea, the vessel pitching and rolling, but not yet breaking the cable. Most of the young clerks, who were Italians, were sick,* and I was alone on the deck when I saw a message coming in, saying that several miles of cable were in progress, and would be rapidly sent out to us. Within a few minutes afterwards the vessel gave one of the sudden plunges which had been repeated through the night, and the cable broke . . .

After this débâcle, one might have thought that the third attempt would have been conducted with almost excessive care. Yet what happened this time was even more ridiculous; somebody forgot the difference between pounds and kilograms, and as a result the weight controlling the brake on the cable was only half what it should have been. So once again the bed of the Mediterranean was festooned with overlapping coils of expensive cable, and once again the supply ran out a dozen miles from the African coast . . .

Yes, the time was undoubtedly ripe for a Royal Commission and for the replacement of the amateur engineers by professionals with a sound scientific training. Such men did exist – Professor Wheatstone, the Siemens brothers, Latimer Clark, for example – but there were far too few of them. The study of electricity was in such a primitive state that no agreed units existed; although it seems incredible, there was still no way of measuring resistance, voltage or current in quantities which would be understood by everybody. The very meanings of these terms were not generally understood; to most people, even those who worked with it, electricity was still a mysterious and almost occult power, and the way in which words such as 'intensity', 'tension', 'quantity', 'rate', 'velocity' were tossed about only added to the confusion. Voltage was defined in terms of so many Daniell's batteries; current by the deflections of whatever instrument the experimenter happened to be using. Volts, ohms and amps still belonged to the future, and one of the witnesses before the committee felt compelled to remark: 'It is a great pity that those who touch upon this question do not make themselves familiar with the laws of Ohm; it would set aside all those absurd discussions that take place.'

There can be little doubt that the man chiefly responsible for changing submarine cable practice from an esoteric art about as successful as rain-making to an exact mathematical science was William Thomson. Though he

*The immunity of the British to seasickness is, of course, proverbial.

was still a relatively young man when he appeared before the committee, he was already famous and was listened to with great respect. One would like to have heard his Scots burr as he remarked, apropos of a proposal by one inventor to make a cable with the strengthening steel wires on the inside: 'It is about as well planned as an animal with its brains outside its skull.'* And on the unfortunate Dr Whitehouse's patent relay, which was intended to write down the telegraphed messages automatically as they were received, he delivered this annihilating verdict: 'I find altogether two or three words and a few more letters that are legible, but the longest word which I find correctly given is the word "be".' It would have been interesting to see how the Whitehouse relay coped with 'Dampfschiffahrts-gesellschaft' (steamship company), which, one witness complained, with a justifiable sense of grievance, was charged as a single word all over Europe according to telegraphic law.

Dr Whitehouse was, of course, one of the chief witnesses. His appearance must have been somewhat embarrassing to all concerned, for half the board of inquiry consisted of his ex-colleagues whose fortunes and reputations he had been so instrumental in damaging. It says much for Professor Thomson's nobility of spirit (if not for his powers of judgement) that he had attempted to shield Whitehouse from the wrath of the directors when the 1858 cable had failed, by stating that he was one of the company's most loyal and devoted servants. But what the directors thought of 'our late electrician' is made very clear by their reply to Thomson, written on 25 August 1858 – even before the cable had given up the ghost:

> Mr Whitehouse has been engaged some eighteen months in investigations which have cost some £12,000 to the company and now, when we have laid our cable and the whole world is looking on with impatience . . . we are, after all, only saved from being a laughing-stock because the directors are fortunate enough to have an illustrious colleague . . . whose inventions produced in his own study – at small expense – and from his own resources are available to supersede the useless apparatus prepared at great labour and enormous cost . . . Mr White-house has run counter to the wishes of the directors on a great many occasions – disobeyed time after time their positive instructions – thrown obstacles in the way of everyone, and acted in every way as if his own fame and self-importance were the only points of consequence to be considered . . .

Yet despite all that had happened, Whitehouse refused to admit that he had made any mistakes, and threw up an imposing smoke-screen of experimental data to support his theories. He would not agree that his giant induction coils,

*But here, as in the case of the Earth's age, the Professor was quite wrong. The proposal was just a century ahead of its time: some modern cables are made in precisely this manner.

with their thousands of volts, had been responsible for the breakdown of the cable, and put forward complicated arguments to 'prove' that signals produced by his coils could be transmitted more rapidly than those from batteries. He made one good point, however, when he tried to throw some of the blame on to Cyrus Field, who had refused to let him have the time he needed for his preliminary experiments. 'Mr Field,' remarked the Doctor, 'was the most active man in the enterprise, and he had so much steam that he could not wait so long as three months. He said, "Pooh, nonsense, why, the whole thing will be stopped; the scheme will be put back a twelve-month."'

It would have been better for the promoters if the scheme *had* been put back for twelve months. As it was, for lack of preparation it was delayed eight years.

One of the most remarkable, as well as most opinionated, characters to appear before the committee was Admiral Robert Fitzroy, FRS. The Admiral was a scientist of no mean repute, being a pioneer of meteorology and the founder of today's system of weather forecasting. However, what had given him a small but certain lien on immortality was the fact that, twenty years before, Captain Fitzroy had set out from England on one of the most momentous voyages of all time – the five-year cruise of HMS *Beagle*, with a shy young scientist named Charles Darwin aboard. The results of that voyage had been published in three volumes, of which Fitzroy had written the first two and Darwin the last.

His career after that had been somewhat chequered. He had been an unsuccessful Governor of New Zealand, infuriating the colonists by supporting the rights of the natives.* Tact was not his strong point, and at one time he even became embroiled in fisticuffs outside a London club; luckily his assaults on his gentle ex-colleague Darwin, whose Evolutionary theory he hated, were purely verbal. Perhaps his brilliant but unbalanced temperament was due to his somewhat unusual ancestry: he was a direct descendant of Charles II and the rapacious royal mistress Barbara Villiers, Duchess of Cleveland. (She could be tactless as well as rapacious; it once took all Charles's powers of persuasion to stop her combining his honeymoon with her confinement.)

Only five years in the future, Admiral Fitzroy was to kill himself in a fit of depression; but there was no sign of any uncertainty or lack of confidence as he threw off his ideas about insulators, the best routes for Atlantic cables, and methods of taking deep-sea temperatures. He wanted to coat the cable not with gutta-percha but with a flexible form of glass or 'vitreous substance' –

*See Hilaire Belloc's advice to the youngest scions of British aristocracy: 'When all else fails, Go off and govern New South Wales.' Which is exactly how the Admiralty's Sea Lords disposed of another difficult colleague – Captain Bligh. The result – surprise, surprise – his *third* mutiny.

a suggestion which had also been made by the Prince Consort. The Admiral pointed out that when it is immersed in water, glass is a much more pliable and manageable substance than when it is in air, and mentioned the extraordinary fact – which no one will believe until they try the experiment for themselves – that a sheet of glass held under water can be cut with an ordinary pair of scissors. Just how this would help submarine cables, Admiral Fitzroy did not explain. He also ventured to *dissent entirely* (his italics) from the theory of *circuits formerly held generally*, and had the novel idea that there was no need for excessive care in making perfect joints when sections of cable were united. He thought that a simple snap-joint like that on a watch-chain would be sufficient, and that the elaborate cleaning and soldering indulged in by electrical engineers was unnecessary.

Admirals, engineers, business men, cable contractors, scientists – for weeks and months they gave their views and experiences to the committee, while the Board of Trade clerks toiled to take down the hundreds of thousands of words of evidence. And then, of all the unexpected people to turn up in Whitehall, there arrived a colonel from Kentucky with a proposal that must have given the Atlantic Telegraph Company some anxious moments.

Colonel Tal P. Shaffner had built many of the first long-distance telegraphs in the United States, including, to use his own words, one 'from the Mississippi river to the western borders of civilisation'. ('That was through Kansas?' 'Yes, it was before Kansas was settled; it was at that time all occupied by Indians.')

The Colonel did not believe that a direct transatlantic cable was an economic proposition, and produced the complete transcript of all the messages passed through the 1858 line to prove his theory. In each direction, the cable had managed no more than a hundred words *per day* – and very few of those words had formed commercial messages, most of them being operating instructions or desperate attempts to find what was going wrong. ('Can you read this?' etc., etc.) According to Shaffner's calculations, a 2000-mile-long submarine cable could never hope to pay for itself; even if it was in good electrical condition, it would be too slow to be of practical value.

Colonel Shaffner's alternative was to have a North Atlantic cable routed from Scotland to the Faeroes, thence to Iceland, thence to Greenland, and finally to Labrador. The greatest length of submerged cable would then be no more than 600 miles, and as all messages would be relayed from the intermediate land stations as quickly as they were received, this 600-mile section would determine the maximum working speed. It would be, as it were, the weakest link in the electrical chain; even so, it would be far superior to a continuous 2000-mile length, for theory indicated that it would be about ten times as fast.

The Colonel had spent a lot of time and money promoting his scheme, had carried out a survey of the route, and had obtained a concession from Denmark for the Faeroes–Iceland–Greenland section of the proposed line. He had done this as early as 1854, and must therefore have been one of the very first men to realise the possibilities of transatlantic telegraphy. But though his scheme appeared attractive on paper, it involved building over-land lines across some of the most desolate regions of the world, and laying submarine cables in waters infested with icebergs. Admiral Sir James Ross, perhaps the greatest polar expert of the day, spoke out strongly against the dangers of drifting ice, and concluded that the direct southern route would be much safer and easier.

If the direct Ireland–Newfoundland route had not eventually succeeded, it seems possible that Colonel Shaffner's scheme might have been tried; indeed, today there is a cable from Scotland to Iceland via the Faeroes, though it has never been continued to Greenland. It turned out that the Colonel underestimated the ability of the submarine engineers and was misled into thinking that *all* 2000-mile-long cables would perform as badly as the first. He was wrong; there was no need to use Greenland and Iceland as stepping-stones, and the gentleman from Kentucky lost his million-dollar gamble.*

Perhaps the most poignant evidence given to the committee was the account of Mr Saward, secretary of the Atlantic Telegraph Company, of his efforts to obtain the £600,000 needed to lay a new cable. He reported sadly:

> I myself have personally waited upon nearly every capitalist and mercantile house of standing in Glasgow and in Liverpool, and some of the directors have gone round with me in London for the same purpose. We have no doubt in-duced a great many persons to subscribe, but they do so as they would to a charity, and in sums of corresponding amount . . .

But the tide was slowly turning. Now that all the evidence had been aired and all the experts had given their opinions, the reasons for the earlier failures were apparent, and it was also clear how they could be avoided. The committee summarised its Herculean labours as follows:

> The failures of the existing submarine lines which we have described have been due to causes which might have been guarded against had adequate preliminary investigation been made into the question. And we are convinced that if regard be had to the principles we have enunciated in devising, manufacturing, laying

*Western Union (see Chapter 11) lost an even bigger one.

and maintaining submarine cables, this class of enterprise may prove as successful as it has hitherto been disastrous.

In other words: we've learned from our mistakes; now we can do the job. It was true enough; but success still lay five years in the future – and at the far side of yet another catastrophe.

9

THE BRINK OF SUCCESS

The first problem was to raise the money. It has been said that nothing is so nervous as a million dollars, and more than that had already disappeared into the Atlantic. Despite the technical evidence, and the fact that improved cables were now being laid in other parts of the world, Cyrus Field now had an exhausting battle before him. Between 1861 and 1864 he was continually travelling between England and America, trying to convince capitalists that next time there would be no failure. His success in his own country is summed up in this passage from his brother Henry's biography of him:

> The summer of that year (1862) Mr. Field spent in America, where he applied himself vigorously to raising capital for the new enterprise. He was honoured with the attendance of a large array of the solid men of Boston, who listened with an attention that was most flattering . . . there was no mistaking the interest they felt in the subject. They went still further; they passed a series of resolutions in which they applauded the projected telegraph across the ocean as one of the grandest enterprises ever undertaken by man, which they proudly commended to the confidence and support of the American public. But not a man subscribed a dollar.

In all fairness, it must be remembered that American big business now had some excuse for its lack of enterprise. The Civil War was raging and a country divided in twain had little energy or spirit for such a project. Moreover, relations between England and the North were still strained by the declaration of neutrality of 14 May 1861, in which the Confederacy had been granted the belligerent rights accorded to a sovereign nation. All Field's tact and remarkable powers of persuasion must have been exercised to the full as he shuttled back and forth across the Atlantic at a rate that would be notable even in these days of air transportation. By 1864, indeed, he had crossed the Atlantic no less than thirty-one times in the service of the company!

It took more than two years to get things moving again, and this time the project was largely financed and wholly carried out by Britain, only about a tenth of the capital coming from the United States. On 7 April 1864, the two contractors who between them had the greatest experience of submarine cable manufacture merged into a single company. Until that date cable core and insulation had been manufactured exclusively by the Gutta Percha Company, and the protective armouring had been largely made by Messrs Glass, Elliott & Co. They now formed the Telegraph Construction and Maintenance Company, which still exists and which, with its associates, has now made most of the submarine cables in the world.

The directors of the new firm, under their chairman John Pender, MP, were so confident of success that they immediately subscribed £315,000 of capital. Field himself had been responsible for raising no less than £285,000 from private investors, and with £600,000 in the bank the great project could now be started once again.

The next problem was to decide the design of the new cable. This time there was no headlong rush to get it manufactured and laid before proper tests had been carried out; everyone knew what that policy had cost. Scores of samples were examined and submitted to every conceivable electrical and mechanical ordeal; the design finally approved had a conducting core three times as large as the 1858 cable, and was much more heavily armoured. It could stand a breaking strain of eight tons, compared with only three for the previous cable, and was over an inch in diameter. Though it weighed one and three-quarter tons per mile, and was thus almost twice as heavy as its ill-fated predecessor, its weight when submerged in water was considerably less. This meant that the strain it would have to bear when being laid was also reduced, owing to the increased buoyancy. Indeed, ten miles of it could hang vertically in water before it would snap under its own weight; this was four times as great a length as could ever be suspended from a cable ship sailing across the North Atlantic, where there could never be more than two and a half miles of water beneath the keel. In every respect, the new cable was a vast improvement over any that had been built before. And yet, despite all the thought, skill and care that had gone into its construction, hidden within it were the seeds of future disaster.

By the end of May 1865, the 2600 miles of cable had been completed. Its weight was 7000 tons – twice that of the earlier cable which had required two ships to lay it. But this time, by one of history's fortunate accidents, the only ship in the world that could carry such a load was unemployed and looking for a job. In the Atlantic cable, the fabulous *Great Eastern* met her destiny and at last achieved the triumph which she had so long been denied.

This magnificent but unlucky ship had been launched seven years before, but had never been a commercial success. This was partly due to the stupidity of her owners, partly to the machinations of John Scott Russell, her brilliant but unscrupulous builder, and partly to sheer accidents of storm and sea.*

*James Dugan's book *The Great Iron Ship* is a valuable and highly entertaining history of this wonderful vessel, but unfortunately repeats the legend that the skeleton of a riveter was found inside her double hull when she was broken up. This story is much too good to be true, and isn't.

Seven hundred feet long, with a displacement of 32,000 tons, the *Great Eastern* was not exceeded in size until the *Lusitania* was launched in 1906, forty-eight years later. She was the brain-child of Isambard Kingdom Brunel, the greatest engineering genius of the Victorian era – perhaps, indeed, the only man in the last 500 years to come within hailing distance of Leonardo da Vinci. Brunel built magnificent stone and iron bridges which are standing to this day (the Clifton Suspension Bridge at Bristol is his most famous, though it was completed after his death) and threw superbly landscaped railways over most of southern England. He was as much an artist as an engineer, and the remorseless specialisation that has taken place since his day makes it impossible that any one man will ever again match the range of his achievements.

Of these, the *Great Eastern* was his last and mightiest. Though she was *five times* the size of any other ship in the world, she was no mere example – as some have suggested – of engineering megalomania. Brunel was the first man to grasp the fact that the larger a ship, the more efficient she can be, because carrying capacity increases at a more rapid rate than the power needed to drive the hull through the water (the first depending on the cube of the linear dimensions, the second only on the square). Having realised this, Brunel then had the courage to follow the mathematics to its logical conclusion, and designed a ship that would be large enough to carry enough coal for the round trip to Australia. (Little more than a decade before, learned theoreticians had 'proved' that it was impossible for a steam-driven vessel even to cross the Atlantic.)

With her five funnels, six masts, and superb lines, the *Great Eastern* still remains one of the most beautiful ships ever built, though the absence of a superstructure makes her look a little strange to modern eyes. It is impossible to write of her without using superlatives; her fifty-eight-foot diameter paddle-wheels and twenty-four-foot screw have never been exceeded in size, and now never will be. This dual propulsion system made her the most manoeuvrable ocean liner ever built; by throwing one wheel into reverse, she could rotate around her own axis as if standing on a turntable.

By 1865, the *Great Eastern* had bankrupted a succession of owners and had lost well over £1,000,000. Put up for auction without reserve, the floating white elephant was knocked down for a mere £25,000 – about a thirtieth of her original cost. The buyers, headed by Daniel Gooch, chairman of the Great Western Railway, had already arranged with Cyrus Field to use the ship for laying the new cables; they were so confident that she could do it that they had offered her services free of charge in the event of failure.

To provide storage space for the huge coils of wire, three great tanks were carved into the heart of the ship. The drums, sheaves and dynamometers of the laying mechanism occupied a large part of the stern decking, and one funnel with its associated boilers had been removed to give additional storage space. When the ship sailed from the Medway on 24 June 1865 she carried 7000 tons of cable, 8000 tons of coal and provisions for 500 men. Since this was before the days of refrigeration, she also became a sea-going farm. Her passenger list included one cow, a dozen oxen, twenty pigs, 120 sheep and a whole poultry-yard of fowl.

Many of the pioneers – one might say survivors – of the earlier expeditions were aboard. Among them were Field himself (the only American among 500 Britishers), Professor Thomson, Samuel Canning, chief engineer of the Telegraph Construction and Maintenance Company, and C. W. de Sauty, the company's electrician. Commander of the ship was Captain James Anderson, but in all matters relating to the cable-laying Canning had supreme authority. Dr Whitehouse was not aboard, even as a passenger.

The division of duties and responsibility on the voyage was somewhat unusual. The Atlantic Telegraph Company – represented primarily by Field, with Thomson as his expert adviser – was the customer for the job, but as the Telegraph Construction and Maintenance Company had put up more than half the capital, made the cable, and chartered the ship, it was not going to let its client interfere with the actual laying operations. So Field and Thomson were virtually passengers – though if the work did not come up to the specifications they had laid down they had, of course, the right to refuse it.

This time, with all the cable for the entire job in a single ship, there was no problem of splicing in mid-Atlantic; the *Great Eastern* would sail straight from Ireland to Newfoundland. Thanks to the presence on board of W. H. Russell (later to become Sir William), the famous war correspondent of the London *Times*, we have a complete record of the voyage, which was later published in a splendidly illustrated volume with lithographs by Robert Dudley.

The shore-end of the cable was landed at Foilhommerum Bay, a wild and desolate little cove five miles from Valentia Harbour. Hundreds of people had gathered to watch on the surrounding hills, which were dominated by the ruins of a Cromwellian fort. The scene was like a country fair, with pedlars and entertainers of all kinds making the most of the occasion. Nothing so exciting had ever happened before in this remote part of Ireland – but the crowds were disappointed in their hope of seeing the *Great Eastern*. There was no need, nor was it safe, for her to come inshore. She lay far out to sea while HMS *Caroline* brought the immensely heavy shore-end of the cable up to the coast and landed it over a bridge of boats.

The shore-end was spliced aboard the *Great Eastern*, and on the evening of 23 July 1865 she turned her bows towards her distant goal. The escorting warships *Terrible* and *Sphinx*,

> which had ranged up alongside, and sent their crew up into the shrouds and up to the tops to give her a parting cheer, delivered their friendly broadsides with vigour, and received a similar greeting. Their colours were hauled down, and as the sun set a broad stream of golden light was thrown across the smooth billows towards the bows as if to indicate and illumine the path marked out by the hand of Heaven. The brake was eased, and as the *Great Eastern* moved ahead the machinery on the paying-out apparatus began to work, drums rolled, wheels whirled, and out spun the black line of the cable, and dipped in a graceful curve into the sea over the stern wheel.

As Russell remarked, 'happy is the cable-laying that has no history'. This laying was to have altogether too much. The next morning, eighty-four miles out, the testing instruments indicated an electrical fault at some distance from the ship. There was nothing to do but haul the cable aboard until the trouble was found. At first sight, this would seem to be a fairly straightforward operation. But with the *Great Eastern* as she was now fitted out, it was not anything of the sort. She could not move backwards and pick up the cable over the stern, where it was paying out, because she would not steer properly in reverse and there was also the danger of the cable fouling her screw. So the cable had to be secured by wire tackle, cut, and transferred the 700 feet to the bow. As Russell describes it:

> Then began an orderly tumult of men with stoppers and guy ropes along the bulwarks, and in the shrouds, and over the boats, from stem to stern, as length after length of the wire rope flew out after the cable. The men were skilful at their work, but as they clamoured and clambered along the sides, and over the boats, and round the paddle-boxes, hauling at hawsers, and slipping bights, and holding on and letting go stoppers, the sense of risk and fear for the cable could not be got out of one's head.

It took ten hours to haul in as many miles of cable. When the fault was discovered, it was a very disturbing one. A piece of iron wire, two inches long, had been driven right through the cable, producing a short circuit between the conducting core and the sea. It might have been an accident; but it looked very much like sabotage.

A new splice was made and paying-out started again. This time only half a mile had gone overboard before the cable went dead. Russell remarked despairingly:

> Such a Penelope's web in twenty-four hours, all out of this single thread, was surely disheartening. The cable in the fore and main tanks answered to the tests most perfectly. But that cable which went seaward was sullen, and broke not its sulky silence. Even the gentle equanimity and confidence of Mr. Field were shaken in

that supreme hour, and in his heart he may have sheltered the thought that the dream of his life was indeed but a chimaera . . .

Luckily, the fault cleared itself; almost certainly it did not lie in the cable, but in the instruments or connections either at Valentia or aboard the ship. 'The index light suddenly reappeared on its path in the testing room, and the wearied watchers were gladdened by the lighting of the beacon of hope once more.'

On the fourth day, 26 July, the *Great Eastern* ran into heavy seas which made it hard for the *Sphinx* and the *Terrible* to keep up with her. As she forged ahead at a steady six knots, hardly affected by the waves which battered her little escorts, the *Sphinx* slowly dropped astern and at last disappeared from view. This was a serious loss to the expedition, because owing to some oversight the *Sphinx* carried the only set of sounding gear.

The next two days were uneventful, and those aboard were able to relax. The literary gentlemen produced a ship's newspaper containing local news and gossip, and it would be hard to improve on this standard of reporting:

> Professor Thomson gave a lecture on 'Electric Continuity' before a select audience. The learned gentleman having arranged his apparatus, the chief object of which was a small brass pot, looking like a small lantern with a long wick sticking out at the top, spoke as follows: 'The lecture which I am about to give is on a subject which has ever been of great interest to the intellectual portions of mankind, and –' The luncheon bell ringing, the learned Professor was left speaking.

For all his erudition, Professor Thomson did not overawe his colleagues and they seem to have looked upon him with affection as well as respect. One of them remarked later: 'He was a thoroughly good comrade . . . he was also a good partner at whist when work wasn't on, though sometimes, when momentarily immersed in cogibundity of cogitation, by scientific abstraction, he would look up from his cards and ask "Wha played what?"'

As the *Great Eastern* ploughed on across the waves, spinning out her iron-and-copper thread,

> there was a wonderful sense of power in the Great Ship and in her work; it was gratifying to human pride to feel that man was mastering space, and triumphing over the wind and waves; that from his hands down into the eternal night of waters there was trailing a slender channel through which the obedient lightning would flash for ever instinct with the sympathies, passions and interests of two mighty nations.

On the afternoon of the seventh day, when 800 miles had been paid out, the alarms went again. The fault was close to the ship, so once more the cable was cut, secured by wire ropes, and hauled round to the bow for picking up.

Thousands of fathoms down we knew the end of the cable was dragging along the bottom, fiercely tugged at by the *Great Eastern* through its iron line. If line or cable parted, down sank the cable for ever . . . At last our minds were set at rest; the iron rope was coming in over the bows through the picking-up machinery. In due, but in weary time, the end of the cable appeared above the surface, and was hauled on board and passed aft towards the drum. The stern is on these occasions deserted; the clack of wheels, before so active, ceases; and the forward part of the vessel is crowded with those engaged on the work, and with those who have only to look on . . . the two eccentric-looking engines working the pickup drums and wheels make as much noise as possible . . . and all is life and bustle forward, as with slow unequal straining the cable is dragged up from its watery bed.

It required nineteen hours of this nervous work before the fault was reached – though it would have taken only a few minutes if suitable equipment had been installed at the stern. The cable was respliced, paying-out commenced once more, and a committee of inquiry started to examine the faulty coils piled on deck.

Concern changed to anger when it was found that the cable had been damaged in precisely the same manner as before, by a piece of wire forced into it. 'No man who saw it could doubt that the wire had been driven in by a skilful hand,' Russell comments, and it was pointed out that the same gang of workmen had been on duty when the earlier fault occurred. The sabotage theory seemed virtually proved, and a team of inspectors was at once formed so that there would always be someone in the cable tank to keep an eye on the workmen.

On the morning of 2 August, the *Great Eastern* had completed almost three-quarters of her task. Back at Valentia, the electricians were receiving perfect signals along the 1300 miles of cable that had been paid out. They could even tell, by the gentle wavering of the galvanometer light-spot, exactly when the ship rolled, for minute currents were induced in the cable by the field of the 32,000-ton magnet as it swung back and forth on the face of the sea.

And then, without any warning, the signals stopped. The hours passed, and still no messages came along that thin thread leading out into the Atlantic. The hours grew into days; a week passed – then two. The *Great Eastern* and her escorts had vanished from human knowledge as completely as if the ocean had swallowed them up.

10

HEART'S CONTENT

In England, the total disappearance of the telegraph fleet caused a storm of controversy and speculation. The *Great Eastern*, said the Jeremiahs, had probably broken her back on an Atlantic roller and gone down with all hands; she had been badly designed, anyway. (It was safe to say this, since Brunel had been in his grave for six years.) Arguments and counter-arguments raged in *The Times*, and in the midst of these the Atlantic Telegraph Company called an extraordinary general meeting. They announced not only their complete confidence in the cable that was now being laid, but stated that they would soon be asking for capital to make a second cable. It was an act of extreme courage, and it was fully justified. Far out in the Atlantic the men of the *Great Eastern* were now proving that they would never accept defeat.

Cyrus Field had been one of the watchers on duty in the cable tank on the morning of 2 August. About 6 a.m. there was a grating noise and one of the workmen yelled: 'There goes a piece of wire!' Field shouted a warning, but it did not reach the officer at the paying-out gear quickly enough. Before the ship could be stopped, the fault had gone overboard.

This time, it was not a complete short circuit; the cable was usable, but no longer up to specification. Though Professor Thomson thought it could still transmit four words a minute – which would be enough to make it pay its way – Chief Engineer Canning decided not to take a risk. If he completed the cable, and the customer refused to accept it, his company would be ruined. In any case, picking up a faulty section of cable was now a routine matter; the men had had plenty of practice on this trip. Canning had no reason to doubt that, after a few hours' delay, the *Great Eastern* could continue on the last 700 miles of her journey. The cable was cut, taken round to the bows, and the hauling-up process began again. While this was going on, one of the workmen in the tank discovered some broken armouring wires on the piece of cable which had been lying immediately below the faulty section; the iron was brittle, and had snapped under the tremendous weight of the coils above it. This, said Russell, 'gave a new turn to men's thoughts at once. What we had taken for assassination might have been suicide!'

The *Great Eastern* was now over waters 2000 fathoms deep, though the exact depth was not known owing to the absence of the *Sphinx* with the only set of sounding gear. Unfortunately, she had neglected to signal Ireland that the cable was about to be cut; if this elementary precaution had been taken, much of the anxiety felt in England during the next two weeks would have been prevented.

From the start, the picking-up process failed to go smoothly. First the machinery gave trouble, then the wind made the *Great Eastern* veer round so that the cable did not come straight over the sheaves. It started to chafe against the ship, and when the picking-up machinery began to work once more, the strain on the cable proved too great for the weakened portion. 'The cable parted . . . and with one bound flashed into the sea . . . There around us lay the placid Atlantic, smiling in the sun, and not a dimple to show where lay so many hopes buried.'

Now began a lonely mid-ocean battle which was to fire the imagination, and excite the admiration, of the world. Samuel Canning, despite the fact that the *Great Eastern* was not fitted with suitable gear, decided to fish for the cable two and a half miles down in the Atlantic ooze. His men had grappled successfully for cables 700 fathoms down in the Mediterranean, but the depth here was three times as great. Even if the cable could be hooked, many doubted if it could stand the strain of being dragged up from such an abyss.

A five-pronged grapnel – 'the hook with which the giant Despair was going to fish for a take worth more than a million' – was attached to five miles of wire rope, and lowered over the side. It took more than two hours to sink to the sea-bed, but at last the slackening of the strain showed that it had hit bottom. The *Great Eastern*, which had steamed several miles into the wind, now shut off her engines and drifted under sail alone: 'the biggest sailing-ship the world will ever see', as Dugan points out. All that night she moved silently downwind, the grapnel far below dragging through the deeper night of the ocean bed. Early on the morning of 3 August the hooks caught in something, and then began the nerve-racking business of hauling in the great fishing-line with its unknown catch.

The grapnel-rope was most unsuitable for the work it was doing (and which no one had ever imagined would be necessary) because it was not in one continuous length but was made up of two dozen sections each 600 feet long, joined together by shackles. These were the weak points of the rope, for when about a mile of it had been drawn in over the bows a shackle parted and rope, grapnel and the cable it had undoubtedly hooked fell back to the sea-bed.

To add to Canning's difficulties, fog settled down and it was impossible to take any observations which would fix the ship's position. However, at noon on 4 August the sun providentially broke through, a sight was taken, and it was found that the ship was forty-six miles from the point where the cable had parted. A large buoy was improvised and dropped overboard, anchored to the

sea-bed by three miles of the cable itself. Now the *Great Eastern* had a fixed
point from which she could work – a signpost in mid-Atlantic, as it were.

No grappling was possible for the next two days owing to an unfavourable
wind, but on 7 August Canning made his second try. It was a repeat of the
earlier performance; the cable was hooked quickly enough, brought half-way
to the surface – and another shackle parted under the strain.

After this mishap, there was not enough wire left on board to reach the
bottom, so 700 fathoms of rope was spliced on to make an improvised line. Bad
weather and high seas held up operations until the 10th; then the grapnel
went overboard, appeared to hook something, but came up too easily. When
it was hauled on deck, it was found that the line had twisted round one of the
flukes, effectively preventing the grapnel from doing its job.

The fourth attempt was made the next day, and on the afternoon of
11 August the cable was hooked again.

> It was too much [wrote Russell] to stand by and witness the terrible struggle
> between the hawser, which was coming in fast, the relentless iron-clad capstan, and
> the fierce resolute power of the black sea . . . But it was beyond peradventure that
> the Atlantic Cable had been hooked and struck, and was coming up from its oozy
> bed. What alternations of hopes and fears! Some remained below in the saloons,
> fastened their eyes on unread pages of books, or gave expression to their feelings in
> fitful notes upon piano or violin . . . None liked to go forward, where every jar of the
> machinery made their hearts leap into their mouths . . .

It was dark and raw that evening, and after dinner Russell left the saloon and
walked up and down the deck under the shelter of the paddle-box.

> I was going forward when the whistle blew, and I heard cries of 'Stop it!' in the bows,
> shouts of 'Look out!' and agitated exclamations. Then there was silence. I knew at
> once that all was over. The machines stood still on the bows, and for a moment every
> man was fixed, as if turned to stone. Our last bolt was sped. The hawser had
> snapped, and nigh two miles more of iron coils and wire were added to the
> entanglement of the great labyrinth made by the *Great Eastern* in the bed of the
> ocean.
>
>   There was a profound silence on board the Big Ship. She struggled against the
> helm for a moment as though she still yearned to pursue her course to the west, then
> bowed to the angry sea in admission of defeat, and moved slowly to meet the rising
> sun. The signal lanterns flashed from the *Terrible* 'Farewell!' The lights from our
> paddle-box pierced the night 'Good-bye! Thank you' in sad acknowledgement.
> Then each sped on her way in solitude and darkness.

The 1865 expedition had been yet another failure – but with a difference. It
had proved so many important points that there could no longer be any
reasonable doubt that a transatlantic cable could be laid. The *Great Eastern*
had demonstrated, through her stability and handling qualities, that she was

the perfect ship for the task; the cable itself was excellent, apart from the brittle armouring which could easily be improved – and, most important of all, it had been shown that a lost cable could be found and lifted in water more than two miles deep. In a sense, therefore, the very failure engendered new confidence. Even so, one feels an admiration almost approaching awe for Cyrus Field and his partners as one considers their next step. They decided not merely to build and lay a completely new cable; when they had done that, they would go back and finish the one they had now three-quarters laid.

To circumvent some legal difficulties unsportingly raised by the Attorney-General on Christmas Eve, it was necessary to float a new company; it was also necessary to raise another £600,000. By early 1866, Field, assisted by Daniel Gooch and Richard Glass (managing director of the Telegraph Construction and Maintenance Company), had succeeded in doing this, and it is a tribute to the confidence that the public now had in them that when they needed £370,000 to make up the necessary capital of the new-born Anglo-American Telegraph Company it was subscribed in two weeks.

One thousand, nine hundred and ninety miles of fresh cable was at once ordered, incorporating various improvements over that used in the previous year. It was slightly stronger, yet lighter when submerged; more important, the brittle armouring had been replaced by a more ductile variety made from galvanised iron.

The arrangements aboard the *Great Eastern* had also been greatly improved. Machinery which could haul in the cable at the stern, so that it had no longer to be transferred to the bows, was the most important innovation. A method of continuous electrical testing had been devised, so that it was now impossible for several miles of cable to be paid out before a fault was detected. No less than twenty miles of wire rope, capable of standing a thirty-ton strain, was made to replace the inadequate grappling-line lost in mid-Atlantic. And the *Great Eastern* herself was given a much-needed spring cleaning, for 'her hull was encrusted with mussels and barnacles two feet thick, and long seaweed flaunted her sides'. The removal of these hundreds of tons of marine growths must have added a couple of knots to her speed, and as the paddles had now been arranged to reverse independently, Samuel Canning had a vastly improved and more manoeuvrable cable-ship under his command when he set out from the Thames on 30 June 1866.

This time, the Admiralty had been able to lend only one ship – HMS *Terrible* – but the telegraph fleet was larger than last year as the company had chartered the *Albany* and *Medway*. The latter carried several hundred miles of last year's cable, as well as 100 miles of heavy shallow-water cable to lay across the St Lawrence.

As Sir W. H. Russell was now playing his more accustomed role of war correspondent, we have to rely on other journalists for an account of this trip.

According to the *London News*, when the massive shore-end of the cable –
weighing eight tons to the mile and looking like an iron bar – was landed at
Valentia over a pontoon bridge of forty fishing boats,

> the ceremony presented a striking difference to that of last year. Earnest gravity and
> a deep-seated determination to repress all show of the enthusiasm of which
> everyone was full, was very manifest . . . There was something far more touching in
> the quiet and reverent solemnity of the spectators than in the slightly boisterous
> joviality of the peasantry last year . . . The old crones in tattered garments who
> cowered together, dudheen [clay-pipe] in mouth, their gaudy shawls tightly drawn
> over head and under the chin – the barefoot boys and girls – the patches of bright
> colour furnished by the red petticoats and cloaks – the ragged garments, only kept
> from falling to pieces by bits of string and tape . . .

Such were the inhabitants of this poverty-stricken region; one can understand
their interest in the magic wire which led to the land where so many of their
countrymen had gone in search of a better life.

Thirty miles out from land, the *Great Eastern* was waiting for the special
section of heavy shore-cable, designed to resist both angry seas and dragging
anchors, to be brought out to her. When the end was lifted aboard,

> quick, nimble hands tore off the covering from a foot of the shore-end and of the
> main cable, till they came to the core; then, swiftly unwinding the copper wires,
> they laid them together, twining them as closely and carefully as a silken braid.
> Then this delicate child of the sea was wrapped in swaddling clothes, covered up
> with many coatings of gutta-percha, and hempen rope, and strong iron wire, the
> whole bound round and round with heavy bands, and the splicing was complete.

And so on Friday, 13 July 1866, the *Great Eastern* sailed again from Valentia
Bay. Those who disliked the date were reminded that Columbus sailed for the
New World on a Friday – and also arrived on one.

At a steady and uneventful five knots, Brunel's masterpiece plodded across
the Atlantic, paying out the cable with clockwork regularity. The only incident
on the entire fourteen days of the voyage was when the cable running out from
the tank caught in an adjacent coil, and there was a tangle which caused a few
anxious moments before it was straightened out.

In England, where the progress of the expedition was known at every
minute, excitement and confidence mounted day by day. In the United
States, however, it was different, for there was no news of what was
happening, nor could there be until the ships actually arrived – if they did.
Some spectators were waiting hopefully in Newfoundland, but, as Henry
Field remarks,

> not so many as the last year, for the memory of their disappointment was too fresh,
> and they feared the same result again.

But still a faithful few were there who kept their daily watch . . . it is Friday morning, the 27th July. They are up early and looking eastwards to see the day break, when a ship is seen in the offing. Spy-glasses are turned towards her. She comes nearer – and look, there is another and another. And now the hull of the *Great Eastern* looms all glorious in that morning sky. They are coming! Instantly all is wild excitement. The *Albany* is the first to round the point and enter the bay. The *Terrible* is close behind. The *Medway* stops an hour or two to join on the heavy shore-end, while the *Great Eastern*, gliding calmly in as if she had done nothing remarkable, drops her anchor in front of the telegraph house, having trailed behind her a chain of two thousand miles, to bind the old world to the new.

No name could be more appropriate than that of the landing-place – Heart's Content. It was

a sheltered nook where ships may ride at anchor safe from the storms of the ocean. It is but an inlet from the great arm of the sea known as Trinity Bay, which is sixty or seventy miles long, and twenty miles broad. (The old landing of 1858 was at the Bay of Bull's Arm, at the head of Trinity Bay, twenty miles above.)

Heart's Content was chosen now because its waters are still and deep, so that a cable skirting the north side of the Banks of Newfoundland can be brought in deep water almost till it touches the shore. All around the land rises to pine-crested heights; and here the telegraph fleet, after its memorable journey, lay in quiet, under the shadow of the encircling hills.

As soon as the *Great Eastern* was anchored, Captain Anderson and his officers went ashore and attended a service in the local church, where the preacher, not very tactfully, addressed them on the text 'There shall be no more sea'. (An edict, according to Kipling's 'The Last Chantey', which caused such a protest in heaven that it had to be rescinded:

> To the Glory of the Lord
> Who heard the silly sailor-folk and gave them back their sea!)

The triumph was marred by a slight annoyance: the St Lawrence cable had been broken, and so there was a delay of two days before the telegraph connection could be completed to the United States. It was not until the morning of Sunday, 27 July, that New York received the message: 'Heart's Content, July 27. We arrived here at 9 o'clock this morning. All well. Thank God, the cable is laid and in perfect working order. Cyrus W. Field.'

On the first day of operation, the new cable earned £1000. At last the sea was giving back the fortunes it had swallowed. Field was thankful, but he had not yet attained his own Heart's Content. There was still one more job to be done; neither he nor the men of the *Great Eastern* could rest while out there in the Atlantic, 700 miles away, the broken end of last summer's cable lay in the icy darkness beneath its tangle of grappling-irons.

11

BATTLE ON THE SEA-BED

So eager was the telegraph fleet to resume its battle with the Atlantic that the *Albany* and *Terrible* left Newfoundland almost immediately, and were back in mid-ocean within five days. It took a little longer to get the *Great Eastern* ready for sea again; 600 miles of the 1865 cable and several thousand tons of coal had to be loaded aboard. The cable had come over in the *Medway*, the coal in a small fleet of colliers sent from England, one of which had foundered on the way.

On 9 August the *Great Eastern* and the *Medway* put to sea again, making a rendezvous with the *Albany* and *Terrible* three days later. The two ships had already marked the line of the lost cable with buoys and then, 'like giant sea-birds with folded wings, sat watching their prey'. The *Albany* had made a brave attempt to lift the cable with her own gear, and had indeed succeeded in hooking it and bringing it some way to the surface before it slipped back into the depths again.

The *Great Eastern* stood off a few miles from the line of buoys and lowered her grapnel on its two-inch-thick wire rope. When it had reached the bottom, she started to drift downwind towards the buoys, in the expectation that, after one or two sweeps, the cable would be hooked. But it was not as easy as that. Again and again the *Great Eastern* drifted back and forth without result. Sometimes Cyrus Field would go to the bow, sit on the rope, and tell by its vibrations that the grapnel was dragging on the sea-bed two miles below. The ocean floor

> proved to be generally ooze, a soft slime. When the rope went down, one or two hundred fathoms at the end would trail on the sea floor; and when it came up, this was found coated with mud, very fine and soft like putty, and full of minute shells. But it was not all ooze on the bottom of the sea, even on this telegraphic plateau. There were hidden rocks lying on that broad plain. Sometimes the strain on the dynamometer would suddenly go up three or four tons, and then back again, as if the grapnel had been caught and broken away. Once it came up with two of its hooks bent, as if it had come in contact with a huge rock . . .

It was not until late on the night of 16 August that the cable was hooked. By morning it had been brought to the surface, and a great cheer went up as the company's lost treasure came back into the light of day.

> We were all struck with the fact that one half of it was covered with ooze, staining it a muddy white, while the other half was in just the state in which it left the tank, which shows that it lay in the sand only half embedded. The strain on the cable had given it a twist, and it looked as if it had been painted spirally black and white . . .

Unfortunately, the cable had been weakened by the strain of lifting, and before it could be properly secured it snapped and fell back into the sea. It had been visible, as if to tantalise its seekers, for just five minutes. It almost seemed as if the expedition's luck had turned against it once more. Day after day, grappling continued without success. Sometimes the cable would be hooked, but each time it broke. There was one bitter disappointment when the *Albany* did succeed in bringing an end aboard – only to find that it came up much too easily. She had merely caught a fragment two miles long, broken off by the earlier attempts at lifting.

Supplies were now beginning to run out, and the *Terrible*, which had been at sea for a month, had to return to base. Her crew were already on half rations, but her captain sailed away with reluctance, 'mourning his fate, like a brave officer who is ordered away in the midst of a battle'.

By the end of August, the remaining ships decided to try new tactics. They moved a hundred miles eastwards, into slightly shallower water, and the grapnel went over for the thirtieth time. Again the cable was caught – but this time it was lifted only half-way to the surface and buoyed there, while the *Great Eastern* moved off a few miles and grappled again. Now that the cable was secured at two points, the strain on it was not so great, and after twenty-four hours' patient hauling the great prize was at last brought aboard.

At once the end was taken down to the electricians' room, the core was stripped, and the instruments were connected to see if Ireland was still at the end of the line. It was possible that all this weary angling had been in vain if the cable had developed a fault somewhere along its length, or had been in any way injured during its year of submergence. A silent crowd gathered to await the verdict; of the many tense moments the *Great Eastern* had known, this was perhaps the most dramatic. As Henry Field describes it:

> . . . the accustomed stillness of the test-room is deepened; the ticking of the chronometer becomes monotonous. Nearly a quarter of an hour passed, and still no sign! Suddenly the electrician's hat is off, and the British hurrah bursts from his lips, echoed by all on board with a volley of cheers . . . Along the deck outside, throughout the ship, the pent-up enthusiasm overflowed; and even before the test-room was cleared, the roaring bravoes of our guns drowned the hurrahs of the crew, and the whizz of the rockets was heard rushing high into the clear morning sky to greet our consort-ships with the glad intelligence . . .

The scene at the other end of the cable was less exuberant yet, in its way, quite as moving. It has been beautifully described in the *Spectator*:

Night and day, for a whole year, an electrician has always been on duty, watching the tiny ray of light through which signals are given, and twice every day the whole length of wire – one thousand two hundred and fifty miles – has been tested for conductivity and insulation . . . The object of observing the ray of light was not of course any expectation of a message, but simply to keep an accurate record of the condition of the wire. Sometimes, indeed, wild incoherent messages from the deep did come, but these were merely the results of magnetic storms and earth-currents, which deflected the galvanometer rapidly, and spelt the most extraordinary words and sometimes even sentences of nonsense. Suddenly, one Sunday morning, while the light was being watched by Mr May, he observed a peculiar indication about it, which showed at once to his experienced eye that a message was at hand. In a few minutes the unsteady flickering was changed to coherency . . . and the cable began to speak the appointed signals, instead of the hurried signs, broken speech, and inarticulate cries of the illiterate Atlantic . . . After a long interval in which it had brought us nothing but the moody and often delirious mutterings of the sea, the words 'Canning to Glass' must have seemed like the first rational words uttered by a high-fevered patient, when the ravings have ceased and his consciousness returns.

The splice was made, and the *Great Eastern* turned once more towards the west. This time, the whole world could follow her progress. She could talk to Europe through the cable she was reeling out; Europe could speak to America through the one she had already laid. There were scenes of tremendous excitement at Heart's Content when, despite an encounter with a severe storm, the *Great Eastern* brought in her second transatlantic cable only four weeks after she had arrived with her first. The long and weary battle was ended. From that day to this, America and Europe have never been out of touch for more than a few hours at a time.

The queen of the seas, her triumph complete, turned eastwards again. The first ship that would exceed her in size was still forty years in the future, and many memories must have passed through Cyrus Field's mind as he said goodbye to his friends. 'As he went overboard, "Give him three cheers!" cried the commander. "And now three more for his family!" The ringing hurrahs of the gallant crew were the last sounds he heard as . . . the wheels of the *Great Eastern* began to move, and that noble ship, with her noble company, bore away for England.'

The word 'noble' was appropriate. Queen Victoria, who together with the Prince Consort had always been extremely interested in the project, immediately conferred knighthoods upon Thomson, Glass and Canning, as well as upon Captain Anderson. Daniel Gooch became a baronet, as did Lampson, deputy chairman of the Atlantic Telegraph Company. Perhaps one should not be carping, as there was honour enough for all, and all deserved it;

but it seems a little odd that a higher distinction was given to the men who provided the money than those who did the work.

Just how well they had done it was proved by a famous experiment carried out at Valentia by the electrical expert Latimer Clark a few weeks after the second cable was laid. He gave orders that the Newfoundland ends of the two cables should be connected together, thus providing a submarine circuit more than 4000 miles in length. And through this 4000 miles he was able to send clear signals, using as a source of power a battery made out of a lady's silver thimble containing a few drops of acid. There is, unfortunately, no record of what Dr Whitehouse, whose five-foot induction coils were now gathering dust, thought of this final refutation of his brute-force theories.

It is a good wind that blows nobody some ill; the achievement of transatlantic telegraphy had been a death-blow to a mighty and now forgotten enterprise on the other side of the globe. Colonel Shaffner's project for a line via Greenland has already been mentioned in Chapter 8; this came to nothing, but an alternative and much more grandiose scheme was well under way when the *Great Eastern* returned to England in triumph. This was the so-called 'Overland Line to Europe', a telegraph circuit which would run from America through British Columbia, Alaska, Siberia and Russia. Instead of 2000 miles of submarine cable there would be 16,000 miles of land-line; the narrow Bering Straits, of course, presented no serious problem at all.

Convinced that the Atlantic cable, even if it could be laid, would be uneconomic, the Western Union Company started work on the Overland Line in March 1864. It chartered ships, organised land expeditions and carried out surveys of the barren and uninhabited regions through which the telegraph would run. Three years of toil and $3,000,000 of cash were poured into the project. The engineers and workmen were still full of enthusiasm, despite the hardships they had endured, when a passing ship brought the news to their remote Siberian camp that there was now not one, but two, cables linking Europe with America.

Robert Luther Thompson, in his historical survey *Wiring a Continent*, has an entertaining account of the way in which the great project collapsed:

They opened a sort of international bazaar and proceeded to dispose of their surplus goods upon the best terms possible. They cut the price of telegraph wire until that luxury was within the reach of the poorest Korak family. They glutted the market with pick-axes and shovels . . . which they assured the natives would be useful in burying the dead, and then threw in frozen cucumber pickles which they warranted to fortify the health of the living . . . They taught the natives how to make cooling drinks and hot biscuits, in order to create a demand for their redundant lime-juice and baking powder. They directed all their energies to the creation of artificial wants in that previously happy and contented community . . . But the market at last refused to absorb any more brackets and pick-axes; telegraph wire did not make as good fish-nets and dog harnesses as the Americans confidently predicted; and lime-juice, even when drunk out of pressed crystal insulators, beautifully tinted with green, did not seem to commend itself to the aboriginal mind . . .

So, like a defeated army leaving its stores scattered over the battlefield, the workmen and engineers trickled home. Yet though they had failed in one enterprise, they had achieved something equally important. They had opened up British Columbia, and they had drawn the attention of the United States to the hitherto ignored region known as 'Russian America'. In the year that the Overland Line was abandoned, the territory through which it would have passed was purchased from Russia, largely at the instigation of Secretary of State Seward. He had to face almost as much opposition from Congress as when he had backed Cyrus Field and the Atlantic cable ten years before; but it is now generally agreed that the United States had a good bargain when it bought Alaska for $7,200,000.

As for Cyrus Field, his life's great work was now completed, though he was still only forty-seven. How he saw that work can best be shown by his own words, from a speech he gave at a banquet arranged in his honour by the New York Chamber of Commerce on 15 November 1866. They are still as timely as when they were delivered more than a century ago:

> As the Atlantic Telegraph brings us into closer relations with England, it may produce a better understanding between the two countries. Let who will speak against England – words of censure must come from other lips than mine. I have received too much kindness from Englishmen to join in this language. I have eaten of their bread and drank of their cup, and I have received from them, in the darkest hours of this enterprise, words of cheer which I shall never forget; and if any words of mine can tend to peace and goodwill, they shall not be wanting . . . America with all her greatness has come out of the loins of England, and though there have sometimes been family quarrels, still in our hearts there is a yearning for our old home, the land of our fathers; and he is an enemy of his country and of the human race, who would stir up strife between two nations that are one in race, in language and in religion.

The year after the cable was opened, Congress made amends for its earlier treatment by giving Field a unanimous vote of thanks and awarding him a gold medal – though owing to the stupidity of a Government clerk it took several years to reach him. He had achieved fame in his own country, which he also served in many other ways. After the Civil War, he had helped to smooth the controversies that developed between England and the United States, and when President Garfield was assassinated in 1881 Field started the fund which raised $362,000 for his dependants. A few years later he tried to launch a subscription to aid Grant, then ill and in financial difficulties, but a letter from the proud old general deterred him.

These acts were proof of Field's generosity, and it is sad to relate that in his own later years monetary and personal troubles came upon him. When he was over seventy, he discovered that some of his business colleagues had depreciated his stocks, and that only a few thousands were left of his once considerable fortune. Yet two years before his death in 1892, at the age of seventy-three, he had the happiness of celebrating his golden wedding surrounded by seven of his children and many more grandchildren.

There are few men who have achieved so much in the face of such overwhelming obstacles. And he had done this without the ruthless brutality which characterised many of the other great financiers of the epoch. According to one of his contemporaries, he was both visionary and chivalrous, but because of his own frankness he sometimes underestimated the selfishness and ingratitude of others.

Sir William Thomson, on the other hand, was to go on to yet greater fame and achievement once the 1866 cable was safely laid. Four years later he succeeded in making an instrument which would automatically record even the feeblest of signals, so that there would be a permanent record on tape. It is hard to imagine what the strain on the telegraph clerks must have been before this problem was solved; they had to sit for hours on end, watching a spot of light jiggling to and fro – and if they took their eyes off it for a moment a letter or a word would be lost. It is hardly surprising that one of the witnesses at the 1861 inquiry stated that quarrelling between the operators was a serious cause of lost time, the clerks sometimes becoming so irritable that they would refuse to work.

In his earlier mirror galvanometer, Thomson had used a beam of light to provide a frictionless, weightless pointer; now he produced a frictionless pen. The heart of his siphon recorder was a very fine glass tube, bent into a U. One end dipped into an ink bottle, while the other was held a fraction of an inch above a moving paper tape. There was no physical contact – and hence friction – between pen and paper; the ink was electrified so that the paper attracted it and it jumped the gap without producing any drag as the pen wrote its dots and dashes in the form of a continuous wavering line. This durable instrument was still in use well into our century.

Thomson was now doing well out of his inventions; it was no coincidence that in the year that he produced the siphon recorder he also bought his yacht *Lalla Rookh*. After that he spent much of his spare time at sea – frequently testing more inventions. One of the most important of these was a new method of taking deep-sea sounding, using piano wire instead of the hemp ropes that had previously been employed. Soundings could now be taken while a ship was under way, for the thin wire was much less affected by the drag of the water. Thomson was no theoretical seaman; he once navigated across the Bay of Biscay using only his new sounding machine, which even the modern echo-sounder has not yet made obsolete. And he revolutionised the design of the mariner's compass, notwithstanding the usual dogged opposition of HM Lords of the Admiralty.

It is also pleasant to record that Thomson's telegraphic activities brought him personal happiness as well as riches; he was a widower when he met his second wife while on an expedition to lay a cable to South America. Throughout the remainder of the nineteenth century his fame steadily increased. In 1892 he became Lord Kelvin of Largs, and when he died in 1907 his long life had spanned the almost unimaginable gulf between the first steam locomotive and the first aeroplane. Yet all that time – thought he never knew it – he had been engaged on a hopeless quest. To the very last he had striven to understand the universe in mechanical terms; it was almost as if he hoped that one day science might be able to produce an engineering blueprint of the atom.

Today we know the futility of that dream; only a dozen years after Kelvin of Largs was laid in Westminster Abbey, the first successful test of the Theory of Relativity showed that the universe was a far stranger place than he had ever imagined.

12

GIRDLE ROUND THE EARTH

With two submarine cables in operation across the Atlantic, there could be no further doubts about the future of this method of communication. From 1866 onwards, cables spread swiftly across the seas and oceans of the world. In 1869 the *Great Eastern* laid her third Atlantic cable – this time one almost 3000 miles long, between France and the United States. In 1870, Britain and India were linked – again by the *Great Eastern* – and the failures of a decade before were redeemed. Previously, it had often taken a week for telegrams to reach India by the overland route, and they had frequently arrived in an indecipherable condition after having been relayed by clerks of many different nationalities. The submarine cable avoided all language and political problems, and London could now get a reply from Bombay within a matter of minutes. A year later, in 1871, Australia was reached by way of Singapore, and in 1874 the first cable was laid across the South Atlantic, connecting Brazil to Europe via the islands of Madeira and St Vincent. Before she had finished her career, the *Great Eastern* was to lay five Atlantic cables.

Few things are duller than a record of steady and uninterrupted progress; when the telegraph fleet anchored in Heart's Content on 27 July 1866, the adventurous, pioneering days were over, and with them the excitement they engendered. From then onwards the story was largely one of straightforward commercial development, as is proved by the fact that when the century ended no less than fifteen cables had been laid across the North Atlantic. The 1865 and 1866 cables lasted for five years before they had to be repaired, but sections of the 1873 cable from Ireland to Newfoundland were still in service after more than a century of operation. Once a well-designed cable has been safely laid in deep water, there are very few things that can stop it working, and apart from accidents its natural span of life is measured in decades. But as we shall see in the next chapter, accidents can and do happen even on the bed of the ocean.

The very longevity of a submarine cable – almost unprecedented for any technical device – has to some extent acted as a brake on the progress of long-distance telegraphy. It costs many millions to lay a trans-ocean cable, and even if somebody invents a much better one ten years later, there is little incentive to abandon a piece of equipment which may give half a century of reliable operation. During their first century, as we shall see later, there were only three major improvements in the design of submarine cables; it was the transmitting and receiving equipment which changed out of recognition, from the days when a telegraph clerk tapped a key at one end of the line, and another watched a needle or a spot of light dancing back and forth at the other.

In the days of manual operation, messages had to be taken down and retransmitted at every station along the cable; there might be six or more repetitions on a long line, with all the possibility of error and delay that they introduced. There was obviously an urgent need for a device which would automatically receive signals as they came from one section of a cable and pass them on again, as good as new, into the next length, however weak and distorted they might have been when they arrived. Merely amplifying or magnifying the incoming signal (even if anyone had known how to do this back in the 1870s) was not enough, because that would also amplify the imperfections the signal had picked up during its journey along the line. After two or three stages of this, it would be impossible to tell a dot from a dash.

What was wanted was an instrument which would carry out the same functions as the human relays – the telegraph clerks. They recognised whether the incoming signal was a dot or a dash, and sent out a fresh signal which was as good as new – *if* the identification had been properly made. It was not until the 1920s that a reliable instrument capable of doing this made its appearance. Its name – the 'regenerator' – describes its function perfectly. It scrutinised each impulse that came along the line, decided whether it was a dot or a dash and then made a fresh dot or dash which was not a mere copy of the incoming one but a brand-new article.

At this point, it should be explained that though the telegraph companies still use Morse Code (as well as other codes), the terms 'dot' and 'dash' are now somewhat misleading for the two basic elements of the code are no longer distinguished by their length. When a Boy Scout sends Morse by sounding a buzzer or flashing an electric torch, he is dealing in the old-fashioned dots and dashes, and an SOS comes out as:

Dit Dit Dit Da Da Da Dit Dit Dit

or

Flick Flick Flick Flash Flash Flash Flick Flick Flick –

the dashes lasting about twice as long as the dots. This is uneconomical and inconvenient for automatic working, and in the normal cable code a dot lasts exactly as long as a dash. The two are distinguished by making a dot a pulse of negative current, a dash a pulse of positive current. So an SOS in cable code would be, in terms of a moving needle or spot of light:

Left Left Left Right Right Right Left Left Left

When a message is sent, for example, from London to Hong Kong, it may be passed through a dozen regenerators in series before it reaches its destination approximately one second later. At each intermediate station – Porthcurno (Cornwall), Carcavelos (Spain), Gibraltar, Malta, Alexandria, Suez, Port Sudan, Aden, Seychelles, Colombo, Penang, Singapore – all the dots and dashes will have been scrutinised and repeated almost faster than the eye can watch the machines operating. And today there is not even a human operator at the end of the line; the message is automatically printed on paper tape, glued to a cablegram form and delivered to the addressee.

One of the most important developments in the early days of submarine telegraphy was a means of sending signals simultaneously in each direction – a useful trick that almost doubled the working capacity of a circuit. This is known as duplex operation, and like many other electrical feats seems somewhat miraculous until you are shown how it is done. The secret lies in making the receiver at your end of the line insensitive to the impulses you are transmitting, while still capable of picking up the incoming signals. When you stop to think about it, you will realise that Nature has done exactly the same thing with your sense of hearing. When you speak, you cannot hear your own voice except as a very faint ghost of the original – as is amply proved by the fact that nobody ever recognises a recording of himself. But you can hear anyone else speaking, even when you are talking at the same time. So can telegraph instruments working on a duplex circuit.

The next development – which in some ways seems even more remarkable – was multiplex working, in which several messages could be sent in the same direction at the same time. Thus one might have a single cable carrying eight separate messages simultaneously – four in each direction. Once again, the trick was simple, though as is usually the case the practical application was much harder than the theory. A rapidly operating switch connected the line to each of the sending instruments in turn; each would have the use of the line for a fraction of a second, and then hand over to the next sender. At the far end, the receiving instruments would be switched in and out at exactly the same rate. It is precisely as if four people with only one telephone between them took turns to speak to four people at the other end of the line, talking for say one minute in strict rotation. By the use of such techniques, it was possible by the 1930s to send up to 400 words per minute across the most up-to-date of the Atlantic cables. This is just about 100 times better than the 1858 cable could do, even at those rare moments when it was working properly.

One of the results of the rapid extension of the submarine telegraph system over the face of the globe was that some very odd and out-of-the-way places, which had previously been no more than names on the map – and sometimes not even that – suddenly became of great commercial and strategic value. Since the rate of working of a cable falls rather rapidly as its length increases, it is important to keep the sections as short as possible, linking them together with the relays or regenerators already described.

By bad luck, there is no suitable island in mid-Atlantic for the convenience of the cable (and airline) companies. The first direct circuit between England and the United States (TAT-3) was not established until 1963. For reasons which are better apparent by looking at a globe rather than a map, for a long time the cables preferred to take the short northern route via Newfoundland, or else go south and make a stop at Fayal in the Azores before continuing their journey.

Such remote pin-points of land as Ascension in the South Atlantic, Fanning, Guam and Midway in the Pacific, and Cocos in the Indian Ocean, have become crossroads of world communications simply by virtue of their geographical positions. More than once this has turned a coral atoll that would seem to be of no use to anyone into a major military objective.

The classic case in World War I was that of the Cocos Islands, junction of the cables from South Africa, the East Indies and Australia. On 9 November 1914 the German cruiser *Emden* put a landing party ashore on the Cocos to destroy the station and cut the cables. It was a Pyrrhic victory; before the line went dead the station transmitted the alarm which brought the Australian cruiser *Sydney* racing to the attack. The *Emden* was sunk, in the first major naval engagement of the 1914–18 war – which gave as big a boost to the morale of the Allies as did the Battle of the River Plate twenty-five years later.

In World War II, the Japanese tried a repeat performance when one of their battleships shelled the island on 3 March 1942. Perhaps remembering the fate of the *Emden*, the raider did not stay to see if the cable station had been destroyed, and thus the British were able to work a bluff which they maintained until the end of the war. The circuit was still intact, but radio messages were sent to the adjacent stations, in plain and interceptible English, ordering them to destroy their instruments because Cocos had been put permanently out of action. At the same time, of course, orders were sent by cable telling them to do nothing of the sort but to ignore the radio instructions. And so the Japanese never bothered defenceless Cocos Island again until the Far Eastern war was over.

Besides the cable stations, the cables themselves have been prime objectives during both world wars. In 1939, the Germans possessed only two cables of their own – one from Emden to the Azores, the other from Emden to Lisbon. Both were cut with neatness and dispatch before the war was twenty-four hours old, in the first move of a battle of wits which was to continue on the sea-bed for the next six years.

It is not hard to cut a cable if you know its approximate position; all you have to do is to trawl at right angles until you hook it. You then have a choice of cutting it where it lies, using the special grapnels that have been designed to do this, or hauling it up to the surface and perhaps reeling it in for your own use. This is obviously only possible if you have command of the seas and can protect your cable-ship from enemy attack. If this is not the case, you will have to do the job from a submarine; such an operation was actually carried out in 1945 when the XE4, a British midget submarine, cut the Saigon–Singapore and Saigon–Hong Kong cables.

This feat – one of the most remarkable operations of the war – was carried out by two divers, Sub-Lieutenants K. M. Briggs and A. K. Bergius. Their tiny four-man craft was towed to the area by a larger submarine, and then proceeded on its own course a few feet above the sea-bed, dragging a grapnel. After several runs the cables were hooked, and the divers left the submarine carrying power-operated cutters. It was a risky operation, for they were working in a strong current at a depth where oxygen poisoning is liable to occur. But they cut the cables successfully, and brought back sections as souvenirs.

To cause the maximum annoyance to the enemy, you should cut his cable in several places, so that when he has hopefully mended one break he finds that he still has some more to locate and splice. The neatest trick of all, however, is to cut his cable in such a way that his testing instruments will not show him where the break is.

Very early in the days of cable-laying, techniques were worked out for locating the approximate position of faults, so that the repair ships would not have to grope blindly along the sea-bed for scores or hundreds of miles. In the case of a cable which has a clean break, so that its conductor is short-circuiting into the sea, the problem is a particularly simple one. The electrical resistance of any cable is known when it is laid down and if a section is chopped off, the resistance of the piece that remains will be reduced proportionately. A measurement made at any point along the cable, followed by some simple arithmetic, would show the location of such a break. (Other types of fault, however, may be much more difficult to locate.)

Any reader with a sufficiently antisocial turn of mind will already have worked out how a submarine cable can be sabotaged so that it is impossible to locate the break by straightforward electrical tests. Instead of leaving a clean cut open to the sea, you should attach to the end of the cable a 'dummy-resistance' which is electrically equivalent to the length that has been severed. The tests will then show that the cable is still just as long as it ever was – but it won't carry any signals.

It is one thing to be able to cut your enemy's cables; it would be better still if you could tap them and read his messages. At first sight – especially in these days of telephone-tapping – this would seem a fairly straightforward problem, at least in shallow water. In practice, however, it would be exceedingly difficult for any eavesdropping submarine to interpret the torrent of electrical impulses passing through a modern cable, even if it could pick them up. And having performed so nearly impossible a feat, it would still be necessary to get the information back to base.

I have been able to find no evidence that submarine cables have ever been successfully tapped, and some telegraph engineers have claimed that such a thing is quite impossible. Even if this is not literally true, it is certain that the security of the cable system has never been seriously threatened. In wartime, all secret signals have to go by cable; after a hundred years, the copper wires along the ocean bed remain the safest messengers mankind has yet discovered.

13

THE DESERTS OF THE DEEP

Before the coming of submarine telegraphy, nothing whatsoever was known of conditions in the ocean depths. To those who gave any thought to the matter, the deep sea was a place of utter mystery, peopled with hideous monsters, and littered with the wrecks and treasure of centuries. It was as unattainable and remote from human affairs as the far side of the moon.

The picture changed as soon as men attemped to lay the first cables in the open sea, for it then became vitally important to gather knowledge about this unseen realm which covers more than half the world. The telegraph-ships had to know the depth of the water beneath their keels, as well as the type of terrain over which they were sailing, sometimes as high as a cloud above the surface of the earth. Their skippers had to be certain that their cables were not draping themselves over unexpected precipices or mountains; it was also important to know whether the sea-bed was covered with rocks or had any other peculiarity that might affect the operation of the cable, or make it impossible to grapple for it if it developed a fault.

When Lieutenant Maury started collecting material for his *Physical Geography of the Sea*, only 180 soundings had ever been taken in the open Atlantic, beyond the shallow waters of the continental shelf. This was partly because no one was particularly interested, and partly because the lowering and raising of several miles of line with a heavy weight on the bottom was a tedious and time-consuming business. Not until steam winches were available to haul up the lines swiftly and effortlessly did deep-sea soundings become practicable; this is not the first time that a simple mechanical invention has had important and unexpected scientific repercussions.

From 1854 onwards, soundings began to accumulate from the oceans of the world, and methods were devised for collecting specimens from the sea-bed by ingenious grabs and scoops. These techniques have now culminated in machines which can bring up core-samples hundreds of feet long, providing the geologists with millions of years of submarine history.

The invention of these new instruments, the rapid development of deep-sea cables, and the great stimulus given to biological studies by Darwin's *Origin of Species*, all reacted together to produce the first great oceanographic expedition – the classic voyage of HMS *Challenger*. Between 1872 and 1875 this 2306-ton corvette with her 400-h.p. auxiliary engine travelled right round the world, bringing back a volume of knowledge which has never been surpassed. The expedition was a joint venture of the Royal Society and the British Navy, and though there were only six civilian scientists on board, led by Professor C. Wyville Thomson, they were ably assisted by highly qualified naval officers. The results of their work filled fifty massive volumes, which are still a mine of marine information to this day.

The main result of the *Challenger* expedition was to revolutionise ideas about life in the ocean abyss. Popular imagination might fill the deep with monsters, but the scientists of the early nineteenth century knew better. Nothing could possibly live in total darkness, at a temperature only a few degrees above freezing-point – and, worst of all, at a pressure of several tons to the square inch.

Challenger proved that the scientists were wrong. There was life at the greatest depths that the dredges and nets could reach. It was carnivorous, for no vegetation could exist thousands of feet below the reach of the last rays of light, and the only source of food was the incessant rain of biological debris from the ocean's upper levels.* On this, and upon each other, preyed legions of nightmare beings – tiny dragons, fish that could swallow creatures several times their own size, phosphorescent squids, sharks with elongated fins which enabled them to rest like tripods on the sea-bed . . .

Such is the alien life that swims and battles above the thin cables that carry men's words and thoughts from land to land. And one thing is certain: even now we have glimpsed only a minute fraction of the menagerie of the abyss. For what would we know of life on the earth's surface if our only information came from dredges let down by helicopters beyond the clouds?

The ocean bed itself is covered deeply with a dense slime or ooze which dries into a hard clay when exposed to air. It is fortunate that this is sufficiently close-packed to support the weight of a submarine cable on its surface, since if cables sank deeply into the ooze, retrieving them for repairs might be impossible. This deposit is largely composed of the skeletons of myriads of minute creatures known as plankton, which serve the same role in the ocean that plants do on land. They are the beginning of the great food chain that terminates in the higher fish (and often in man himself); when they die their chalky or siliceous skeletons, which are miracles of microscopic design, slowly drift to the sea-bed, where they form layers thousands of feet in thickness. Out in the Atlantic basin, indeed, the layers of sediment have been found to be as much as 12,000 feet thick. Such deposits must have taken not millions but scores of millions of years to accumulate. Their discovery, which is quite a

*The amazing discovery, in the 1980s, of biosystems nourished by chemicals spewed from deep-ocean thermal vents proved once again that Nature has more imagination than most scientists.

recent one, was a final death-blow to the legend of lost Atlantis. They prove that no continent can have existed in the Atlantic much later than the time of the great reptiles – ages, therefore, before the coming of Man.

This endless rain of tiny skeletons, to which must also be added the mud of the continents which the world's great rivers forever sweep into the sea, has long ago blurred and buried all the minor irregularities of the ocean bed. But the floor of the ocean is not a featureless plain; it is wrinkled with submerged mountains, scarred with trenches and valleys, puckered here and there with mysterious flat-topped plateaux. The mid-Atlantic contains the greatest mountain range on earth, 10,000 miles long and 500 miles wide, occasionally breaking the surface at such spots as the Azores, where Pico rears 7000 feet into the sky out of waters 20,000 feet deep.

It was the northern foothills of this mid-Atlantic range that the surveys of the 1850s revealed, and which Lieutenant Maury christened 'Telegraph Plateau'. Such a label is much too neat (though it was excellent propaganda at the time); the best that can be said about this 'plateau' is that it contains no exceptionally deep trenches that might be a hazard to cable-laying operations.

Sheer depth is not a serious problem for a well-designed cable, but any abrupt irregularities are an obvious danger, for a cable might be slung across a submarine canyon and subjected to a strain which would eventually snap it. Moreover, in regions where the sea-bed plunges suddenly into great depths there is a strong liability to seismic disturbances. The rocks of the Earth's crust are under such enormous strain in such unstable areas that occasionally something gives, and the result is a submarine earthquake. Such an event caused great alarm in Australia in 1888, when three cables to the continent snapped simultaneously and the country lost contact with the outer world. Not unreasonably, it was assumed that the cables had been cut by an enemy, and the Navy was promptly mobilised to meet the expected crisis.

The danger of earthquakes is one that might have been anticipated; indeed, from the earliest times attempts were made to avoid laying cables through regions where there was liable to be volcanic activity. But a more subtle peril was not discovered until quite recent years, and is still something of a mystery. On 18 November 1929 a vast submarine convulsion in the North Atlantic snapped most of the cables between Europe and America. But they did not break simultaneously; they went one after another as if some disturbance was moving along the sea-bed. It is believed now that what broke the cables was a 'turbidity current' – a submarine avalanche of silt-laden water triggered off by the earthquake, and travelling initially at about fifty miles an hour. In any event, it took six months to repair the damage, and the loss to the cable companies was over £1,000,000.

Perhaps the most extraordinary accident that has ever happened to a submarine cable occurred near Balboa in April 1932. The repair ship *All*

America had been sent to mend a break in water 3000 feet deep, and when – with considerable difficulty – she hauled up the damaged cable the cause of the trouble came with it. A forty-five-foot sperm whale had become hopelessly entangled in the iron coils, which were wrapped around its lower jaw, flippers and flukes.

This was very annoying for the cable company (not to mention the unfortunate whale), but it gave most valuable information about the habits of these great animals. The sperm whale is known to feed on the giant squid, which it hunts in the darkness along the ocean bed, but many naturalists had found it hard to believe that an air-breathing mammal could possibly descend several thousand feet in search of its prey. Yet here was one that had established a diving record of 3240 feet before it met an enemy it could not conquer, and was drowned in the ensuing struggle. Did it mistake the iron cable for the tentacle of a giant squid? It seems possible, though we shall never know for certain. Nor do we know yet to what depths these supreme divers can descend, and how they manage to avoid the physiological problems which limit human explorers of the sea.

To deal with all the accidents that can occur to submarine cables a fleet of repair ships is kept in readiness scattered over the oceans of the world. These ships are quite small vessels – about 2000 tons – as they do not have to carry the heavy loads of their big sisters, the cable-layers. Their job is a skilled, humdrum and frequently unpleasant one, for they may have to operate in most adverse weather conditions.

Today, recovering a damaged cable is no longer the uncertain affair that it was in the days of the *Great Eastern*'s heroic fishing contest. When a break has been reported by the shore stations, and its location found as accurately as possible by electrical measurements, the repair ship proceeds to the spot and puts down a marker buoy so that it has a reference point from which to work. Then it starts dragging operations with a grapnel chosen according to the nature of the sea-bed. If the bottom is sandy, a rigid grapnel is used, with prongs which plough beneath the surface; if the cable lies on rock, the grapnel used is a sort of flexible snake with hooks along its length. In deep water, where the cable might not be strong enough for lifting in its entirety, a 'cutting and holding' grapnel is employed; this cuts the cable soon after it has been grappled, so that only one end is brought up at a time.

It is possible to tell from the instruments recording the strain on the grapnel-rope whether or not a cable has been hooked. But the officer-in-charge has a more sensitive method of detection; he analyses the vibrations coming up the rope by sitting on it, and many old hands claim that this technique gives much more accurate information than any instrument. There were pioneers of aviation who claimed to be able to fly by the seat of their pants; the men of the cable-ships were working on this principle a hundred years ago.

Once the ends of the faulty cable have been secured, it is then a routine matter, as long as the weather co-operates, to locate the trouble and splice in a new section. Many of the older cables contain literally hundreds of repairs; sometimes, indeed, about all that can be left of the original cable is its route.

The battle against corrosion, ships' anchors, marine borers, dragging trawls and even sharp-toothed fish is a never-ending one of which the world knows nothing. Improved materials, as we shall see in the next chapter, have tilted the battle in the cable companies' favour, but anyone who has dealings with the sea must always be prepared for trouble. Sometimes it can be anticipated, but sometimes there are accidents which no one in their senses would ever have imagined. Consider this entry which a disgruntled but somewhat unimaginative operator once inscribed in the log of a telegraph station overlooking the Red Sea – and remember that it refers to the shore-end of a cable, weighing perhaps ten tons in all: 'At 5 minutes past 8 a.m. the cable suddenly disappeared through aperture and has not been seen since.'

What had happened? Well, laying had just started, and the cable-ship was less than a mile from shore when the paying-out mechanism jammed. The ship continued on its course – and, despite the strain, the cable did not snap. The whole length, right the way back to the telegraph hut, took off after the ship. One hopes that the engineers, when they had gone back to the beginning and started laying the cable again, had the grace to send a testimonial to its manufacturers.

14

The Cable's Core

There are two key substances without whose existence the development of submarine cables – and indeed of electrical engineering – would have been impossible. One, copper, has been known since the beginning of civilisation. The other, gutta-percha, was introduced into Europe less than ten years before the laying of the first cable beneath the English Channel.

Copper, either in a relatively pure state or in the form of its alloy bronze, was the first metal man ever learned to work. For thousands of years it was prized for its mechanical properties, yet today those are far less important than its electrical ones. Only silver is a better conductor than copper (by about 10 per cent), and using that for electrical wiring is scarcely an economic proposition. However, it has been done in at least one case where money was literally no object. During the development of the atomic bomb, it was necessary to construct the largest electromagnet ever built in order to separate the isotopes of uranium. The magnet was over a hundred feet across, and providing copper for such a monster would have created a serious drain on the United States' supplies of this vital material. Some genius therefore proposed using the silver which was lying in the Treasury vaults, pointing out that it would be at least as safe inside the closely guarded confines of Oak Ridge. So the US Treasury handed over 15,000 tons of the precious metal to go into the magnet windings; it got over 99.9 per cent of it back when the isotope separator was dismantled and its coils melted down again.*

It is fortunate for the communications industry that copper is not yet as expensive as silver; even as it is, the telegraph companies have been engaged for more than a hundred years in a running fight against thieves who specialise in stealing their lines and selling them for scrap. As long ago as 1823 Sir Francis Ronald, whose primitive telegraph system has already been mentioned, clearly envisaged the rise of this parasitic trade and gave his advice for dealing with people who might dig up even buried cables: '. . . render their

---

*A. H. Compton, who tells this story in his book *Atomic Quest*, says that the Assistant Secretary of the Treasury was not unduly perturbed at being asked for half a billion dollars' worth of silver, but was distressed when the Army used the phrase '15,000 tons'. 'Young man,' he reprimanded the colonel who made the request, 'when we talk about silver the term we use is ounces.'

difficulties greater by cutting the trench deeper; and should they still succeed in breaking the communication by these means, hang them if you can catch them, damn them if you cannot, and mend it immediately in both cases'.

When the first Atlantic cable was constructed, no one realised that the conductivity of copper was greatly influenced by the presence of impurities. The contractors supplied what they considered the best grade of copper, but they were concerned only with its gauge (diameter) and its ductility or freedom from brittleness. As long as the metal was mechanically good, that was all that mattered. Copper was copper, wasn't it?

Not as far as the electrical or telegraph engineer is concerned. To him, copper with a trace of arsenic or sulphur is no better a conductor than iron. Nowadays, we can go into a radio or hardware store and buy, without giving it a second thought, copper which is purer than anything the early Victorian scientists could make in their laboratories. The wire which carried the first messages across the Atlantic would have been rejected with indignation by any electrical contractor today.

Being able to carry electricity where you want it to go, with a minimum of loss through resistance, is only half the problem. Providing an efficient insulator to stop it from leaking away proved even more difficult in the early days of telegraphy, and it is hard to see how the industry could ever have developed if gutta-percha had not turned up at the exact moment when it was needed.

Strictly speaking, gutta-percha is not an insulant – nothing is – but is merely a very bad conductor. In actual figures, it is a poorer conductor than copper by a factor of some 1,000,000,000,000,000,000,000,000. This means, to put it in another way, that a square of gutta-percha half a million miles on a side would not let as much electricity pass through it as a piece of copper only one inch square, assuming that the thickness of each sample was the same.

Gutta-percha is a substance much more familiar to our grandparents than it is to us, for it has now been largely replaced by the many synthetic plastics that modern science has produced. The gum of a tree found in the jungles of Malaya, Borneo and Sumatra, it was introduced into Europe in 1843, and its remarkable properties were at once recognised. Indeed, it was the first natural thermo-plastic ever to come into general use. Unlike rubber, it is not elastic, being hard and solid at room temperatures. However, in hot water it becomes as malleable as putty, reverting to its original hardness when cold again. This makes it extremely easy to mould it into any desired shape, and in the 1850s an extraordinary variety of gutta-percha articles came on to the market, such as dolls, ear-trumpets, 'chamber utensils for use in mental homes', pin-cushions, inkstands, chess-men 'not liable to be broken even if thrown violently on the ground' and lifebuoys for ocean voyagers. ('No emigrant ought to be unprovided with them for he can, at the end of his voyage, use the material for shoe-soles.')

Curiously enough, one of the early uses of gutta-percha was in *non*-electric communication over a distance, by means of speaking tubes. It is impossible to keep a straight face while reading the testimonials and advertisements for these. One would give a good deal to see the Barrett family, on a day's outing from Wimpole Street, employing one of the 'small and cheap Railway Conversation Tubes, which enable parties to converse with ease and pleasure, whilst travelling, notwithstanding the noise of the train. This can be done in so soft a whisper as not to be overheard even by a fellow-traveller. They are portable, and will coil up so as to be placed inside the hat.' And in the omnibuses – horse-drawn, of course – 'the saving of labour to the lungs of the Conductor is very great, as a message given in a soft tone of voice is distinctly heard by the Driver'.

Somehow it is difficult to picture a cockney conductor speaking in a soft tone of voice, even with benefit of the Gutta-Percha Apparatus. But it was a boon to doctors, one of whom wrote:

> I have had the tubing carried from my front door to my bedroom, for the transmission of communications from my patients in the night. I have brought it to my pillow, and am able with the greatest facility to hold my communication with the messenger in the street, without rising to open the window, and incurring exposure to the night air.

(Ah, that deadly 'night air'! How it terrified our forefathers!)

And what a picture of a bygone age this report conjures up:

> The Gutta-Percha Hearing Apparatus fitted up in Lismore Cathedral, for the use of HIS GRACE THE DUKE OF DEVONSHIRE, has most fully answered the purpose for which it was required. The tubes are conveyed from the pulpit to His Grace's pew (under the flagging, and altogether out of sight), and although their length is between thirty and forty feet, he is able, with their assistance, to hear distinctly every word.

Poor duke; he must often have cursed the March of Science.

Yet it was a very different form of communication which gutta-percha was to make possible. The great Michael Faraday was the first to realise that this new material might be the answer to the unsolved problem of electrical insulation in the presence of water. Rubber had already been tried, but was found to perish far too swiftly. The first cross-Channel cable, that of 1850, was coated with gutta-percha and nothing else; there was no armouring of any kind, so that it was in fact a wire rather than a cable. All subsequent cables, for the next eighty years, were insulated with the same material or its derivatives; not until the late 1930s did a fundamentally new insulant arrive on the scene – again just when the electricians needed it.

The long reign of gutta-percha was ended by an unexpected laboratory development, which is almost a classic example of the way in which pure scientific research, with no particular thought of a practical application, can produce revolutionary results. For years the submarine cable companies had been trying to improve the electrical qualities of the insulant that Nature had provided, and they had made substantial advances. But in 1933 a group of scientists at Imperial Chemical Industries, working in an entirely different field, produced a substance electrically far superior to anything that is found in the natural world – a substance which has not only had profound effects on communications, but which has also brought many changes in the home.

The ICI scientists took the cheap and common gas ethylene – C_2H_4 – and compressed it under more than 1000 atmospheres. This is a pressure greater than that found at the bottom of the deepest ocean, and the result was startling. The invisible gas turned into a waxy solid, and when the pressure was released it remained a solid. This new substance, which had never existed in the world before, was christened polyethylene – a name which was itself rapidly compressed to polythene. It was produced just in time to provide the thousands of miles of radar and high-frequency insulation used in World War II. So priceless was it, and so well kept the secret of its manufacture, that at one time the Germans' only source of polythene was crashed Allied bombers. The single small factory which produced the world's entire output thus had the distinction of supplying friend and foe with this wonderful new substance.

Today, polythene is familiar to everyone in the shape of hygienic, unbreakable containers and transparent plastic bags. We make far more things out of it than the Victorians ever did from gutta-percha; and will posterity consider our products just as amusing as great-grandfather's Emigrants' Lifebuoys and Railway Conversation Tubes seem to us?

I think not, because they will be cursing us – for inventing materials which Nature cannot recycle.

2

VOICE ACROSS THE SEA

15

The Wires Begin to Speak

On the morning of 4 August 1922 the entire telephone system of the United States and Canada closed down for one minute in a farewell tribute to the man who had brought it into existence, and who was at that moment being lowered into his grave on Cape Breton Island, Nova Scotia. Today, the overland radio link of the transatlantic telephone passes the very mountain bearing Alexander Graham Bell's tomb, and it is equally appropriate that the eastern end of the circuit is in his native Scotland.

The telephone was perhaps the last of the simple yet worldshaking inventions that could be made by an amateur working with limited resources. It has sometimes been stated that had Bell understood anything about electricity, he would never have attempted to make such a ridiculous device, as any real expert would have known at once that it couldn't possibly work.

This is both untrue and unjust: Bell knew exactly what he was doing, though he was surprised to discover that it could be achieved by such simple means. If we try to forget that we know the answer, and put ourselves back into the last century, every one of us would probably decide that the transmission of speech over long distances would require highly complicated equipment – even if it could be done at all. For human speech is a most complex phenomenon by any standards, and fantastically so as compared with the simple dots and dashes of the telegraph code. Graham Bell was more thoroughly aware of this than most men, for he was a professor of elocution, as his father and grandfather had been before him.

When we speak, we launch into the air a rapidly and continually varying pattern of pressure waves. The frequency (rate of vibration) of those waves covers a very wide range. In normal speech, it extends from a lower limit of around fifty cycles a second for a deep bass up to 5000 cycles a second for a high soprano – a range, in other words, of a hundred to one, or almost seven octaves.

Moreover, in speech we are never dealing with single, pure sounds, such as those obtained from a tuning fork or an unstopped violin string. Dozens of different frequencies exist together at the same time, and their unbelievably complex sum makes up an individual human voice. We recognise each other's voices because our ears can detect and analyse all these frequencies, just as by a similar sort of analysis our palates can tell whether we are drinking milk or brandy or beer. If human beings communicated in pure musical notes, like talking tuning forks, we could exchange information as rapidly as we do now – but we should never know to whom we were speaking, if we had to judge by sound alone, with no other sense to aid us.

Any method of speech transmission, therefore, requires that a wide band of frequencies be carried from one spot to another without distortion. Fortunately for the telephone engineer, we can understand each other, and recognise each other's voices, even when the upper and lower frequencies are missing, and the range needed for intelligible speech is thus reduced to the more manageable figure of 200 to 2000 cycles a second. Only if we need high-fidelity reproduction – which the telephone has certainly never claimed to give – must we worry about the extreme ends of the frequency range.

Though the matter is now only of historic interest, it is worth noting that speech can be sent quite surprising distances by purely mechanical means, without the aid of electricity. We have already mentioned speaking-tubes, which still have limited applications in ships' engine-rooms and elsewhere, but during the 1880s 'wire telephones' of much greater range were introduced in a desperate attempt to evade the Bell patents. These are still sometimes met as children's toys, but are otherwise extinct. They consisted of nothing more than a pair of light diaphragms with a metal wire joining their centres; the speech vibrations were transmitted along the wire, which did not have to be taut or straight and could even be laid on the ground or under water. Ranges of up to five kilometres were possible, but 500 metres was nearer the practical limit. At one time attempts were even made to arrange switching systems, so that different subscribers could be put in touch with each other; one can only marvel at such misguided ingenuity.*

Surprisingly enough, the actual word 'telephone' came into existence before Graham Bell was born; it was used by Professor Wheatstone as early as 1840 to describe a device he had made for conveying musical notes short distances through wooden rods. By the 1870s, dozens of inventors all over the world were trying to achieve the electrical transmission of speech, and it was only a matter of time before someone succeeded. In fact, the unlucky Elisha Grey took *his* design for a telephone to the American Patent Office on the same day as Bell, but an hour or two later – to the subsequent great profit, needless to say, of the legal profession, which did very well indeed out of the telephone.

There can be no doubt, however, that Alexander Graham Bell was the first

*Now that I read this passage again, more than thirty years after it was written, the long-forgotten 'wire telephone' appears almost like an acoustical parody of the very latest technology – fibre optics (Chapter 42).

man to produce, patent and publicly demonstrate a practical telephone; though others had come very near this, their work had not been published or carried through to a successful conclusion. Bell received the fame, and his rivals are now only footnotes in the history books. There are no second prizes in the race for any great invention or discovery.

Alexander Graham Bell was born in Edinburgh in 1847, but when two of his brothers died of tuberculosis and he was threatened with the same disease, the family moved to Canada. Bell was then twenty-three, and as he was seventy-five when he died one can assume that the cure was successful. He settled first at Brantford, near Toronto, then moved to Boston, where he became Professor of Vocal Physiology – a high-sounding phrase for teacher of voice production and elocution. It was at Boston that the telephone was invented in 1876,* and Bell made the basic discovery that led to it while he was working on a quite different project, which he had christened the harmonic telegraph. It is worth looking at this device, because the principle underlying it is employed, in a much more sophisticated manner, throughout the whole area of modern telecommunications.

Bell was trying to perfect a method of sending several telegraph messages simultaneously over a single wire. His plan was to use a series of vibrating steel reeds, each tuned to a different musical note, as the sending instruments, and to have reeds tuned to the same set of notes at the receiving end. It was easy enough to convert a musical note into an interrupted electric current; a make-and-break contact on the vibrating reed was sufficient to do that. All the signals would be transmitted together along the line, but each reed at the receiving end would respond only to currents of its particular frequency, and would ignore all the others. The messages would thus be sorted out according to their characteristic frequency – exactly as we separate radio stations by tuning between them.

On the afternoon of 2 June 1875, Bell was adjusting one of the reeds of the receiver while his assistant, Thomas A. Watson, in a room about sixty feet away, was looking after the transmitter. The sending reed had stuck, and Watson tried to get it going again by plucking it. He didn't succeed; what had happened was that the make-and-break contacts had become welded together, and a *continuous* current was flowing instead of the normal interrupted one.

At the same moment that Watson was plucking the recalcitrant reed, Bell had his ear pressed against its opposite number in the other room. He heard, faintly but clearly, the ghostly echo of the twanging spring, and in that instant the telephone was born – though it would be many months before it spoke

*On 10 March 1976 AT&T arranged two days of celebrations at MIT, and I was asked to deliver the concluding address, 'The Second Century of the Telephone'. It will be found in *The View from Serendip* (Victor Gollancz; Random House, 1978).

intelligible words.* Bell realised at once what had happened; though only a single musical note had been transmitted, the principle had been demonstrated. Other frequencies could be transmitted by the same means – including the wide band of them that constitutes speech.

After this, the development of the telephone was largely a matter of working out details. The instrument which Bell finally produced was extremely simple; it consisted essentially of an iron diaphragm placed within the field of a horseshoe magnet. The diaphragm, set vibrating in the field of the magnet by the pressure waves of speech, generated corresponding fluctuations of current which were transmitted along the line. An identical instrument at the other end converted the electric variations back into sound.

The Bell instrument still survives virtually unchanged in countless telephone receivers, and most radio speakers are also its lineal descendants. As a transmitter, however, it was inefficient, and it was soon superseded, after a lengthy patent war, by the carbon microphone invented by Edison – also still in common use, in one form or another.

Once invented, the telephone spread over the face of the world with remarkable speed. It was of such universal value and so simple to use (a contemporary advertisement remarked, 'Its employment necessitates no skilled labour, no technical education . . .') that there can be very few inventions in history which came into everyday use so swiftly. Within ten years there were well over 100,000 telephones in the United States alone; within twenty-five years there were a million, and when Bell was laid to rest, thirteen million instruments were silenced.

The adoption of the telephone was, of course, immensely assisted by the fact that the telegraph, using very similar techniques and equipment, had been in use for thirty years, and it was relatively simple to work the telephone over many of the existing lines. Had the telephone been invented first (an improbable but not impossible event) it would have taken much longer for it to have come into general use, if only for the reason that no one would have believed in it.

When William Preece, the Engineer-in-Chief of the British Post Office, heard about the new invention, he was confident that he could expose Bell as a fraud. Having unaccountably failed to do this, he denied that the telephone had any practical value, saying three years later: 'I have one in my office, but more for show . . . if I want to send a message . . . I employ a boy to take it.'†

We are not concerned here with the story of the telephone's swift and

---

*I still smile at a cartoon I saw many years ago showing Mr Watson holding the primitive receiver to his ear and saying: 'Sorry, Mr Bell – I keep getting the "Busy" signal.'

†You will meet several variants of this story: I am indebted to Paul Nahin's book on Heaviside (see next chapter) for this definitive quotation. Sir William, as he later became, also distinguished himself by proving mathematically that electric lighting was completely impossible.

uninterrupted rise to its present dominating position in social and business life, but a few dates and highlights are worth recording. One now-forgotten episode is the incredible Edison's equally incredible answer to the Bell patent. As already remarked, Edison had an excellent transmitter, even simpler than Bell's; it worked on the principle of variable resistance. The speech vibrations picked up by a diaphragm varied the pressure on a piece of carbon, and this changing pressure produced a resistance – and hence a current – which fluctuated in sympathy with the original speech.

When the Western Union Telegraph Company tried to introduce this brilliantly simple device it at once ran into difficulties. A transmitter was no use without a receiver – and the Bell Company's lawyers were standing in the background waiting to serve the writs if their instrument was employed for the purpose. When he was informed of this situation, Edison – who was busy with half a dozen other inventions at the same time – promised to deliver a receiver which would work on entirely different principles from Bell's. He produced it *five days* later; it generated sounds from the friction of a platinum contact against a rotating cylinder of chalk, and the user had to keep turning a handle if he wished to hear what the party at the other end of the line was saying. Naturally enough, this clumsy and complicated device did not last for very long, and when the Edison and Bell interests were merged the great inventor was able to turn his mind to less sterile pursuits than patent-busting.

As an historical curiosity, we might mention that in 1878 Professor Hughes produced a microphone which probably represents the ultimate in simplicity for any scientific instrument. It consisted, believe it or not, of three ordinary nails – and nothing else. Two of the nails were laid side by side, and the third rested across them like the rung of a ladder. When an electric current was passed through this H-shaped arrangement, it became an extremely sensitive detector of sounds or vibrations. Even a fly walking past it could be heard in a telephone receiver connected to the circuit. The minute tremors, causing the points of contact of the nails to move, produced current variations which were turned into audible sound.

Once he had made his great invention, Bell seemed to lose interest in the telephone; probably the prolonged litigation it inspired disenchanted him, as well it might. His fame and fortune were secure, and he spent the rest of his long life experimenting in various branches of science. Among these was aviation, though of somewhat static kind. Anyone who is still a boy at heart will feel a little envious of the fun Bell must have had when, in 1907, he built the largest kite the world had ever seen. Fifty feet long and twelve feet high, it consisted of 12,000 small triangular wings which formed a great honeycomb. It was able to lift a man to a height of 150 feet; its passenger was the unfortunate Lieutenant Selfridge, who a few months later had the sad distinction of being the first man to be killed in an aeroplane.

One of Bell's most valuable public services was his sponsorship of the struggling National Geographic Society, of which he became president in 1898 before handing over to his son-in-law Gilbert Grosvenor. In 1965 I had the pleasure of introducing Bell's direct descendant, now NGS President Gilbert (M.) Grosvenor to some of Sri Lanka's many attractions. (See 'Ceylon: The Resplendent Land' by Donna K. and Gilbert M. Grosvenor, *National Geographic*, April 1966.)

Within a few years of Bell's patent, the world's great cities had become festooned with a cobweb of overhead telephone wires, often installed by bitterly competing companies. War to the soldering iron was not at all uncommon between them, as linesmen destroyed their rivals' circuits in feats of aerial sabotage.

The overhead lines have gone, at least in the cities, but the telephone exchanges remain as the nerve centres without which the telephone itself would be useless. In the early days many of the operators were boys, but this arrangement did not last for long – probably owing to the working of that curious mathematical law with which all efficiency experts are familiar: 'One boy equals one boy: two boys equals half a boy; three boys equals no boy at all.' Girl operators soon took over entirely; perhaps the telephone did almost as much as the typewriter to emancipate women and to give them independence. It is amusing to read, in the *Pall Mall Gazette* for 6 December 1883, a description of a London exchange which ends as follows:

> The alert dexterity with which at the signal given by the fall of a small lid about the size of a teaspoon the lady hitches on the applicant to the number with which he wishes to talk is pleasant to watch. Here indeed is an occupation to which no 'heavy father' could object; and the result is that a higher class of young woman can be obtained for the secluded career of a telephonist as compared with that which follows the more barmaid-like occupation of a telegraph clerk.

It was obvious that attempts would be made, at the earliest possible date, to link together the telephone systems of Britain and the Continent, and thus to achieve with the new instrument what had been done years before with the telegraph. The first Anglo-French telephone cable was laid in 1891: it was little more than a slightly modified telegraph cable, which was good enough for the job over the relatively short distance involved. But when attempts were made to establish submarine telephone links over greater distances – such as from England to Ireland – the engineers ran into trouble. The problems which had plagued the first submarine telegraphs were reappearing, in a far more severe form. We have already seen how the electrical sluggishness of the early telegraph cables delayed and distorted the signals passing through them. To some extent, this can be overcome by slowing down the rate of working, but obviously no such solution is possible for a circuit which has to carry speech, not code. If you halve the working speed of a telegraph cable, you halve its earning power – but it can still function. A telephone cable which can only transmit speech at half the rate at which a man can talk is, on the other hand, completely useless.

The problem was solved, as far as cables of a few score kilometres in length were concerned, by the work of Oliver Heaviside, a brilliant but highly eccentric mathematical genius whose name is now remembered in quite a different connection. The 'Heaviside Layer' of the upper atmosphere became familiar in the 1920s as a result of long-distance radio – though there have been people who spelled it 'Heavyside' and thought it was a description, not a name. Less well known, except to specialists, is Heaviside's remarkable work in mathematics and communications. And still less well known is the man himself; of all the characters who enter this story, he is surely the most entertaining, for he belongs to that gallery of English eccentrics of whom Lewis Carroll is the patron saint.

16

The Man before Einstein*

All the events of Oliver Heaviside's quiet life can be summed up in a few paragraphs. He was born on 18 May 1850 – three months before the laying of the first submarine cable – and died seventy-five years later on 3 February 1925. He was almost entirely self-taught, never married, and for much of his life was virtually a recluse, living a hermit-like existence and seeing few visitors.

After working as a telegraph operator in Denmark during his teens, Heaviside returned to his parents' home in his early twenties and never went out into the world again. He produced his most important scientific papers during the 1880s, and his method of working is not one to be recommended. A lover of heat, he would close the doors and windows of his room, light gas fire, oil stove and pipe, and calculate away into the small hours while the temperature rose to the nineties and the oxygen was slowly depleted. Most of his life Heaviside suffered from ill health; in the circumstances it is hardly surprising, and one wonders that he did not suffer the same fate as Émile Zola – death by carbon monoxide poisoning.

After his parents died in 1896, Heaviside lived completely alone for twelve years. Then he moved to a house in Torquay, Devon, where he spent the remaining seventeen years of his life. For some time he was looked after by a friendly relative – his brother's sister-in-law – but the strain of caring for a genius eventually proved too much for this kind soul, and after eight years she left Oliver to his own devices.

But though Heaviside was undoubtedly a difficult person, quite a few friends penetrated his armour of reserve. From 1919 to the end of his life he was watched over by a local policeman, PC Henry Brock, who ordered his groceries and whose daughter delivered them to the house. Heaviside expressed his gratitude in voluminous letters, illustrated by many sketches; unfortunately, none of these survived Constable Brock's death in 1947.

*Since this chapter was written, an engaging biography of this remarkable man has been written by Paul J. Nahin: *Oliver Heaviside: Sage in Solitude* (IEEE Press, 1988). Heaviside's protracted war with the British Post Office's pig-headed Engineer-in-Chief, William Preece, is a perfect – and tragi-comic – example of the eternal conflict between 'practical man' and theoretical genius.

Though poor, Heaviside was never destitute. Many individuals and organisations did their best to help him, but few succeeded. His early tiffs with conservative mathematicians had embittered a naturally shy and retiring personality, and the fact that he was slightly deaf also cut him off from society. Attempts to aid him financially were foiled by his stubborn independence; he frequently resembled, to borrow Shaw's famous description of Mrs Patrick Campbell, 'a sinking ship firing on its rescuers'.

Heaviside was certainly not a neglected genius; long before his death his great contributions to electromagnetism and telecommunications had been fully realised and he had received that highest of scientific honours, a Fellowship of the Royal Society. (Professor Bjerknes, the great Norwegian meteorologist, once remarked: 'I proposed Heaviside for the Nobel Prize; but, alas, it was a hundred years too early.')

The Institution of Electrical Engineers (my own amiable and tolerant Thames-side employer, 1949–50) made particularly determined efforts to help and honour him, with fair success. In 1921 it instituted its highest award, the Faraday Medal, and Heaviside was the first recipient. With some trepidation, the President of the IEE called on the old man, and later gave this account of his reception:

> Heaviside lived entirely alone in a pleasant house in Torquay – a house decaying from long neglect. I found him waiting in the weed-covered drive in an old dressing-gown, armed with a broom, trying rather vainly to sweep up the fallen leaves. He was pleased to see me in a queer, shy way and took me through a furniture-laden hall, all covered with dust . . . He vigorously criticised the wasteful expenditure on the leather-covered vellum document which accompanies the medal, but was consoled by the medal being of bronze and not of gold . . .

One of the few visitors who saw him fairly regularly in later years has recorded the perils of accepting Oliver's hospitality:

> I had first to help him find gas-leaks with a lighted candle. We patched up a flexible leaky gas tube and then he made tea. He put the whole of the contents of a new quarter-pound packet of tea into the teapot. I had to drink the potion, which he had fortified with a heavy dose of condensed milk . . . He provided a good cup for my wife and a slop basin for me. Most of his crockery had gone the way of all crockery. A sheet of *The Times* formed the table-cloth . . .

Though he was an eccentric, Heaviside was certainly no ogre. In his old age he was described as strikingly handsome, with brilliant eyes, a most remarkable head of white hair, and the gracious manners and bearing of 'a gentleman of the old school'.

It is satisfying to record that he ended his days in more comfort than he had lived. Found unconscious by the faithful Constable Brock one January evening, he was taken to hospital (the ambulance was the first automobile he had ever ridden in!) and quickly revived. A great favourite of the nurses, he was full of fun and enjoyed the good food; but his seventy-five years were too much for him and he died four weeks later.

So much for the man; his uneventful life is wholly overshadowed by his work, which appeared in a long series of technical papers and three massive volumes entitled *Electromagnetic Theory*. Many of his results were obtained by a mathematical technique (the Operational Calculus) which caused a minor scandal when he published it, for the purists were unable to prove to their satisfaction that Heaviside was justified in using his equations in the way that he did.

To put it briefly, Heaviside treated mathematical operators as if they were quantities. The familiar signs of ordinary arithmetic, i.e. $+$, $-$, $\times$, $\sqrt{}$ are all *operators*: they have no values in themselves, but are merely orders or instructions. More complex operators are the differential and integral signs met with in calculus, and Heaviside was particularly concerned with the first of these. When such entities occur in equations, they are normally associated with the quantities which they modify, but Heaviside left them up in the air, forming in effect equations which consisted solely of operators which had nothing on which they could operate. This was as bad as writing sentences containing all verbs and no nouns or even pronouns (try it and see how far you get), so it is not surprising that Heaviside's fellow mathematicians were up in arms. But the method worked – usually; though as Sir Harold Jeffreys has remarked: 'Heaviside got many wrong answers, but by amazing ingenuity and industry in calculation he was able to find his mistakes. The fact that he succeeded, however, is no guarantee that everyone else could do so . . .'

Such unorthodox techniques did not make it easy to follow Heaviside's mental processes, and to one scientist who protested that his papers were very difficult to read he made the now classic retort: 'That may well be – but they were much more difficult to write.'

In his researches into the very foundations of physics, Heaviside became aware that mass and energy were equivalent long before this was generally realised by the scientific world. By 1890 he had already arrived at a rigorous proof of the famous relationship $E = mc^2$, thus anticipating Einstein's more general formulation of this law by some fifteen years. This is perhaps his most astonishing – and least-known – achievement.

Also like Einstein, Heaviside spent the last years of his life working on a Unified Field Theory that should weld together electricity, magnetism and gravitation. He had incorporated his results in Volume 4 of his *Electromagnetic Theory* – but they were never published, and despite extensive searches the manuscript of this volume has never been found. It is known to have existed, for Heaviside submitted it to an American publisher, who understandably baulked at the £1000 advance he demanded.

And here is a tantalising enigma that may never be solved – like the mystery of Einstein's dying words, which escaped into the unknown because the nurse at his bedside knew no German. There must, surely, have been a copy of the manuscript in Heaviside's house when he was taken to hospital, but no one thought of looking for it at the time. Unfortunately, when the announcement of Heaviside's death was broadcast by the BBC, an enterprising burglar broke into the empty house. He could not have found much of value (and how bitterly Constable Brock must have regretted being unable to perform one last duty for his old friend!) but many books and papers were stolen and scattered. Perhaps one of the keys for which the world's physicists have searched in vain for a generation was lost on that February night in 1925.

However this may be, Heaviside left enough behind him to secure his place in mathematics and, above all, communications theory. As Lord Kelvin had done thirty years earlier, he tackled the problem of the current flowing in a long submarine cable, but he was concerned now with the complex and high-speed impulses of speech, not the relatively slow ones of telegraphy. To work satisfactorily, a telegraph cable must be able to transmit between one and two hundred impulses a second, and a certain amount of distortion can be tolerated, since the pulsed signal can be reshaped or regenerated by suitable receiving equipment and made as good as new. To transmit speech, however, at least 2500 impulses a second must be handled, with no appreciable distortion. The low frequencies of the male voice at its gruffest, the high frequencies of an indignant soprano – all must travel along the line with equal facility.

Needless to say, in general they do nothing of the sort, and there are two effects which make it impossible to send speech for any great distance through a submarine cable. The first is attenuation, or the inevitable fading out of the signals as they pass along the line. To make matters worse, the higher frequencies fade out more rapidly than the lower ones – an effect which also occurs with sounds in everyday life. If you hear a brass band a long way off (which is where many people prefer it) all that you can make out at first is, in Omar's phrase, 'the brave music of a distant drum'. It is not until the band comes nearer that you can distinguish the higher-pitched instruments such as the fifes. Even in the air, the low frequencies carry better, and this effect is much exaggerated in a submarine cable.

To some extent, this tendency could be counteracted by 'boosting' the higher frequencies, thus making up for their increased losses. This is what we do when we turn up the 'treble' or 'top' control of a hi-fi set, in an attempt to correct the characteristics of a recording or the deficiencies of a loud-speaker. However, there eventually comes a point when there is nothing left to amplify, and no amount of boosting is then of any use.

A subtler, and even more serious, form of distortion is caused by the fact that the different frequencies also travel at different speeds through a cable. This effect, luckily, does not happen with sounds propagated through the air. If it did, the results would be extremely odd. Music would be impossible; at a symphony concert, if all the instruments simultaneously sounded a note at the middle of their registers, the audience would hear the piccolos first, then the violins, then the cellos, and the double basses and contra-bassoons last of all. Even speech would be impossible, unless we agreed to converse with each other at a constant distance. If I spoke the word 'Nonsense', by the time it reached you the 'sss' at the end would have overtaken the lower-pitched 'nnn' at the beginning, and the word would have turned into the thing it described.

These peculiar effects are caused almost entirely by the excessive electrical capacity of submarine cables, which we have already mentioned in Chapter 5, where a cable was compared to a hosepipe which takes a definite length of time to fill up, so that one has to wait before anything comes out of the far end.

However, a cable also possesses another electrical characteristic, known as inductance. The mechanical equivalent of this is inertia; an electrical circuit, like a solid object, has a certain sluggishness, and takes some time to respond when an impulse is applied to it. A submarine cable has very little inductance, and at first sight this might seem to be a good thing. However, when he had completed his mathematical analysis Heaviside discovered, no doubt to his surprise, that if one *deliberately* increased the inductance of a cable its transmission characteristics would be improved. What happens cannot be explained in non-mathematical terms, but we may say that a cable's inductance and its capacity tend to counteract each other. By correct adjustment, indeed, they can cancel out completely, and the result is what Heaviside called a 'distortionless line' – that is, one in which all frequencies travel at the same speed and suffer the same attenuation or fading.

It was ten years or more before the engineers appreciated and accepted this peculiar result; perhaps they were as suspicious of Heaviside's equations as the pure mathematicians were, though for different reasons. But eventually it was proved by experiment that submarine cables could be greatly improved by deliberately adding inductance to them, either by inserting coils at intervals along their length, or by winding iron wire around the central conductor.

This discovery of Heaviside's, put into practice by Michael Pupin in America and Krarup in Denmark (Heaviside still being a prophet without much honour in his own country), made submarine telephony possible over distances of a few hundred kilometres. Inductive loading, as it was called, was also applied to telegraph cables, increasing the traffic they could carry by up to five times – a fact of enormous commercial importance. Even before his death, Heaviside's equations were earning thousands of pounds a day. There is big money in mathematics: but seldom for mathematicians.

By the late 1920s, improved insulating materials and special alloys for inductive loading had made it possible to think seriously of a telephone cable across the Atlantic. The pioneer in this field was Dr E. O. Buckley of the Bell Telephone Laboratories; between 1928 and 1931, in conjunction with the British Post Office, he carried out a series of experiments with sample cables off the coast of Ireland and in the Bay of Biscay. Unfortunately, one cable could carry only a single conversation for such a distance and this made the project uneconomic. To improve the performance, the use of amplifiers in the cable was considered; these were first visualised as sunken globes, anchored to the sea-bed, and carrying batteries for six months' operation.

Here was the germ of the idea which was to lead, a generation later, to the submerged repeaters of today's Atlantic telephone cables. But nothing came of the scheme at the time, for two main reasons. The first was the economic uncertainty of the 1930s, which made it unlikely that such a technical gamble would pay; the other was the development of radio, which provided an entirely new and unexpected method of long-distance communication, besides giving the submarine cables the greatest challenge of their career.

At this point, therefore, we have to make a wide detour into a field which would have seemed as miraculous to the pioneers of Atlantic telegraphy as their enterprise appeared to many of their contemporaries. The human voice spanned the Atlantic by radio forty years before it made the same journey by cable, and the submarine telephone system could never have been built without the use of many techniques developed for radio.

17

Mirror in the Sky

The existence of radio waves was first discovered by the great mathematical physicist James Clerk Maxwell, sitting in his Cambridge study and writing equations. He proved theoretically that when an electric current oscillates in a conductor, it throws off waves which travel through space at the speed of light, and which in fact differ from light merely by possessing much longer wavelengths and hence lower rates of vibration.

Maxwell did not live to see his equations triumphantly verified. He died in 1879 at the early age of forty-eight; eight years later, in a series of classic experiments, a young German scientist named Heinrich Hertz became the first man to generate and detect the waves which were to revolutionise communications and to change patterns of culture and society over all the world.

Ironically enough, Hertz did not believe that his work – important though it was to the understanding of the physical universe – would have any practical consequences, and specifically pooh-poohed the idea that radio waves could ever be used for signalling purposes. This kind of blindness to the results of their own work is not uncommon among physicists (as well as other people). Lord Rutherford, the first man to split the atom and unravel its structure, used to laugh at imaginative journalists who wanted to know if atomic energy would ever be harnessed. 'We'll always have to put more energy into the atom than we'll ever get out of it,' he stated categorically – and missed refutation at Hiroshima by exactly the same number of years that Maxwell missed confirmation by Hertz.

It is seldom that a single man dominates an important and rapidly expanding field of technology, but for thirty years Marconi was the colossus of radio. He was scarcely out of his teens when he succeeded in sending radio waves for a distance of about a kilometre near Bologna, Italy, and two years later – in 1896 – he moved to England, where many of his most famous experiments were carried out, frequently in connection with the British Post Office.

Very early in the development of the art, it was discovered that radio transmitting and receiving equipment could be tuned, so that one could choose the station one wished to listen to, and ignore all others. We take this so much for granted that it is hard to realise that someone had to discover it; the credit is due to Sir Oliver Lodge, who first demonstrated the principle in 1897.

As the twentieth century dawned, radio (or wireless, as most people then called it) rapidly extended its range, and in 1901 it leaped the Atlantic. Flying a receiving antenna from a kite in Newfoundland, Marconi was able to pick up Morse signals transmitted from Poldhu, Cornwall.

Now here was a first-class mystery. If radio waves behaved like light, there was *no* way in which they could bend round the curve of the earth. A searchlight in Cornwall, no matter how powerful, could not be seen more than a few score kilometres out in the Atlantic; after that distance its rays would have arrowed on out into space, high above the falling curve of the world.

In 1902 Oliver Heaviside (and, simultaneously, Kennelly in the United States) proposed an explanation which seemed almost as far-fetched as the facts. They suggested that, at a very great altitude in the atmosphere, there was a reflecting layer which turned radio waves back to earth, preventing them from escaping into space. As it seemed most unlikely that Nature should be so considerate to the communications industry, and it was also hard to see what could create a layer with such peculiar properties, scientists were slow in accepting this explanation. Not until 1924 – only two months before Heaviside's death – did Appleton and Barnett prove conclusively that the upper atmosphere contained not only one reflecting layer but at least two. Today thousands of rockets – and scores of astronauts – have flown through the ionosphere, and many of its secrets have been uncovered.

The early radio workers had been hampered by two serious deficiencies in their equipment: their methods of detecting the waves were very insensitive and cumbersome, and they had no way of amplifying the signals when they had been received. Radio was still in the pre-crystal-set stage. The first major breakthrough came in 1904 when Fleming invented the diode valve, the primitive ancestor of countless billions of electron tubes. The name 'valve' was accurate enough; the diode allowed signals to pass in one direction, but not in the other. It turned the rapidly varying radio waves into audible signals – but it could not amplify them.

That essential step came in 1907, with de Forest's invention of the triode. By feeding the faint impulses to a wire-mesh grid strategically placed inside Fleming's diode, de Forest made the overwhelmingly important discovery that it was possible to amplify signals to an almost unlimited extent. The triode ushered in the electronic age, and was therefore one of the truly epoch-making inventions of history – comparable only to the transistor half a century later. In the field of communications, where it received its first use, the triode and its more complex successors gave radio the basic tool needed for its swift development. Once the means for amplifying faint and rapidly varying electric currents had been discovered, armies of ingenious engineers, with Marconi well in the forefront, worked out the rest of the radio technology and built up the most swiftly expanding industry the world has ever seen.

The early experimenters, once they had got over their surprise at discovering that radio waves could bend round the earth, quickly investigated the laws controlling their propagation. They found that the longer the wave, the greater the range at which it could be received; for his transatlantic experiments, Marconi used waves about a kilometre in length. These long waves needed correspondingly huge antenna systems for their radiation and reception, and a long-wave radio station was a most impressive sight, with arrays of towers a hundred metres high and covering square miles of ground. Until the 1920s, these immense installations appeared to be the only means of establishing round-the-world radio circuits. The short waves, being of no use except for local communication, were handed over to the amateur experimenters or 'hams', who accepted them grudgingly, protesting at the injustice of their treatment. They did not know it, but they were rather like Oklahoma Indians being fobbed off with a piece of unwanted desert that just happened to be soaked with oil.

In the early 1920s, the ham operators made a discovery which brought the governments and communications firms back into the short-wave field in a hurry. The early tests on these waves had shown that their range was very limited, and also somewhat variable; they faded out a few scores of kilometres from the transmitter. What no one had dreamed was that they came in again, often loud and clear, *thousands* of kilometres away, after being reflected down from the ionosphere.

It is not surprising that it took some time to discover this. After all, if one was carrying out tests between, say, New York and Washington, one would hardly bother to place additional receivers in Greenland and Peru on the off-chance that signals could be picked up there. Not until the world was well covered with enthusiastic amateurs busily searching the radio spectrum and trying to beat each other's distance records did the unexpected pattern of short-wave reception come to light.

In 1924 Marconi, with great technical and commercial courage, decided to exploit the possibilities of the short waves. At that time the world's long-distance radio links employed waves of five to ten kilometres in length, generated at very high power levels and broadcast from huge and expensive antenna systems. Marconi believed that much better results could be obtained far more cheaply by using waves a thousand times shorter – metres, not kilometres – in length.

The rest of the world was sceptical; though short waves could be received over vast distances, reception was erratic and apparently unpredictable.

Marconi hoped to overcome this by using beam systems, so that most of the radio energy would be sent in the desired direction and not broadcast wastefully over the whole of space. Only with the relatively small antenna arrays which the use of short waves made possible could this be done economically; attempts to make directional antennae on the long waves had resulted in systems up to fifteen kilometres in length, and of poor efficiency at that.

Marconi's gamble was brilliantly successful, and during the period 1927–8 Britain was linked by short waves with Canada, India, South Africa and Australia. The new radio service was so efficient, in fact, that it was a serious threat to the existing submarine cables. In 1928, therefore, the British cable and radio interests were merged into one body – Cable and Wireless Ltd. – which for half a century dominated international communications. C. & W. was a typically British compromise between private industry and state control. The Government was represented on the board of the company, and had a right to take it over in time of war. It is a considerable tribute to the company that this right was not exercised in 1939–45.

We have already mentioned Marconi's spanning of the Atlantic in 1901, when the letter S (dot dot dot) was transmitted from Cornwall to Newfoundland. It was not until 1915 that the human voice made the same journey, this time in the opposite direction. After a long series of experiments with the transmitter of the United States Naval Wireless Station at Arlington, the American Telephone and Telegraph Company picked up intelligible speech via a receiver at the top of the Eiffel Tower. The experiments were carried out under difficulties, for the Eiffel Tower was the centre of the French military communications system and the antenna could be spared only for a ten-minute interval in the small hours of the morning. After several months of patient waiting and adjustment of the apparatus, occasional words were picked up, and the first complete sentence was received at 5.37 a.m. on 23 October 1915. For the record, the spoken words which blazed a trail for some many millions of others across the Atlantic were 'Hello, Shreeve! How is the weather this morning?'

The first commercial radio-telephone service between New York and London opened in February 1927, using a wavelength of some 6000 metres – about four miles. This was sixty-one years after the establishment of the submarine telegraph, and fifty-one years after the invention of the telephone. From that date until the laying of the first submarine telephone cable in 1956, radio was the only means of sending speech across the Atlantic.

Unfortunately, it was not a wholly reliable means. Though great improvements were made in transmitters and receivers, nothing could be done about the third link in the chain – the ionosphere itself. When conditions were good, transatlantic speech was of excellent quality, with little distortion or interference. But all too often the radio beams picked up most peculiar noises, like the sounds of cosmic frying-pans. These were usually no more than annoying, but sometimes they could obliterate the signal. There might be periods of hours, or even days, when radio-telephony was quite impossible, and the resulting delays were both infuriating and expensive to the customers. The Atlantic telephone service was in much the same position as the early airlines; it could never guarantee to be working at any particular time – it all depended on the weather. The weather in this case, however, was not something that concerned the first few kilometres of the atmosphere, but the last few hundred.

The study of the ionosphere is one of the most intricate branches of modern science, as well as one of the most important both from the practical viewpoint and from the light it throws on the universe around us. To look at it in any detail would take us far outside even the generous limits of divagation set for this book, yet it is necessary to say something about the ionosphere's causes and idiosyncrasies to understand why, after a thirty-year battle, the telephone engineers turned at last from the upper atmosphere back to the depths of the sea.

The ionosphere is neither a simple nor a stable structure; it consists of three main layers, the lowest (E layer) about 125 kilometres up, the higher (F and F2) layers ranging round the 250–400-kilometre level. The designations E and F, incidentally, were given by Appleton, who was the first man to discover that there was more than one layer. With laudable foresight he started at the letter E in case any further layers turned up nearer to the ground – as indeed they have.

We know now that the chief agency producing these layers is the flood of ultraviolet light falling upon the Earth's atmosphere from the sun. Ultraviolet light is generally regarded as being health-giving, and so it is – in weak and feeble doses. The raw rays from the sun, however, would destroy all terrestrial life within minutes if they reached the surface of the Earth; fortunately for us, they are filtered out many kilometres above our heads. And as a by-product of this filtering process they electrify (ionise) the atmosphere, spending their energy in tearing electrons from the widely spaced atoms of oxygen and nitrogen they encounter.* Air which is strongly enough electrified reflects (or, more accurately, refracts) radio waves, just as air under suitable conditions of temperature reflects light waves and thus produces mirages.

Since the ionosphere is maintained by sunlight, it naturally changes in density and altitude between day and night, summer and winter. It is possible to allow for this effect to a considerable extent, by varying the wavelength

*Little did I imagine that, some thirty years after these words were written, this obscure piece of electrochemistry would make world headlines via the 'ozone hole'.

employed, but there are limits beyond which no such technical tricks are of any avail.

As in the lower atmosphere, the sun is both the creator and the disturber of the weather. It maintains the ionosphere, but sometimes it tears it to pieces by blasts of intense ultraviolet radiation emerging from violent explosions on the solar surface. Some of these are associated with sunspots, which vary in frequency over an eleven-year cycle, so that at one period the face of the sun may be freckled with dark whirlpools many times the size of the Earth, while at another it may be completely unmarked. It is at the times of peak activity that the ionosphere is most disturbed, and radio communication correspondingly upset.

We may think of the ionosphere, therefore, as an earth-englobing mirror which pulsates with the days and the seasons, which is seldom smooth or perfectly reflecting, and which is sometimes shattered into fragments which may take hours or days to re-form. Such a mirror would not be very satisfactory for ordinary use, and it is rather surprising that the radio engineers have been able to take as much advantage of it as they have.

But before we abandon the stormy heights of the ionosphere and turn again to the calm stillness of the ocean bed, let us recall one immeasurable debt which civilisation owes to the scientists who probed these electrified layers. In 1925, Merle A. Tuve and Gregory Breit, working at the Naval Research Laboratory near Washington, developed a pulse technique which gave direct measurements of the ionosphere's height above the ground by measuring the time that it took for radio echoes to return to earth. This, of course, was the basis of radar, the weapon that won the Battle of Britain and, later, the Battle of the Atlantic. Without radar, pioneered by Sir Robert Watson Watt and a handful of co-workers in the late 1930s, the Luftwaffe would have destroyed the far smaller Royal Air Force, the invasion of Britain would have gone ahead, and today we would be living in a very different world.

Compared with radar, such developments as rockets, jet propulsion and even atomic energy had little effect upon the progress or outcome of World War II. And radar evolved directly from the pulse-and-echo method of sounding the ionosphere – that remote and invisible layer whose very existence was still unsuspected only a lifetime ago.

There are still foolish people who insist on asking the use of pure scientific research. Nothing could have seemed more detached from everyday life than attempts to measure the electron density a hundred kilometres up in the sky. Yet from this work came the decisive weapon which won the greatest of wars, and changed the course of history.

18

TRANSATLANTIC TELEPHONE*

We have seen how the telephone spread swiftly over the world within a few years of Graham Bell's invention in 1876. But long-distance telephony – even on land – was not practicable until forty years later, when the problem of amplifying speech currents was solved by de Forest's triode tube. It had been a fairly easy matter to boost the fading pulses along a telegraph line by means of the relay or repeater, but doing the same thing for the telephone had baffled the best brains in the business for decades. The problem had been completely solved by the 1940s, when any long-distance call was amplified by banks of electronic tubes at repeater stations about fifty kilometres apart; without such amplification, it would have faded below hearing after a few hundred kilometres.

Radio technology also played an important role by permitting hundreds – or even thousands – of simultaneous conversations to be carried on a single conductor, each using a different frequency (a technique known as 'carrier frequency transmission'). Without the public realising it, much of the telephone system was really wired radio, the 'wire' itself being the now familiar coaxial cable with its single central conductor. How this would have puzzled old-timers like Bell and Edison, accustomed to hundreds of separate insulated wires, each carrying its own private conversation!

The coaxial cable (the noun has already been jettisoned, and the adjective contracted to 'coax') can handle an enormous range of frequencies. The lead-in to your TV set carries signals oscillating at hundreds of millions of cycles a second, and could manage several billion for short distances – the equivalent of a million separate telephone conversations without mutual interference.

The three basic elements in modern long-distance telephony, therefore, are the coaxial cable which provides the physical link, the repeater stations every fifty kilometres or so which boost the signals to make up for the losses in

*The 1958 and 1974 editions of *Voice across the Sea* devoted five chapters to the design, manufacture and laying of TAT-1. Despite three decades of technological advances, many of these details are still of interest, so I have condensed some of the highlights into this chapter. For the complete story, see the series of papers which appeared simultaneously in the *Bell System Technical Journal* and the *Journal of the Institution of Electrical Engineers* for January 1957.

the line, and the terminal equipment which merges (at the sending end) and sorts out (at the receiving end) the thousands of messages passing along the single copper core.

With properly designed repeaters, spaced at the right intervals, there is no practical limit to the distance over which telephone conversations can take place. Certainly distance is no physical limitation (though it may be an economic one) to telephony on the land surface of our rather small planet. Indeed, it is most unlikely that any planets could exist, anywhere in the cosmos, whose antipodes could not be put in touch with each other by virtually the same equipment which is used when New York talks to San Francisco, or London talks to Rome.*

Soon after World War II, and as a direct result of developments in radar, the coaxial cable was challenged by a major rival – the microwave link. Everyone is now familiar with the tall towers, crowned with enigmatic horns or parabolic reflectors, which now rear from the roofs of telephone exchanges or stand in lonely isolation on remote hilltops. These repeater stations are connected together not by copper wires but by narrow beams of radio waves, so sharply focused that, could they be observed by the naked eye, they would look like searchlights. The towers must, therefore, be close enough to 'see' each other, which is why they are situated on the highest possible ground. Usually they are about as far apart as the repeaters used in the coaxial cables – say forty or fifty kilometres – but much greater separations are possible in mountain areas.

The great advantage of microwave links is that they can leap effortlessly across country through which it would be very difficult and expensive to bury a cable. The obstacles to land-lines, incidentally, are not always geographical. Grasping farmers can be as big a nuisance as marshes, rivers and ravines, but the microwave beam ignores them all. And they will not support a thriving black market in stolen copper – no trivial problem in developing countries.

Whether we use coaxial cables or microwave towers, therefore, the maximum length of a single link in a telephone chain carrying a large number of simultaneous conversations is about fifty kilometres. After this distance, the signals need amplifying again if good-quality speech is to be transmitted. This does not matter on land, but it means that any large expanse of water is an apparently insuperable barrier to telephone circuits.

Although by the 1950s specially designed cables could have carried a limited number of conversations up to 300 kilometres in a single jump, this was only a tenth of the distance needed to span the Atlantic. So the obvious solution was to have a string of amplifiers all across the ocean, boosting the signals before they were lost in the background of noise. This was simple

*Cables containing thousands of pairs of wires must still be used in urban areas where there are large numbers of subscribers very close together; the carrier-frequency systems are essentially for long-distance work.

enough in theory, but the practical difficulties were so great that for a long time there seemed no hope of overcoming them. The 1950 telephone repeaters were the size of large filing cabinets and required very reliable power supplies of several different voltages. And the vacuum tubes on which they depended had limited life-spans; it would not be easy to replace them a couple of kilometres down on the sea-bed.

Designing telephone repeaters which would function faultlessly for decades at the bottom of the Atlantic, under pressures of tons to the square centimetre, must have appeared such a formidable problem that almost any reasonable alternative would have been accepted. There are in fact two, and it is worth looking at them if only to see why they were turned down.

A telephone circuit from Europe to America could be built almost entirely overland – *if* it went across the USSR. The only submerged section would be under the Bering Straits, and this could be spanned quite easily with a single length of cable. As we have seen in Chapter 11, this route was attempted in 1864, after the failure of the first Atlantic telegraph. One argument raised against it in the 1861 inquiry was all too valid a century later: 'The principal objection would be the internal regulations, and the political character of Russia.' Even in today's slightly saner world, such a roundabout route through appalling territory would not be an economic proposition.

So it had to be the Atlantic, and one way of bridging it which was seriously discussed was a string of high-flying aircraft (or dirigibles), establishing line-of-sight radio contact round the curve of the Earth. About five such relays would have done the trick, but the capital and running costs would have been enormous, since stand-by aircraft (and crews) would have been needed, and the operational problems would have been severe. Yet it could have been done, had there been no alternatives; and this is essentially the solution which, only a few years later, the communications satellites were able to provide in a much more elegant way. In the 1950s, however, the only practical answer was the submerged repeater; and the challenge was met by a unique combination of American, Canadian and British engineering skills.

When, in November 1953, the British Post Office, the Canadian Overseas Telecommunication Corporation and the American Telephone and Telegraph Company signed the contract to build the first transatlantic telephone cable, they had already accumulated many years of experience with submerged repeaters of various types, though in circuits far shorter than the one now proposed. The Post Office had laid a repeater in the Irish Sea, between Anglesey and the Isle of Man, as early as 1943, after five years of experimental work. This was followed by other repeaters in telephone cables to the Continent, but all of these were laid in fairly shallow water, and could not have withstood the enormous pressure existing at the bottom of the Atlantic.

In the United States, on the other hand, interest had been focused from the beginning on repeaters which could be laid in the deep ocean. Since the 1930s, advances in electronics had caused the Bell System to think seriously about transatlantic cables with submerged repeaters, and a great deal of experimental work had been done on the development of the very reliable components which would be needed. In particular, long-duration tests had been carried out on vacuum tubes to discover, and if possible eliminate, causes of failure. When TAT-1 was being designed, the Bell engineers could point proudly to tubes that had been running continuously for seventeen years. No wonder that they preferred not to switch to the relatively untried transistors.

All this work culminated in 1950 with the laying of a telephone cable between Key West (Florida) and Havana (Cuba), a distance of about 220 kilometres. Six repeaters were used, some of them at depths of almost two kilometres. From the beginning, this cable was regarded as a model of the proposed Atlantic cable, and its performance was therefore watched with extreme care. When it had given two years of trouble-free service plans went ahead on the far more ambitious project, and consultations were started between the technicians of the British Post Office and AT&T.

The fundamental problem, of course, was the design of the submarine repeaters. These had to contain wide-band amplifiers consisting of vacuum tubes and their associated circuits, to boost the faint incoming signals by a factor of a million before sending them on their way into the next section of coaxial cable. They would have to be sealed in completely watertight containers, with casings which could stand the pressure at depths of up to four kilometres. This meant that they would be massive and heavy – which presented a major problem in cable-laying, especially in deep water.

The British had manufactured repeaters encased in stubby, rigid tubes about the size and shape of torpedoes, and the cable-ship had to be brought to a full stop when it was time to splice one into the cable. This did not matter in the shallow waters for which these units were designed, but when a great length of cable was being paid out, as would be the case in the open Atlantic, stopping the ship introduced very serious danger of kinking. The spiral wires which provide armouring tend to untwist slightly when several kilometres of cable hang freely down from the ship. When the paying-out is steady and continuous, this untwisting spreads itself uniformly along the cable without causing any harm; but stopping the ship can result in kinks which may distort the cable or even, in extreme cases, tie it in knots. It is quite astonishing what a piece of cable which looks as rigid as an iron bar can do during its brief period of freedom on the way from the ship's tanks to the sea-bed; sometimes knots are produced that could hardly be bettered by a kitten playing with a ball of wool.

To prevent such disasters, the Bell System engineers set themselves a challenging goal. They designed repeaters which were *flexible*, so that they were virtually part of the cable and could be paid out with it; there would be no need to stop the ship in order to make a splice. A section of cable holding such a repeater looks rather like a boa constrictor after a light lunch; only a barely perceptible bulge shows that anything unusual has taken place.

It was hard enough to build vacuum-tube-based equipment that could function on the sea-bed for decades without attention; packing it into an armoured cylinder only a few centimetres across, *and capable of bending round a drum only two metres in diameter* (the size of the paying-out sleeves on the cable-ship) made the design even more difficult. Worse still, the extremely small diameter of the deep-water flexible repeaters meant that they could transmit signals in one direction only; there was simply not room for the circuits that would allow two-way working. The much bulkier British repeaters, on the other hand, could work in both directions.

Faced with these two different approaches, a neat compromise was reached. The Bell repeaters would be used for the Atlantic crossing, even though this would mean laying two cables – one to carry speech from east to west, the other to carry it from west to east. The British Post Office repeaters would be used in the shorter and shallower sea-crossing from Newfoundland (where the transocean cable would come ashore) to the Nova Scotia mainland, and because they could amplify signals passing in both directions only a single cable need be laid in this section. From Nova Scotia the service would be continued to Canada and the United States by land-line and microwave links.

The critical task of laying the cable was undertaken by the British Post Office's 8050-ton *Monarch*, the only ship able to carry 4000 kilometres of cable. This was stored in four huge circular wells or tanks, twelve metres in diameter; each tank could hold a thousand tons of cable, stacked in horizontal layers one above the other. The coiling of such a mass so that it could be paid out smoothly without kinks or tangles at up to fifteen kilometres an hour is a highly specialised skill – as anyone who has ever engaged in a struggle with a demoniacally-possessed garden hose will agree. And the crew must have had some tense moments when the bulges in the cable which contained the repeaters (each costing about as much as a dozen Cadillacs) bent into improbably sharp curves as they slid over the paying-out gear.

A hundred and two of these repeaters were successfully laid on the bed of the Atlantic, fifty-one in the eastbound and fifty-one in the westbound cable, at intervals of about sixty kilometres. Each contained three specially developed vacuum tubes (pentodes) and about sixty resistors, capacitors and other components. At a casual glance, the circuit of a contemporary radio set would have looked more complex; but appearances would have been deceptive.

To make up for the losses in the sixty kilometres of cable leading into it, each repeater has to amplify the incoming signals approximately a million times, and this bring us to what is undoubtedly the most awe-inspiring statistic in the whole enterprise. Since there are fifty-one repeaters in the circuit, this means that the total amplifications along the line is given by the colossal figure of a million multiplied by itself fifty-one times – or 1 followed by 306 zeros!

Let us pause to contemplate this number for a moment. It would be a gross understatement to call it astronomical – there is no quantity, anywhere in the natural cosmos, that begins to compare with it in magnitude. The number of grains of sand on all the shores of Earth? That's too small even to bother about. If the whole world were made of sand, the total number of grains could be written out in half a line of type; there would only be about thirty zeros in it, not 300. The number of electrons in the entire cosmos? Well, that's a little bigger; there may be as many as a hundred digits in it – but that's still not within hailing distance of ten to the power of 306.

This truly stupendous number appears twice in the mathematics of the Atlantic telephone cable. It is not only the total amplification (or gain) produced by the repeaters, but also the total loss (or attenuation) along the line, which these repeaters have to counteract. So the engineers had to perform a kind of balancing act, designing and adjusting the overall circuit so that the losses precisely equalled the gains. You will appreciate now why there was no possibility of establishing a multi-channel transatlantic telephone cable without repeaters. The total energy output of all the stars in the cosmos would not be sufficient to give a measurable signal, after it had been divided by a factor of ten – 306 times in succession.

And yet, incredibly, men are now dreaming of a cable across the Atlantic *without a single repeater*. This possibility has been raised by the fibre optics revolution (Chapter 42); perhaps it will happen about the time we go back to the Moon.

19

THE DREAM FACTORY

The one place in the world which has turned most scientific dreams into multi-billion dollar industries is AT&T's famed Bell Telephone Laboratories. Although this account of my first visit to Bell Labs was written more than thirty years ago, I have left it completely unchanged. I do so with a perfectly clear conscience, for two reasons.

First, it records a classic era in communications technology which now seems as remote, in some respects, as the age of Edison and Marconi. Yet only a few years later, as recounted in Chapter 29, Bell Labs was to see some of its finest hours.

Secondly, my friend Jeremy Bernstein has written an excellent book *Three Degrees above Zero* (Scribners, 1984) which brings the story up to the traumatic date of 24 August 1982, when Judge Harold Greene's divestiture order partitioned AT&T, but left it retaining its 'Jewel in the Crown' – the Bell Labs. I strongly recommend Jeremy's book for anyone who wishes to know more about the past – and probable future – of this unique organisation.

(For another Bernstein safari, not to New Jersey but to slightly more distant Sri Lanka, to 'profile' me for the *New Yorker*, see his essay 'Out of the Ego Chamber', in *Experiencing Science* (Basic Books, 1987). I am happy to record my indebtedness to Jeremy for inducing me to climb the Sacred Mountain, Adam's Peak – and thus helping to inspire *The Fountains of Paradise*.)

It would be interesting to know what young Graham Bell, toiling away in his couple of small rooms with his single assistant, would have thought of the group of immense laboratories that now bears his name, and which played so important a role in transatlantic telephony. At first sight, when one comes upon it in its surprisingly rural setting, the Bell Telephone Laboratories' main New Jersey site looks like a large and up-to-date factory, which in a sense it is. But it is a factory for ideas, and so its production lines are invisible.

The plural form 'laboratories' is correct, since the physical plant is in four separate locations, one in down-town New York and the other three in New Jersey. However, 'Bell Labs' is invariably used as a singular noun, like 'United

States', so we will conform to this convention even if the resulting grammar sometimes looks a little odd.

Bell Labs is not unique, either in the United States or elsewhere, as nowadays many other great industrial organisations sponsor pure scientific research and what has been neatly called 'creative technology'. However, it is the largest entity of its kind, and probably the most famous. At the moment it has a staff of some 17,000, of whom about 7000 are scientists or engineers, and it costs its parent body, the American Telephone and Telegraph Company, a modest $600,000,000 a year.

AT&T can afford it. If most of us were asked to name the company with the largest capital assets in the world, we would probably plump for Ford or General Motors or Metropolitan Life. In fact, AT&T heads the list, its annual revenue alone adding up to the awe-inspiring total of twenty-three billion dollars ($23,000,000,000).* Bell Labs is in no small measure responsible for this.

The Laboratories has a divided allegiance, since half its stock is owned by the Western Electric Company – builders of most of the equipment for the enormous Bell Telephone System. Much of the Labs' work is concerned with design and development in the communications field – which today includes radio, TV, radar, missile guidance, and the whole explosively expanding empire of electronics. But its most important and most interesting activity is nothing more or less than discovery.

This is not something that can be planned and produced by a given delivery date. No executive vice-president can say: 'We'll have twenty basic scientific discoveries in the next financial year.' The only thing that can be done is to catch one's scientists (preferably young), pay them enough money to keep them from worrying about the rent, and give them pleasant offices where they can study whatever happens to interest them. This is expensive, and there is no guarantee at all that the results will be of the slightest commercial value, either today or a hundred years hence. But that twenty-three billion suggests that the gamble is well worth taking for any organisation that can afford it.

During the half-century since the Labs' formation in 1925 its workers have accumulated two Nobel Prizes, and pioneered such revolutionary devices as crystal oscillators and filters, waveguides, and negative feedback amplifiers, each one of which has created entire new fields of electronics. Negative feedback, for example, was invented in 1930 and is now the principle upon which every hi-fi amplifier in the world is designed. And without waveguides, modern radar would be impossible.

In the realm of basic research, perhaps the most important of the hundreds of scientific discoveries flowing from the Labs was that of electron diffraction –

*1974 figure. In 1989, five years after the splitting-up of the Bell System, it was around $50,000,000,000.

for which Davisson won a Nobel Prize in 1937 – and cosmic radio noise, which Karl Jansky detected in 1932, and which would certainly have gained him a Nobel award if anyone at the time had had the slightest idea of its importance. The first discovery proved that the particles making up what is naïvely called solid matter have the property of waves; the second founded, a dozen years later, the vast new science of radio astronomy, which has revealed a new and unsuspected universe around us.

In recent years, the most dramatic example of the way in which research for its own sake can pay off to an extent beyond all computation was the discovery of the transistor at Bell Labs in 1948. This wonderful little device, which earned the Labs its second Nobel Prize, arose from fundamental research by Brattain, Bardeen and Shockley into the way in which electricity flows through certain substances known as semiconductors. These are materials (frequently crystalline) which, though much poorer conductors than metal, let electricity leak through them at a rate which takes them out of the insulating class. Sometimes they conduct better in one direction than in another; the classic example of this was the old crystal and cat's-whisker detector which was the heart of so many radios in the 1920s. Though it made a rather unexpected come-back during the war in certain types of radar equipment, the crystal detector vanished completely from the radio field. It could detect signals, but it couldn't amplify them – and the electronic tube or valve could do both.

Then came the discovery that, in the right circumstances, certain types of crystal could amplify, and also possessed very great advantages over conventional tubes (extremely small size, low current consumption, absence of heating, ruggedness). The name 'transistor' was coined (by John Pierce, of whom more anon) to describe such a device, and a revolution in electronics started which in a few years was to change the world. Its first impact was in the small but important field of hearing aids, which promptly shrank to invisible size and reduced their battery consumption to a fraction of its former value. Then came portable radios that were really portable, 'giant' computers that could fit into filing cabinets; and before long there will be more tiny transistorised devices watching over our safety, supervising our industrial processes, providing our communications and entertainment, than there will be human beings on the surface of this planet.

And it all started because three inquisitive scientists, for reasons best known to themselves, wanted to find out what happened when they passed an electric current through minute pieces of the obscure and unimportant element germanium.

Much of the excitement and stimulus one gets from a visit to the Bell Labs comes from the realisation that one is watching the birth of the future. It is impossible to guess which particular project will turn out to be of revolutionary importance, and which will amount to nothing more than an unnoticed letter tucked away at the back of the *Physical Review*. As examples of the sort of things the Bell Labs scientists get involved in, here are some choice specimens from over sixty papers listed in a single issue (January 1957) of the *Bell System Technical Journal*. Take a deep breath . . .

Quenched-In Recombination Centres in Silicon.

The Dipole Moment of NF3.

Observation of Nuclear Magnetic Resonances via the Electron Spin Resonance Line.

Energy spectra of Secondary Electrons from Mo and W for Low Primary Energies.

Ballistocardiographic Instrumentation.

Refined Theory of Ion Pairing.

A Developmental Intrinsic-Barrier Transistor.

Theory of Plasma Resonance.

Artificial Living Plants.

How's that last one again? At least it's intelligible, but what does it mean?

To avoid fruitless speculation, perhaps I should explain that the last paper was a piece of very long-range thinking (see E. F. Moore in the *Scientific American* for October 1956), concerning the possible creation of mechanical 'plants' – for want of a better word – which would go foraging over land or sea, collecting and processing the materials needed for mankind, and reproducing themselves in the process. Moore is a colleague of Claude Shannon, another uninhibited thinker we shall meet in a minute.

Since this is an age, alas, of Secret Science, it is inevitable that a great deal of the work going on at the Bell Labs is highly classified. As you walk along the corridors past workshops, store-rooms, offices and laboratories, every so often you come across locked and sealed rooms bearing un-welcome notices, and sometimes patrolled by, surprisingly, unarmed guards. It is a fairly (though not completely) safe bet that what is going on in such places is not of fundamental scientific interest. Improving the intelligence of missiles, the security of communications systems or the accuracy of radar sets is of great military importance and may have valuable consequences in other fields, but in the long run what really matters is the work that seems to have no practical applications at all.

A Chinese writer once remarked that all human activity is a form of play. He would have considered this theorem proved beyond all doubt, at least as far as scientific activity is concerned, could he have accompanied me on my various visits to Bell Labs and watched its denizens entertaining themselves with some of the gadgets they had built. Perhaps the most thought-provoking of these was Claude Shannon's mechanical mouse. It was at first sight somewhat surprising to find one of the most eminent mathematicians in the United States, and a founder of Information Theory (the mathematical basis of communication – using that word in its most general sense), playing with a small toy mouse that had obviously come from the local dime store, but there was a method in his madness.

Shannon's mouse is a highly sophisticated animal. It lives inside a metal maze, through the labyrinths of which it wanders in a random search-pattern until, by pure trial and error, it comes to the end of the maze and is 'aware' of its arrival when its whiskers close an electric circuit. If you then take it back to the beginning of the maze, it will now head straight to its goal in an apparently intelligent and purposeful manner, without making any mistakes or going up any blind alleys. To put its behaviour in anthropomorphic terms, the mouse has 'remembered' which of its blundering trials was successful, and has 'forgotten' all the others.

And what is the point of this? Well, to some extent the mouse represents the behaviour of an automatic telephone selector looking for the desired circuit once a number has been dialled. But the implications of the mouse are very much wider, for though its accomplishment is a relatively trivial one, it is the prototype of a machine that can learn by experience. It is thus something quite new, and not merely a robot that can do only what it has been told. True, one might say that Shannon has 'taught' it to learn – but when he drops it into the maze it is on its own. And is the human brain anything more than a machine that can learn by experience as it blunders through the maze of life?

Machines that can mimic intelligent behaviour are not only of great philosophical interest and possible practical importance, but they are extremely stimulating (and frequently frustrating) to anyone who comes up against them. It is, for example, somewhat humiliating to be out-guessed by a pile of electronics the size of a small filing cabinet, as happened to me on my last visit to Bell Labs. This particular machine depends for its operation on the fact that a man is incapable of behaving in a completely random manner; everything we do has a pattern, conscious or unconscious. Thus if you are asked to call a random series of heads and tails, it is impossible for you to do so.

The machine I pitted myself against was told, by the pressing of the appropriate switch, whether I called heads or tails, and had to guess what my next call would be. When I tried to be clever and called a continuous series of heads, it took only three or four moves for my adversary to realise what I was doing and to predict that I would continue to call heads. When I switched back to tails it stayed in the heads groove for only a couple of calls before chasing after me.

In a short run, a man might beat the machine. In a sufficiently long one, however, he would have given it enough statistical information for it to predict his strategy. And there are implications in that last word ranging all the way from business through social relations to international politics.

After such esoteric devices, it might be a relief to mention two perfectly straightforward projects I encountered, which have immediate practical applications understandable by everyone. The first was a programme to see if anything can be done to improve the design of something that had been taken for granted by the whole world for a generation.

The familiar telephone handset seems about the ultimate in functional design. But nothing human is perfect, and there may be room for improvement here. If you had never seen a telephone before, but had merely been told what it had to do, how would you design it? This was the question that a team at Bell Labs had asked itself, and it had produced dozens of answers. Some of them looked like anything but telephones; there were flower vases, pieces of abstract sculpture, salt-shakers, table cigarette-lighters . . . Perhaps the most interesting specimen had the calling dial built neatly into the handset itself, and not forming part of the base and cradle. Microphone, earpiece and dial formed one compact unit that fitted snugly in the hand; the Museum of Modern Art would have loved it.

A second project had equally universal applications; it involved psychology, and an obscure branch of mathematics known as the Theory of Partitions. This may seem heavy artillery to bring to bear on a trivial problem, viz. how do you remember a telephone number?

Large cities like London and New York have so many subscribers that seven-figure numbers are necessary. In both cases, words are used as part of the identification, but they are purely an aid to memory, since each letter merely stands in for a number. The mechanism behind the dial knows nothing of letters – only the digits 1 to 0. However, the number of reasonable names for exchanges is limited; sooner or later we may have to use nothing but digits, and perhaps even seven will be insufficient. When that happens, how is the non-mathematical man-in-the-phone-booth to remember such numbers as 3952841 or still worse, 96821473? A lot of people have difficulty in carrying the existing numbers from the telephone directory to the dial, and as for keeping them in their heads . . .

The answer seems to be that these long numbers must be broken up into segments; the problem is to decide where the break or breaks shall occur. A seven-digit number, it is rather surprising to find, can be split (partitioned) in no less than thirty ways – without, of course, altering the order of the digits, which would turn it into something else. To give an example, the number 1234567 can be written, spoken and – most important – carried in the head as

123–4567

12–34–567

1234–567

and in twenty-seven other ways you may care to work out for yourself. The dash represents a verbal or mental pause, and only field studies and Gallup Polls can decide where the public prefers to have these pauses. A little reflection will show that this is very far from a trivial matter; an incorrect decision could greatly increase the percentage of wrong numbers dialled and the general irritation among the telephone-using public.

I have just found among my own memories a perfect example of the way in which this partitioning works. Though I've not used my RAF airman's number for fifteen years, it is still available on demand because I stored it away in my brain not as 1097727 but as 109–77–27. Yet my shorter officer's number, though used over a longer and more recent period, has vanished completely; I remembered it as a complete six-digit entity, and now it would probably take deep hypnosis to bring it back.

So much, then, for a few of the hundreds of projects under way at any one moment at the Bell Labs. They are probably not representative, but merely happen to be ones I have encountered personally. However, they do give some idea of the immense range of activity and the general intellectual ferment which takes place when enough scientists are locked up together, with or without definite problems to tackle.

But before we go on to the specific project which is the main theme of this book, and which is perhaps the most daring technical feat yet attempted by the organisation, I cannot leave Bell Labs without mentioning one more device which I saw there, and which haunts me as it haunts everyone else who has ever seen it in action.

It is the Ultimate Machine – the End of the Line. Beyond it there is Nothing. It sat on Claude Shannon's desk, driving people mad.

Nothing could look simpler. It is merely a small wooden casket the size and shape of a cigar-box, with a single switch on one face.

When you throw the switch, there is an angry, purposeful buzzing. The lid slowly rises, and from beneath it emerges a hand. The hand reaches down, turns the switch off, and retreats into the box. With the finality of a closing coffin, the lid snaps shut, the buzzing ceases, and peace reigns once more.

The psychological effect, if you do not know what to expect, is devastating. There is something unspeakably sinister about a machine that does nothing – absolutely nothing – except switch itself off.

At one time, versions of Shannon's diabolical device were on sale as a toy, though I have not seen any around lately. They would make perfect retirement gifts for unsuccessful chief executives.

20

'WIRELESS'

It is very hard for me to realise that a whole generation has arisen that has never even seen one of the key inventions of our century – the vacuum tube, or 'valve', as we British preferred to call it, which made long-distance telephony possible and ushered in the Age of Radio.

Picturesquely but not inaccurately described as a 'red-hot hairpin in a bottle', the vacuum tube changed human society as fundamentally as those other great inventions we now take for granted – the wheel, the stirrup, the plough, the horse-collar, the lathe, the number zero, the printing-press, double-entry book-keeping, the joint-stock-company . . . Unlike these, its reign lasted for less than a human lifetime, though in some form or other, such as the giant rectifiers used in power-stations, it may well exist indefinitely.*

I can still remember, after more than sixty years, our family's very first wireless set. It was a wooden box about the size of a small TV set, but instead of a screen the face it presented to the user was a sloping sheet of insulating black plastic ('ebonite'). On this were mounted three dully glowing glass tubes, a pair of flat, tightly wound coils which could be opened or closed like a clam-shell, and several knobs, which we twiddled hopefully in search of the one station that was on the air. (Daventry – wavelength 1500 metres, if my memory is correct.) Reception was through bulky earphones, connected through a couple of metres of flex to small brass pillars; loudspeakers still lay in the future.

Every home sufficiently affluent to possess a wireless could be easily identified. Some twenty metres from the house there would be a pole from which was suspended, via glass insulators, a catenary of bare copper wire, connected by a down-lead to the set itself. Flagpoles at the bottom of the garden supporting long, swaying 'aerials' were as much a symbol of the late twenties as satellite dishes will be of the nineties. These too will pass . . .

Children of the transistor age will hardly believe that it required three separate types of battery to satisfy the demands of the primitive wireless sets, and it was a constant struggle to make sure that they were all working

---

*The vacuum tube is still omnipresent, of course, in the form of TV picture tubes and VDUs. But even here it is threatened by solid-state devices. I give it another ten years.

simultaneously. First there was the low-voltage but heavy-current 'wet' battery, which by keeping the tube's minute heater coil (or filament) red-hot ensured an ample supply of electrons. It was a single two-volt cell, identical with those that are grouped in threes or sixes to make an automobile battery. Every week or two it had to be carried, dripping dilute sulphuric acid (I can still remember the taste on my fingers) to a local garage to be recharged.

Battery Number Two was a bulky (and expensive) affair about the size of a small shoe-box. It could provide more than a hundred volts, but at very low current, so it posed no danger to life and limb. (Though anyone foolish enough to test it in the traditional manner by *licking* wires attached to the terminals would be very, very sorry.) It had to be replaced every month or so, after it had worn itself out dragging streams of electrons across the vacuum between negative filament and positive anode.

On their journey, the electrons passed through a third electrode, de Forest's grid – a mesh of fine wires, upon which was impressed the minute, fluctuating voltages of the Nine O'Clock News or whatever. Being critically placed in the electron stream, the grid controlled the current through the tube, and thus the incoming signals were amplified. To operate most efficiently, the grid had to be maintained at around six volts – and that required yet a third source of power, the 'grid bias' battery. Luckily, that required so little current that it lasted for months.

A whole generation of junior electrical engineers gained its basic training trouble-shooting those three batteries. If any one of the trio was sick, the wireless would be speechless.

All this may seem very primitive – even primeval – but there was a magic in conjuring music and voices from the sky which our sophisticated age, sated with wonders, would find it hard to match. And what is perhaps equally important, the equipment needed to perform this miracle could be cheaply and easily built. Only the vacuum tubes, earphones and batteries had to be purchased, and everything could be fixed on a small piece of board. If it didn't work the first time, rewiring took only a few minutes. Your personal computer, however user-friendly it may be, will not permit such enjoyable liberties, which can only be attempted by the sort of people who have well-equipped laboratories and write mind-boggling articles for *Byte* magazine.

No wonder that a technology which gave its users such undreamed-of powers, yet was basically cheap and simple, attracted not only the professionals of the communications and entertainments industries, but a vast army of hobbyists. Most were content merely to listen with their home-built sets, but thousands – eventually, millions – decided to play a more active role. As was described in Chapter 17, during the 1930s myriads of amateur radio operators ('hams') established a global network, talking to each other first by the dots and dashes of Morse Code, later by voice. Their Bible was the *Amateur Radio*

Handbook, and their exploration of the ether had consequences which no one could possibly have anticipated. They discovered one of the very few natural resources of this planet which could never be exhausted, and never – except for brief moments – polluted.

As Wordsworth said, 'Bliss was it in that dawn to be alive'. And to have been a ham was very heaven, for a new heaven was indeed waiting to be explored – the electromagnetic spectrum.

21

EXPLORING THE SPECTRUM

Light is something which, like the air we breathe, we take for granted. To the ancients – when they thought about it at all – light was a total mystery. Some philosophers even believed that we observe the world around us by means of particles *emitted* by our eyes – acting, presumably, like miniature radars.

Not until Newton's experiments with optics in 1666 – which alone would have been sufficient to establish his fame – was there any progress in understanding the nature of light. In a series of classic experiments with a glass prism, Newton proved that ordinary 'white' light is actually a composite or blend of all possible colours – a fact which the familiar rainbow had demonstrated to an uncomprehending humanity since time immemorial. (Or at any rate since the Ark grounded on Mount Ararat, if the Old Testament's science correspondent is to be believed.)

Fundamental though Newton's discovery was, his towering reputation blocked further progress in optics for almost 200 years, because he believed that light was composed of *particles*, not waves. Though we now know that, paradoxically, there is truth in both viewpoints, for most everyday applications – certainly for radio – the wave theory is the only one that matters.

Early in the nineteenth century, in a series of very simple experiments that Newton might well have performed himself if he hadn't been looking in the wrong direction, it was proved that light consists of waves. Colours were distinguished – and identified – by virtue of their wavelength, red light having about twice the wavelength of blue light.

Those lengths are, by everyday standards, extremely small. Obviously they have to be, otherwise the world we see would look very grainy, like one of those TV special effects where everything is chopped up into coloured squares. Blue light has a wavelength of about forty, and red light about seventy, *millionths* of a centimetre. Since light travels at the colossal speed of 300,000,000 metres (or 3×10^{10} centimetres) a second, the number of waves that flashes past an observer in this same time – i.e. its frequency – is enormous. Simple arithmetic gives the frequency of red light as 400 million, million (4×10^{14}) and blue light as 7×10^{14} vibrations per second.

These numbers are, of course, beyond the grasp even of national budget directors, yet they define a mere fragment of the spectrum of all possible radiations. During the nineteenth century, it was discovered that 'visible' light was far from the only kind of light that exists. Beyond the extreme violet is the shorter ultraviolet, perceived by some insects but not by us. Beyond the red is the longer infra-red, detectable (when it is sufficiently intense) as heat.

According to Maxwell's equations (Chapter 17), light was simply the visible manifestation of a vibrating electromagnetic field, free from gross matter and hurtling through space at a characteristic velocity (set by the original specifications of the universe) of 300,000 kilometres a second. This raised an interesting possibility. The Victorians knew how to make vibrating (or oscillating) electromagnetic fields – but their Leyden jars and wire-wound coils were hard put to produce frequencies of more than a few thousand per second. They couldn't possibly attain the staggering hundreds of millions of millions of cycles per second to generate visible light. But if Maxwell was correct, they should produce *something*, even at far lower frequencies. It was this argument that led Hertz, working at a more modest few thousand million cycles per second to the discovery of radio waves. His name is now immortalised in the unit of frequency: 1 hertz = 1 cycle/second; 1 megahertz (or Mh) = 1,000,000 c/s; 1 gigahertz (Gh) = 1,000,000,000 c/s, and so on.

Physicists and engineers rushed into this new-discovered territory like arms-dealers and missionaries into a virgin continent. Although Hertz discounted any practical applications of his discovery (after all, the telephone had already been invented, and who would ever need anything better?) others were more far-sighted. It was not long before dots and dashes were being transmitted for hundreds of metres – and, in the last decade of the century, for kilometres.

Two countries, Russia and Italy, honour one of their citizens as 'the inventor of radio'.* In 1895 Aleksandr Stepanovich Popov built a primitive detector that could receive the pulses from Nature's own transmitters, thunderstorms, and the next year he generated his own signals and used them to send Morse Code for short distances. By 1899, working with the Russian Navy, he had achieved ship-to-shore ranges of fifty kilometres.

Quite independently, and almost simultaneously, Guglielmo Marconi was conducting his own experiments. He took out the first patent for wireless transmission as early as 1896, and until his death in 1937 continued to play a pioneering role in the field. And unlike all too many pioneers, Marconi achieved both fame and profit, because he possessed an unusual constellation of talents. He was not only a brilliant engineer/physicist, but also an excellent business man, organiser – and promoter. He recognised the value of

---

*The British never bothered. But for the record: in 1884 Oliver Lodge had signalled by radio, and had perfected the detector used until the end of the century. Deciding that there was no future in wireless, he turned his attention to something of more practical value – psychic research.

publicity, as was shown by his bridging of the Atlantic in 1901 by the three dots of the letter S.

Eleven years later, in the early hours of 14 April 1912, there would be an even more dramatic demonstration of this wonderful new medium, when John George Phillips also tapped out three dots in the *Titanic*'s 'Marconi Room' as he sent out the first SOS in history. From that moment, the future of wireless telegraphy was assured, and wireless *telephony* would not be far behind. And some crazy inventors were even dreaming of wireless *vision* . . .

Although radio waves travel at almost a million times the speed of sound waves, both have dimensions on the human scale – unlike visible light, where the crests and troughs are unresolvable thousandths of a centimetre apart. Perhaps the best way of appreciating this is by considering the familiar piano keyboard.

Middle C (the first white one to the left of the keyhole, for two-fingered performers like myself) has a frequency of approximately 256 hertz, or cycles a second.* This corresponds to a wavelength of 134 centimetres or about five feet. So you could comfortably hold a middle C note between your outstretched arms, if it would stay still. Going down one octave to the next C (128 Hz) doubles the wavelength, to 268 centimetres, or ten feet. The lowest C on the piano (32 Hz) has a wavelength of no less than forty feet. In the other direction, of course, each octave means a doubling of frequency and a corresponding halving of wavelength. The piano's top C note (4096 hertz) is only eight centimetres, or three inches, long – easily spanned by thumb and forefinger.

For most radio applications it is more convenient to work with frequencies, as is shown by your local programmes listings, and the graduations on the tuning dials of all modern sets. However, vibrations per second are not units that come naturally to us, whereas lengths are, thanks to the skills acquired by our arboreal ancestors. (If they couldn't judge the distance to the next branch, they weren't likely to become ancestors.) And by an odd but convenient coincidence, the wavelengths covered by the piano are the same as those in the most valuable part of the radio spectrum. Hertz's pioneering experiments were carried out round the left-hand end of the keyboard; VHF, FM and TV stations operate around the middle; radars and communication satellites over on the right. The analogy between sound waves and radio waves is even more striking when one considers that an organ pipe and a radio antenna of the same length would also tune to waves of the same length – though their frequencies would differ by a million.

And *tuning* was the secret of exploiting the electromagnetic spectrum; we now take this for granted, but the first wireless receivers were tone-deaf, and

*Actually, 261.63. But Sir James Jeans's classic *Science and Music* also gives 256, and I find such a nice round number – 2^8, or binary 100000000 – impossible to resist.

picked up a whole range of wavelengths simultaneously. The engineers therefore had to invent devices which could imitate the human ear in its ability to discriminate pitch; until then, only one transmitter could operate at a time. If another was switched on, the two would shout each other down, unless the louder prevailed.

In 1900 Marconi filed his landmark patent, No. 7777, which allowed operators to select the wavelength they wished to receive, and ignore all the others. Very soon, as many as five stations could be on the air at once; I sometimes think that's just about the right number.

22

Beyond the Ionosphere

Several times in human history, new lands have been suddenly opened up for exploitation, and settlers have rushed in to stake their claims. The most famous example – now enshrined in popular mythology – is that of the American West. (Movie buffs may have noticed my indebtedness to Hollywood for the title of this book.)

The territory carved up in the electromagnetic 'land rush' of the twentieth century was of a kind that could not have been imagined in earlier ages. What would a typical Victorian robber baron have thought, had he been told that there was an unexploited natural resource worth not billions but *trillions* of dollars, completely invisible and untouchable – and a hundred kilometres overhead?

The ionosphere also has another unique characteristic; it is the only terrestrial resource which can never be exhausted. If all the world's radio transmitters closed down today, it would be just as intact as when the sun's rays first created it, before life began on Earth. (Indeed, it might well be that life could *not* begin, until it was created, and blocked out the deadlier radiations from space.)

Local radio stations, serving a limited area, do not need the ionosphere to reflect their signals back to Earth; in fact, it can sometimes be a nuisance, causing interference from distant sources, especially at night. It was only with the establishment of global radio telecommunications that this natural mirror in the sky became of enormous commercial and political importance – though not until fortunes had been wasted in pursuit of the 'long-wave' mirage.*

For half a century, the medium and short radio waves have carried much of mankind's business, news and entertainment. They will probably always play an important role in telecommunications, because no useful technology is ever completely abandoned. But their dominance ended on 4 October 1957 – the last day on which planet Earth had only a single moon.

Much of the remainder of this book is concerned with the communications revolution brought about by satellites, and it has been my good luck to be

*Long-wave systems are still employed for at least one special application – contacting nuclear submarines at moderate depths.

involved in this from the earliest days. The 'Brief Prehistory' which follows is therefore highly personal, and I have made no attempt (not that I would have succeeded very well) to play the role of a completely distinterested and impartial observer. I hope, in fact, that my occasional asides and comments may provide more entertainment than the usual carefully sterilised technological *rapportage*.

Over the last thirty years I have written several versions of the comsat story, filling in more details as I recalled them, or was reminded of them by others. What is perhaps the most complete is the address I gave on receiving the Eighth Marconi International Fellowship Award in 1982, the citation of which reads: 'For first specifying in detail the potentialities and technical requirements for the use of geostationary satellites for global communications; for other innovations in communications and remote sensing from space throughout a lifetime of promoting the benevolent use of advanced space technology.'

Here it is, exactly as it was delivered in the historic Ridderzaal (Hall of the Knights) at The Hague on 11 June 1982, when HRH Prince Claus of the Netherlands presented the Award.

3

A Brief Prehistory of Comsats

23

In the Hall of the Knights

Your Royal Highness, Mrs Marconi Braga, my kind hosts from Philips, distinguished guests . . .

My great pleasure in receiving this award is at least doubled by the knowledge that it has already been won by two very good friends, who deserved it far more than I do.

Dr John Pierce was the first engineer-scientist to publish a detailed technical analysis of communications satellites. Even more important, he was the driving force behind the pioneering practical demonstrations with Echo and Telstar. He and Dr Harold Rosen – who played a similar role with the first geostationary comsats* – are the true fathers of satellite communications. That title has sometimes been given to me, but honesty compels me to disclaim it. I am not the father of comsats – merely the godfather.

The other friend, whom I'm delighted to see here today, is my northern neighbour Dr Yash Pal. I've known Dr Pal since the early days of the Indian SITE project [see Chapter 33], which he directed so brilliantly after the untimely death of its founder, Dr Vikram Sarabhai – whose work he is still continuing as Secretary-General of Unispace. By a happy chance, I was in Ahmedabad when Dr Pal received notification of *his* Marconi Award, and was wondering how best to utilise it. Yash, I'd like to resume that discussion, just as soon as convenient . . .

I am not indulging in false modesty – a concept which all my friends would reject with hysterical laughter – when I say that my contribution to satellite communications was largely a matter of luck. I happened to be in the right place at the right time. In the winter of 1944-5, World War II was obviously coming to an end, and one could think once more about the future. Dr Wernher von Braun – another good friend, whom I miss badly – had demonstrated that big rockets were practicable, to the grave detriment of London as target, and The Hague as launch pad. The time was ripe to think about reviving the British Interplanetary Society, which had been in suspended animation since 1939.

*From now on, comsat stands for communications satellite, and COMSAT means Communications Satellite Corporation.

But how could one possibly raise money for such a fantastic enterprise as space travel? Pre-war estimates by the BIS had suggested that a lunar expedition might cost the truly astronomical sum of one million dollars, and it was ridiculous to imagine that governments would spend such awesome amounts on purely scientific projects. We would have to find the money ourselves; was there any way in which rockets could earn an honest living? Rocket mail had been suggested, but that seemed a rather limited application, and it might take some time to overcome the poor advance publicity generated by the V2 . . .

I was pondering these matters in my spare time as an RAF radar officer, while helping to run the Ground-Controlled Approach (GCA) system invented by Dr Luis W. Alvarez and his Radiation Lab team [see Chapter 24]. This operated at the then fantastically high frequency of ten gigahertz, producing beams a fraction of a degree wide. I can recall, with some embarrassment, using the dear old Mark 1 to fire single pulses at the rising Moon, and waiting for the echo three seconds later. (Obviously, the available power would have been orders of magnitude too low.)

So communications and astronautics were inextricably entangled in my mind, with results that now seem inevitable. If I had not proposed the idea of geostationary relays in my *Wireless World* letter of February 1945, and developed it in more detail the following October, half a dozen other people would have quickly done so. I suspect that my early disclosure may have advanced the cause of space communications by approximately fifteen minutes.

Or perhaps twenty. My efforts to promote and publicise the idea may have been much more important than conceiving it. In 1952 *The Exploration of Space* introduced communications satellites to several hundred thousand people – including John Pierce, whom I first met in May of that year, and did my best to turn into a space cadet. (He was already one in secret, but as Director of Electronics Research at Bell Labs, he had to conceal such unfortunate aberrations.) When he published his influential 'Orbital Radio Relays' in May 1955, he had never even seen my own paper of a decade earlier; but of course he had no need of it – the mere suggestion was enough to an engineer of John's calibre.

From today's vantage point, it's amusing to note that 'Orbital Radio Relays' was published in *Jet Propulsion*, the journal of the American Rocket Society. Not long afterwards, the ARS became the American Institute of Aeronautics and Astronautics; but in 1955 there was not the slightest mention of space flight in the society's Byelaws. Even the word 'rocket' was to be avoided as too Buck Rogerish; only 'jet propulsion' was respectable . . .

In complete contrast, the British Interplanetary Society was only interested in space travel, and would have been quite happy to abandon rockets as soon as someone got round to inventing antigravity. I am not claiming that one viewpoint is superior to the other. The world needs uninhibited thinkers not afraid of far-out speculation; it also needs hardheaded, conservative engineers who can make their dreams come true. They complement each other, and progress is impossible without both. If there had been government – and dare I say industrial? – research establishments in the Stone Age, by now we would have had absolutely superb flint tools. But no one would have invented steel.

Let me end by sharing with you a discovery I've just been delighted to make, by pure luck – or serendipity, to use the now over-popular word derived from the ancient name for Sri Lanka. It links the pioneering days of European astronautics with the great man whose memory we have now gathered to honour.

Back in 1939, the British Interplanetary Society was always alert for publicity, and for several weeks we waged verbal war against sceptics in the dignified pages of the BBC's *The Listener* – until the editor finally declared that 'this correspondence is now closed'. I had completely forgotten that the controversy was triggered by a radio talk, 'Myself and Life', by Dr W. E. Barnes, then Bishop of Birmingham. It contains words as relevant today as when they were spoken forty-three years ago:

> It cannot be true that the earth is the only planet upon which life exists . . . On other planets of other stars, there must be consciousness; on them there must be beings with minds . . . some far more developed than our own . . . wireless messages from such remote conscious beings must be possible. The only time I met Marconi, he told me of his search for such messages. So far we have failed to find them.
>
> (*The Listener*, 9 February 1939)

Yes, we have failed. But one day we will succeed. And then Marconi's last and greatest dream will have been fulfilled.

24

'YOU'RE ON THE GLIDE PATH – I THINK . . .'

Forty years before my invitation to The Hague, I was on the other side of the North Sea, scanning the coast of Nazi-occupied Holland with the newly invented microwave radar, and wearing an RAF officer's uniform that was even newer. The heart of our three-gigahertz transmitter was the most important secret of the war – the cavity magnetron, invented in 1940 by Boot and Randall at Birmingham University. This generated centimetre-length radio waves of unprecedented power, and so made possible the airborne radar sets which won the vital Battle of the Atlantic.

When Britain's chief scientific adviser Sir Henry Tizard carried the first experimental magnetron to America, the face of war was changed over a weekend (that of 28–30 September 1940), at a meeting which established the Massachusetts Institute of Technology's famous Radiation Laboratory. Sir Henry's unprepossessing block of copper was later called the most valuable cargo ever to reach the shores of the United States: although the atomic bomb ended the war, without the magnetron it might well have been lost before the Manhattan Project could have got under way.

Yet – and this is one of history's biggest 'ifs' – Japanese scientists had made and tested an identical device *a year before the British*. If they had followed up their invention, we would now be living in a very different world.

One day in 1941 I was called to Group Headquarters and grilled by Wing-Commander Edward Fennessey (later Managing Director of Post Office Telecommunications). Presumably he was satisfied with my replies, for soon afterwards I found myself on an airfield in Cornwall with a bunch of wild young scientists and engineers from the Radiation Lab. They were demonstrating a brand-new radar system called GCA (Ground-Controlled Approach) designed, for a change, to do something constructive. It could *talk* aircraft down, instead of shooting them down.

The leader of the team, and GCA's inventor, had just left for the United States, on a mission that no one was supposed to know anything about. When I caught up with Luis Alvarez some ten years later, he had helped to build the atomic bomb and was well on the way to his Nobel Prize. I have often wondered what the inventor of dynamite would have thought of this ironic coincidence.

Working with the GCA team had a decisive influence on my life. For the first time, I got to know some *real* scientists, and I was also exposed to the most advanced electronic technology. Many years later (in 1963) I was to dedicate my only *non*-science-fiction novel, *Glide Path*, to Alvarez and his colleagues. I am now in touch with only two – Lt Noel Jolley, whose GCA unit did yeoman service in the Pacific theatre, and Dr Charles (Bert) Fowler, who later became chairman of the Pentagon's influential Defense Science Board.

Luis himself died in 1988, after a spectacular career which involved building gigantic particle-accelerators, discovering a 'cold-fusion' nuclear reaction which may yet have practical applications (despite recent false alarms), and using cosmic rays to prove that there are no hidden chambers in the Great Pyramid. However, his most famous contribution came at the end of his life, when with his geologist son Walter he proposed that the extinction of the dinosaurs and many other species some sixty-five million years ago was caused – or at least hastened – by the impact of a giant meteorite. Although in one of his last letters to me he stated that this was no longer a 'hypothesis' but an indisputable fact, some geologists are still looking for more mundane explanations.

Because GCA was such a key element in my thinking about communications satellites, I would like to quote at some length from a technically correct but not altogether serious article I published in *The Aeroplane* for 23 September 1949. As the title suggests, in those pioneering days pilots sometimes took a good deal of persuasion before they would follow our radioed advice.*

The one and only Mark 1 GCA unit had been hand-built at MIT, and was intended purely for demonstration purposes, to prove that the 'talk-down' principle would work with all kinds of pilots and aircraft. It occupied two large trucks (the operational Mark 2 employed a single truck and trailer) and was probably the most complex electronic device in existence at that time.

The Mark 1 was undergoing tests in the States, apparently without arousing any great excitement, when it was discovered almost accidentally by a visiting British defence scientist, Dr Richard Grey. He at once realised its importance and succeeded in 'capturing' the whole equipment and loading it aboard a British battleship. He also kidnapped Dr Alvarez and his team, whisking them to the United Kingdom on a priority so high that they crowded Bob Hope off the flying-boat at Shannon. I'm sorry I've forgotten the crack that Bob made when he was 'bumped'.

The equipment was reassembled at Elsham Wolds, then a bomber station,

*The full version of '"You're on the glide path" . . .', my address at the Marconi Award ceremony, and much technical material only lightly touched upon in this volume, will be found in *Ascent to Orbit: A Scientific Autobiography* (John Wiley, 1984).

where the first trials were successfully accomplished. Unfortunately it was not long before some genius decided that the weather at Elsham was altogether too good, and that since GCA was supposed to be a blind-approach system, it ought to go to a station more or less permanently closed by weather conditions. So the unit was moved to Davistowe Moor, in the dreariest depths of Yorkshire.

I only saw this aerodrome in the rainy season, which probably does not last the entire year, but when I arrived on the scene, as a raw technical-officer-under-training, we found the American scientists amplifying their already excellent vocabularies over expiring transformers, and complaining bitterly that their gear wasn't built for underwater operation. At night, when the equipment closed down and cooled off, the all-pervading mist would creep gleefully into every cranny, depositing moisture in high-voltage circuits, so that brief but spectacular firework displays would ensue in the morning. Luckily the unit was removed to St Eval, near Newquay, Cornwall, before the whole apparatus became waterlogged; and it was here that the Mark 1 saw most of its service with the RAF.

Testing an experimental blind-approach system on operational stations had its disadvantages. We had our own little flight of Oxfords and Ansons, which were liable to be making approaches on odd runways – and even *downwind* on the runway in use – when flying control was trying to land an aircraft. This did not help our popularity.

To make matters worse, since there were no proper hard standings for the apparatus, the big GCA trucks and their satellite fleet of service trucks, NAAFI vans and visitors' cars had to be sited on one of the out-of-use runways, near the main intersection. All too often, a change of wind would demand a hasty retreat by the entire unit – a move which we resisted tooth and nail, since it required readjusting the controls and uncoupling all our cables. There were so many of these, an inch or more thick, linking the two vehicles that the site sometimes looked like a rendezvous for amorous squids; but eventually, we got so streamlined that we were able to change positions in about twenty minutes.

The flying-control officers became quite used to seeing what appeared to be an advanced party from a circus proceeding up the runway, turning on to an intersection, and then proceeding to pitch camp with sublime indifference a hundred yards from the edge of the runway in use. Once we miscalculated and found a squadron of Spitfires taking off behind us: luckily, our twenty-ton trucks did some rapid footwork and skipped on to the grass in time.

Some of the GCA sites were in more reasonable places, on outlying pieces of perimeter track, and one was surrounded by a tasteful tableau of crashed Liberator bombers. We were always very careful to explain to visitors that they had managed to get that way without any help from us.

The original American team was still with us, for the early part of the time, at St Eval, although Dr Alvarez had now returned to the States. Incidentally, Alvarez was very far from the popular conception of a high-powered scientist. He had a pilot's licence, and was one of the best, as well as perhaps the first, of GCA controllers.

According to legend, he would calmly continue talking an aircraft down to earth even when cathode-ray tubes were popping in all directions, frenzied mechanics were crawling under his legs and smoke was gently circling from his meter panels. Moreover, he was an expert at breaking down 'sales resistance' – of which there was plenty in those days, particularly from exponents of rival systems.

When Dr Alvarez returned to America, some of us guessed the reason; but we did not know until a long time later that he was one of the atom bomb team on Tinian in August 1945. His deputy, Dr George Comstock, remained in charge until the rest of the team returned. Our dearest memory of George is of him on his last night in England, lying in bed, avidly reading something called *The Gamma Ray Murders*.

With the assistance of the Americans, we trained a team of RAF mechanics, operators and controllers who were later to form the nucleus of the GCA empire. But we were now very much on our own, and could no longer run to experts when anything went wrong – as it very frequently did. It had never been intended that the laboratory-built Mark 1 should be used steadily, month after month, for training and for innumerable demonstrations in a foreign country – and run by people who hadn't watched it grow up from a blueprint.

We sometimes thought that everyone in the RAF above the rank of group-captain visited us at one time or another. They usually went away thoughtful, if not convinced. There were times when the crowd in the control truck was so thick that mere air commodores had to sit outside on the grass, waiting their turns. The operators grew quite accustomed to working with a packed mass of humanity breathing down the backs of their necks.

They also grew quite accustomed to the sudden disappearance of all signals as we switched off to forestall some incipient breakdown. If the weather was dirty and we had an aircraft up at the time, that was just too bad: it would have to ask someone else the way home. As we often pointed out to the OC Flying, it was easy enough to get more aircraft and pilots – but there was only one GCA, and we couldn't take risks with it. He rather stubbornly refused to see our point of view.

At St Eval, we made every imaginable mistake, and quite a few others, mastering the technique and developing the RT patter that has now become universally familiar. Nothing could be taken for granted, and we had to learn by trial and error. No one, for example, seemed sure of the best glide path:

anything between two and five degrees was suggested for different types of aircraft. Changing the glide path involved mechanical rearrangements in a Heath-Robinson apparatus full of gears, clutches, solenoids and selsyn motors. As the GCA was not sited at touch-down, but well up the runway, the radar operators 'saw' a distorted picture of the aircraft's approach: the glide path in fact appeared on the screen as a hyperbola instead of a straight line.

This distortion was corrected by most peculiar cams, based on a spiral co-ordinate system: these revolved once during every approach, except when they fell off their shafts. Changing a glide path meant changing a cam, but one day the wrong cam was accidentally left in the machine, so that we brought a heavy bomber down a fighter glide path. Nevertheless, the pilot reported an excellent approach, so we decided not to pamper our clients any more, and therefore *everyone* came down at 3½ degrees, whether they knew it or not.

The biggest operating boob we ever made on the Mark 1 might have had serious consequences, had our aircraft not wisely carried observers who kept an eye open while the pilot was obeying our instructions, and could break off the approach if anything was obviously wrong. One day, the passenger in the aircraft was a civilian scientist whose progress from station to station was always marked by the trail of mislaid secret documents he scattered in his wake. It was his first approach on GCA, and any faith he had in the system was somewhat shattered when he found his aircraft descending into the sea some miles off the coast, while the controller was saying, 'On the runway, one mile to go, coming along very nicely . . .' He stood it as long as he could, then tapped the pilot gently on the shoulder and suggested that the depressingly damp scenery below bore little resemblance to Runway 320.

It turned out later that the inexperienced radar operators had picked up the wrong aircraft, and were tracking someone who was making a normal visual approach – so was indeed 'coming along very nicely', while our own aircraft had been missed altogether. The mistake was, in the long run, a fortunate one, as it focused attention on the problem of identification and resulted in improvements in control techniques. But it was quite a while before we lived it down.

St Eval was one of the first airfields to be fitted with FIDO (Fog Investigation Dispersal Operation), and the installation was a colossal one, burning a thousand gallons of petrol a *minute*. Not only was there a double row of burners the whole length of the main runway, but various sheets of flame branched out at right angles as well. When the whole affair was going full blast, it lit up most of Cornwall and caused confusion among the fire brigades for fifty miles around.

For a long time, attempts were made to arrange a combined GCA–FIDO landing, but they were spoiled by persistently good weather. At last we got what we wanted – a drizzling fog with practically zero visibility. It was so bad in fact that the aircraft could never even have taken off without FIDO's assistance.

At midnight, all was ready. The scene might have come from Dante's *Inferno* – there were great sheets of fire roaring on either side, clouds of steam rising into the mist, and a heat like that from an open furnace beating into our faces* – for we were only about a hundred feet from the nearest burners. The aircraft was standing by, waiting to take off with the station commander aboard, and in the GCA trucks the cathode-ray traces were scanning normally, building up the radar pictures on the screens. At that precise moment, the turning-gear that rotated the search (360 degrees of vision) aerial decided it had had enough, and crunched to a halt, shedding half its teeth in the process.

Our overall traffic-control system was thus completely blind: but the aerials of the landing system were still scanning, giving us a picture some thirty degrees wide, centred on the runway, and pointing downwind. It was decided to risk it by keeping the aircraft in the narrow thirty-degree sector (one twelfth of the sky!) and using the landing system, which was now all we had, both for control and approach.

As soon as the aircraft took off, it of course promptly vanished into our 330-degree blind sector, but we immediately turned it through 180 degrees and it soon reappeared. It was allowed to fly downwind for a few miles – we dared not let it go too far, as the landing system had a range of less than ten miles – and then whipped it round for an approach. The pilot was unable to land on this run: he found himself at the edge of the runway, but visibility was so bad that he could see only a single line of FIDO burners and didn't know *which* side of the runway he was on! So the manoeuvre had to be repeated, and luckily the second approach was successful, despite the attempts of the FIDO-induced gale to push the aircraft off course.

That exploit was also one of the last highlights of the Mark 1's career. It had already run for six months longer than it had ever been intended to operate, and we are very proud of the fact that in the days before it was finally dismantled, it was working as well as it had ever done, thanks to extensive overhauls and partial rebuildings. But the operational Mark 2s were now on the way, and the GCA team was moving to a new airfield all (or nearly all) of its very own.

The Mark 1 made the trip, but was never reassembled, and finally perished

*I never expected to witness such a scene again – but the burning oilfields of Kuwait brought it back vividly.

in a cannibal orgy. A long time later, I came across the gutted and derelict vehicles in a parking lot, and had a quiet weep inside them, remembering some of the happiest as well as some of the most exasperating hours of my life. *Requiescat in pace.*

25

'How I Lost a Billion Dollars in My Spare Time.'*

My contribution to communications satellites began rather modestly near Stratford-upon-Avon in the spring of 1945. Here I was peacefully engaged – the whole of my war was a very peaceful one, I am thankful to say – in training airmen and airwomen to maintain and operate the Mark 2 GCAs now coming from the production line. Though the work was fascinating, it left me plenty of time to think about space flight, my chief interest since I joined the British Interplanetary Society in 1935. (It also gave me time to write science fiction, but that is another story – see *Astounding Days*.)

Owing to the war, the BIS was in a state of suspended animation – not that this made much difference as far as the rest of the world was concerned. The society had been founded by a remarkable man, the engineer P. E. Cleator, in 1933, and at its peak had achieved a membership of little more than a hundred. (Today it is about 4000.) A hard core of a dozen enthusiasts kept in touch, by correspondence and occasional meetings, throughout the war.

By early 1945 the European conflict was over and the end was dimly in sight; so we began to make plans for our post-war activities. I was thus simultaneously involved in electronics, astronautics – and science fiction, now taken much more seriously by the general public ever since the V2 had demonstrated that long-range rockets were a practicable proposition. (Despite the opinions of numerous 'experts', one of whom stated categorically: 'My family has been making fireworks for a hundred years. I can assure you that no rocket will ever cross the English Channel.')

Taking a rather more optimistic view, I wrote a letter to the British magazine *Wireless World*, which published it in its February 1945 issue under the heading 'V2 for Ionospheric Research?'. I pointed out that the rockets falling on London at that very moment could be used 'in an immediate post-war research project' to carry scientific instruments to the E1 and F1 layers. With the development of a second stage, orbital velocity could be reached, and it would be possible to have an instrumented payload:

*I apologise for this facetious title, which I originally used almost thirty years ago. Though I don't take it very seriously, it's too good to waste.

circling the Earth perpetually outside the limits of the atmosphere and broadcasting information as long as the batteries lasted, since the rocket would be in brilliant sunlight for half the time, the operating period might be indefinitely prolonged by the use of thermo-couples and photoelectric elements.

Both of these developments demand nothing new in the way of technical resources; the first and probably the second should come within the next five or ten years. However, I would like to close by mentioning a possibility of the more remote future – perhaps half a century ahead.

An 'artificial satellite' at the correct distance from the Earth would make one revolution every twenty-four hours, i.e., it would remain stationary above the same spot and would be within optical range of nearly half the earth's surface.

Three repeater stations, 120 degrees apart in the correct orbit, could give television and microwave coverage to the entire planet. I'm afraid this isn't going to be of the slightest use to our post-war planners, but I think it is the ultimate solution to the problem.

That 'perhaps half a century ahead' (i.e. 1995!) certainly makes me look a dyed-in-the-wool conservative. But please remember that when I wrote this letter, the war in Europe was still in progress, and after that no one could guess how long it would take to deal with Japan. And, of course, I was still thinking in terms of large, manned space stations: the transistor and its progeny still lay in the future.

Another person who was thinking on similar lines was the late George O. Smith, radio engineer and science-fiction writer, whose *Venus Equilateral* series started with 'QRM-Interplanetary' in the October 1942 *Astounding Science Fiction* and continued through thirteen stories in three years. They concerned a radio relay station at the Trojan position sixty degrees ahead of Venus, positioned there to maintain communications between Earth and Venus when the sun blocked the direct path between the two planets. As I wrote in my introduction to *The Complete Venus Equilateral* (Ballantine Books, 1976): 'Though there had been many tales about "space stations" long before the Venus Equilateral series (Murray Leinster's "Power Planet" is a classic example from the early thirties), George Smith was probably the first writer – certainly the first technically qualified writer – to spell out their uses for space communications. It is therefore quite possible that these stories influenced me subconsciously.' (Appropriately enough, the person who pointed this out to me is another long-time science-fiction fan: Dr John Pierce, who makes frequent appearances in this book.)

At this point, a few more historical footnotes are in order. I have sometimes been credited with the discovery of the stationary orbit itself, which of course is ridiculous. No one could have 'discovered' this, since its existence was perfectly obvious from the time of Newton (if not of Kepler!). I will be astonished if it has not often appeared in astronomical literature – perhaps when Asaph Hall discovered the satellites of Mars in 1877. The small outer moon Deimos is not far beyond the stationary orbit, and Phobos is well inside it.

The Russian pioneer Tsiolkovski took the concept for granted but did not develop it; radio, of course, was in its infancy when he was writing around the turn of the century. Not until 1928 did the somewhat shadowy and mysterious Austrian Captain H. Potocnik, writing under the name Hermann Noordung, develop the engineering aspects of the manned space station in great detail – and placed it in the stationary orbit! He naturally assumed that there would be radio links between Earth and station.

Though I was quite unaware of this in 1945 (never having seen his books at the time, still less dreaming that he would be my house-guest six years later), Hermann Oberth appears to have been the first person specifically associating space stations and communication. In his first book, *The Rocket into Planetary Space* (1923), he did so in a very interesting way:

> With their powerful instruments they would be able to see fine detail on earth and could communicate by means of mirrors reflecting sunlight. This might be useful for communication with places on the ground which have no cable connections and cannot be reached by electric waves. Since they, provided the sky is clear, could see a candle flame at night and reflection from a hand mirror by day, if they only knew where and when to look, they could maintain communications between expeditions and their homeland, far distant colonies and their motherland, ships at sea . . . The strategic value is obvious especially in the case of war in areas of low population density . . .

This quotation (translation by Willy Ley, from his *Rockets, Missiles and Men in Space* (Viking, 1968)) is truly impressive, but is also a reminder of the primitive state of radio at the beginning of the 1920s, before the enormous and unexpected potential of short waves had been discovered. Willy Ley once remarked to me, 'Do you realise why Oberth never invented the radio relay satellite? Because when he was writing, the radio telegraphy stations had long-wave antennas that covered square kilometres of ground.' However, this hardly seems a good enough explanation, in view of the fact that even by 1923 Oberth had conceived of orbiting solar reflectors a hundred kilometres across, to melt icebergs and alleviate winter in high latitudes!

On 25 May 1945 I composed a four-page memorandum setting out in concise form the whole concept of geostationary relay satellites, and carefully typed the four or five carbon copies which was all that my Remington Noiseless Portable could manage. (Does anyone remember carbon paper – or want to?) The top one I sent to businessman Ralph Slazenger (of the well-known sporting goods firm), who had joined us in our attempts to revive the British Interplanetary Society. Luckily, he kept it carefully and many years later returned it to me in immaculate condition. It is now in the National Air and Space Museum, Washington, DC; for the 1979 World Advisory Radio Conference (WARC 79) in Geneva, INTELSAT reproduced several thousand copies, so perfectly that they cannot be distinguished from the original. As Exhibit A at the INTELSAT stand, I signed these for hours on end for visiting VIPs.

This short memorandum was the precursor of the more detailed paper, prepared for a possibly sceptical audience, which I dispatched to *Wireless World* on 7 July 1945. Although some of the editorial board argued that they were not publishing a science-fiction magazine, it appeared in the October issue under the heading 'Extra-Terrestrial Relays'. This may well have been one of the first appearances of the now familiar term 'E.T.' in print; the new title was certainly more informative than my original, 'The Future of World Communications'.

The proofs arrived a few days after Hiroshima, and I promptly added an over-enthusiastic postscript about the impact of nuclear energy upon astronautics. It actually took nineteen years before the first atomic rocket was run under full thrust (Rover, Phoebus, 1964) – and the programme was then abandoned after more than a billion dollars had been spent on it. But one day, work will be resumed; some form of nuclear propulsion will be essential for the large-scale exploration of the solar system.

The paper, which is given in the Appendix, ran to four pages and four diagrams. It will probably be remembered when all my fiction is forgotten.

I have, of course, often been asked why I never attempted to patent the idea. The answer is simple – lack of imagination. Not for a moment did I dream, in those final months of the war, that the first crude comsat (SCORE, December 1958) would be orbiting within thirteen years, and that commercial operations would start within twenty. I now know that, in all probability, I could not have patented the idea in 1945 even if I had made the effort. A lawyer friend, who also tries to earn an honest living writing science fiction, once looked into the matter and summed up his conclusions in a story-article 'The Lagging Profession' (originally published in *Analog*, January 1951, later reprinted in the sixth *Annual of the Year's Best SF*).

As far as I can understand the legal mind, and the labyrinthine intricacies of patent law, I gather from my friend Leonard Lockhard's* thesis that (a) I couldn't have patented comsats in 1945; (b) if I had succeeded, the patent would later have been declared invalid, and (c) if it had been valid, it would have been worthless. In support of this argument, so encouraging to all would-be inventors, he quoted the remarkable case of Moffett v. Fiske.

Admiral Fiske was foolish enough to take out a patent for the torpedo-

---

*Actually Theodore L. Thomas, author of some excellent science-fiction stories, whose hospitality I often enjoyed during my lecture-touring days in the fifties.

carrying aeroplane, back in 1912. The Navy (need I say 'of course'?) would have nothing to do with such a crazy idea, and was a little shaken when the admiral sued many years later and was awarded $198,500. But, alas, the case was reversed on appeal, the higher court arguing that the admiral should not have been granted his 1912 patent because at that date there was no aeroplane capable of carrying a torpedo, and no torpedo capable of standing the shock of being dropped from an aeroplane. It was useless for the poor admiral to claim that such developments were a matter of only a few years, and that events had fully vindicated him. He didn't collect, and merely proved the truth of the statement that 'a patent is nothing more than a licence to sue (or be sued)'. It is fatal to be too far ahead of your time, and nowadays, 'too far' is about five years.

Even if I had slipped a patent past the examiners in 1945, there is another poignant aspect of the situation. The life of a patent is seventeen years; so it would have expired just as the Communications Satellite Corporation was being set up . . .

Yet I am quite sure that there were all sorts of loopholes that I might have exploited if I had been a better business man, and if I had realised just how quickly astronautics was going to get off the ground. Perhaps I could have registered a few trademarks (COMSAT, for example . . .) and otherwise made an expensive nuisance of myself, to intercept a few of the billions of dollars soon to be invested in the sky.

But I am not particularly bitter about having missed the boat – or the rocket – and my equanimity is certainly not due to any nobleness of character. I feel that I've received everything due to me in terms of recognition from the people who really matter – starting with the Franklin Institute's award of its 1963 Stuart Ballantine Medal. This gold medal (for developments in communication) had previously been awarded to John Pierce, Claude Shannon, and the teams that invented the transistor, the maser, and the laser. In such company, I felt something of an impostor.

For the people who deserve the real credit for communications satellites are those who had to convert my paper plans into hardware that will function flawlessly for months and years on end, thousands of miles above the Earth. I risked nothing except a few hours of my time; but other men have risked their reputations and their careers.

26

'IF YOU GOTTA MESSAGE . . .'

Whether or not Sam Goldwyn really did tell his script-writers 'If you gotta message, use Western Union', I have always regarded this as excellent advice. The prime duty of fiction is to entertain, not to instruct – and still less to propagandise. In this respect, the greatest of all science-fiction writers may serve as a useful warning. H. G. Wells, someone once wittily remarked, 'sold his birthright for a pot of message'. Given the problems and abuses which H. G. tirelessly attempted to rectify, it was a noble fault, but one that I have always tried to avoid.

Nevertheless, I must confess that I have sometimes used fiction to advertise causes which seemed of importance or value – notably that of space travel. When H. G. Wells wrote *The First Men in the Moon*, he was certainly not trying to promote astronautics – but I was attempting exactly that with *Prelude to Space* (written in 1947, just ten years before Sputnik 1, and published in 1951). And as one of the rationales for space research, in Chapter 4 I stressed the potential of satellites for communication, through the voice of 'Interplanetary's' public relations manager: 'The great radio and television companies *had* to get out into space – it was the only way they could broadcast television over the whole world and provide a universal communication service.'

I went into much more detail the next year (1952) in *Islands in the Sky*: writing in the Early Neo-Electronic Age, before the advent of the transistor, this is what I imagined comsats would look like:

. . . we were only a few minutes behind schedule when we came sweeping into the orbit of Relay Station Two – the one that sits above latitude 30 East, over the middle of Africa. I was now used to seeing peculiar objects in space, so the first sight of the station didn't surprise me in the least. It consisted of a flat rectangular lattice-work, with one side facing Earth. Covering this face were hundreds of small, concave reflectors – the focusing systems that beamed the radio signals to the planet beneath, or collected them on the way up. We approached cautiously, making contact with the back of the station. A pilot who let his ship pass in front of it was very unpopular – as he might cause a temporary failure on thousands of circuits, as he blocked the radio beams. For the whole of the planet's long-distance services, and most of the radio and TV networks, were routed through the relay stations. As I looked more closely, I saw that there were two other sets of radio reflector systems, aimed not at Earth but in the two directions sixty degrees away from it. These were handing the beams to the other two stations, so that altogether the three formed a vast triangle, slowly rotating with the turning Earth . . .

The short-short stories 'Special Delivery' and 'Freedom of Space' (now in the collection *The Other Side of the Sky*) have a similar background. They formed part of a sextet written at the beginning of 1957, which thanks to some high-speed revision I was able to update for publication in the London *Evening Standard* within a few days of the world's first satellite, Sputnik 1 (4 October). 'Special Delivery' recounts a mini-disaster in the pioneering days on the geostationary frontier, involving a robot carrier of the type now used routinely to supply the Mir and Souyez space stations. 'Freedom of Space' deals with a matter which is not yet of great practical importance: but it will be . . .

Both stories are given here exactly as they appeared during the first month of the Space Age. Please remember that the events they purport to describe are now a decade behind us, in some parallel universe. Further proof of a slogan I once suggested for my trade union, the Science Fiction Writers of America: THE FUTURE ISN'T WHAT IT USED TO BE.

SPECIAL DELIVERY

I can still remember the excitement, back in 1957, when Russia launched the first artificial satellites and managed to hang a few pounds of instruments up here above the atmosphere. Of course, I was only a kid at the time, but I went out in the evening like everyone else, trying to spot those little magnesium spheres as they zipped through the twilight sky hundreds of miles above my head. It's strange to think that some of them are still there – but that now they're *below* me, and I'd have to look down toward Earth if I wanted to see them . . .

Yes, a lot has happened in the last forty years, and sometimes I'm afraid that you people down on Earth take the space stations for granted, forgetting the skill and science and courage that went to make them. How often do you stop to think that all your long-distance phone calls, and most of your TV programmes, are routed through one or the other of the satellites? And how often do you give any credit to the meteorologists up here for the fact that weather forecasts are no longer the joke they were to our grandfathers, but are dead accurate 99 per cent of the time?

It was a rugged life, back in the seventies, when I went up to work on the outer stations. They were being rushed into operation to open up the millions of new TV and radio circuits which would be available as soon as we had transmitters out in space that could beam programmes to anywhere on the globe.

The first artificial satellites had been very close to Earth, but the three stations forming the great triangle of the Relay Chain had to be 22,000 miles up, spaced equally around the equator. At this altitude, and at no other, they would take exactly a day to go around their orbit, and so would stay poised for ever over the same spot on the turning Earth.

In my time I've worked on all three of the stations, but my first tour of duty was aboard Relay Two. That's almost exactly over Entebbe, Uganda, and provides service for Europe, Africa, and most of Asia. Today it's a huge structure hundreds of yards across, beaming thousands of simultaneous programmes down to the hemisphere beneath it as it carries the radio traffic of half the world. But when I saw it for the first time from the port of the ferry rocket that carried me up to orbit, it looked like a junk pile adrift in space. Prefabricated parts were floating around in hopeless confusion, and it seemed impossible that any order could ever emerge from this chaos.

Accommodation for the technical staff and assembling crews was primitive, consisting of a few unserviceable ferry rockets that had been stripped of everything except air purifiers. 'The Hulks', we christened them; each man had just enough room for himself and a couple of cubic feet of personal belongings. There was a fine irony in the fact that we were living in the midst of infinite space and hadn't room to swing a cat.

It was a great day when we heard that the first pressurised living quarters were on their way up to us – complete with needle-jet shower baths that would operate even here, where water – like everything else – had no weight. Unless you've lived aboard an overcrowded spaceship, you won't appreciate what that means. We could throw away our damp sponges and feel really clean at last . . .

Nor were the showers the only luxury promised us. On the way up from Earth was an inflatable lounge, spacious enough to hold no fewer than eight people, a microfilm library, a magnetic billiard table, lightweight chess sets, and similar novelties for bored spacemen. The very thought of all these comforts made our cramped life in the Hulks seem quite unendurable, even though we were being paid about a thousand dollars a week to endure it.*

Starting from the Second Refuelling Zone, 2000 miles above Earth, the eagerly awaited ferry rocket would take about six hours to climb up to us with its precious cargo. I was off duty at the time, and stationed myself at the telescope where I'd spent most of my scanty leisure. It was impossible to grow tired of exploring the great world hanging there in space beside us; with the highest power of the telescope, one seemed to be only a few miles above the

*This dates the story more than any of the technical details. Remember the 1957 dollar?

surface. When there were no clouds and seeing was good, objects the size of a small house were easily visible. I had never been to Africa, but I grew to know it well while I was off duty in Station Two. You may not believe this, but I've often spotted elephants moving across the plains, and the immense herds of zebras and antelopes were easy to see as they flowed back and forth like living tides on the great reservations.

But my favourite spectacle was the dawn coming up over the mountains in the heart of the continent. The line of sunlight would come sweeping across the Indian Ocean, and the new day would extinguish the tiny, twinkling galaxies of the cities shining in the darkness below me. Long before the sun had reached the lowlands around them, the peaks of Kilimanjaro and Mount Kenya would be blazing in the dawn, brilliant stars still surrounded by the night. As the sun rose higher, the day would march swiftly down their slopes and the valleys would fill with light. Earth would then be at its first quarter, waxing toward full.

Twelve hours later, I would see the reverse process as the same mountains caught the last rays of the setting sun. They would blaze for a little while in the narrow belt of twilight; then Earth would spin into darkness, and night would fall upon Africa.

It was not the beauty of the terrestrial globe I was concerned with now. Indeed, I was not even looking at Earth, but at the fierce blue-white star high above the western edge of the planet's disc. The automatic freighter was eclipsed in Earth's shadow; what I was seeing was the incandescent flare of its rockets as they drove it up on its 20,000 mile climb.

I had watched ships ascending to us so often that I knew every stage of their manoeuvre by heart. So when the rockets didn't wink out, but continued to burn steadily, I knew within seconds that something was wrong. In sick, helpless fury I watched all our longed-for comforts – and, worse still, our mail! – moving faster and faster along the unintended orbit. The freighter's auto-pilot had jammed; had there been a human pilot aboard, he could have overridden the controls and cut the motor, but now all the fuel that should have driven the ferry on its two-way trip was being burned in one continuous blast of power.

By the time the fuel tanks had emptied, and that distant star had flickered and died in the field of my telescope, the tracking stations had confirmed what I already knew. The freighter was moving far too fast for Earth's gravity to recapture it – indeed, it was heading into the cosmic wilderness beyond Pluto . . .

It took a long time for morale to recover, and it only made matters worse when someone in the computing section worked out the future history of our errant freighter. You see, nothing is ever really lost in space. Once you've calculated its orbit, you know where it is until the end of eternity. As we watched our lounge, our library, our games, our mail receding to the far horizons of the solar system, we knew that it would all come back one day, in perfect condition.

If we have a ship standing by it will be easy to intercept it the second time it comes around the sun – quite early in the spring of AD 15,862 . . .

FREEDOM OF SPACE

Not many of you, I suppose, can imagine the time before the satellite relays gave us our present world communications system. When I was a boy, it was impossible to send TV programmes across the oceans, or even to establish reliable radio contact around the curve of the Earth without picking up a fine assortment of crackles and bangs on the way. Yet now we take interference-free circuits for granted, and think nothing of seeing our friends on the other side of the globe as clearly as if we were standing face to face. Indeed, it's a simple fact that without the satellite relays, the whole structure of world commerce and industry would collapse. Unless we were up here on the space stations to bounce their messages around the globe, how do you think any of the world's big business organisations could keep their widely scattered electronic brains in touch with each other?

But all this was still in the future, back in the late seventies, when we were finishing work on the Relay Chain. I've already told you about some of our problems and near-disasters; they were serious enough at the time, but in the end we overcame them all. The three stations spaced around Earth were on longer piles of girders, air cylinders, and plastic pressure-chambers. Their assembly had been completed, we had moved aboard, and could now work in comfort, unhampered by space suits. And we had gravity again, now that the stations had been set slowly spinning. Not real gravity, of course; but centrifugal force feels exactly the same when you're out in space. It was pleasant being able to pour drinks and to sit down without drifting away on the first air current.

Once the three stations had been built, there was still a year's solid work to be done installing all radio and TV equipment that would lift the world's communications networks into space. It was a great day when we established the first TV link between England and Australia. The signal was beamed up to us in Relay Two, as we sat above the centre of Africa, we flashed it across to Three – poised over New Guinea – and they shot it down to Earth again, clear and clean after its 90,000-mile journey.

These, however, were the engineers' private tests. The official opening of the system would be the biggest event in the history of world communication – an elaborate global telecast, in which every nation would take part. It would be a three-hour show, as for the first time the live TV camera roamed around the world, proclaiming to mankind that the last barrier of distance was down.

The programme planning, it was cynically believed, had taken as much effort as the building of the space stations in the first place; and of the problems the planners had to solve, the most difficult was that of choosing a compère or master of ceremonies to introduce the items in the elaborate global show that would be watched by half the human race.

Heaven knows how much conniving, blackmail, and downright character-assassination went on behind scenes. All we knew was that a week before the great day, a non-scheduled rocket came up to orbit with Gregory Wendell aboard. This was quite a surprise, since Gregory wasn't as big a TV personality as, say, Jeffers Jackson in the US or Vince Clifford in Britain. However, it seemed that the big boys had cancelled each other, and Gregg had got the coveted job through one of those compromises so well known to politicians.

Gregg had started his career as a disc jockey on a university radio station in the American Midwest, and had worked his way up through the Hollywood and Manhattan night-club circuits until he had a daily, nationwide programme of his own. Apart from his cynical yet relaxed personality, his biggest asset was his deep velvet voice, for which he could probably thank his African blood. Even when you flatly disagreed with what he was saying – even, indeed, when he was tearing you to pieces in an interview – it was still a pleasure to listen to him.

We gave him the grand tour of the space station, and even (strictly against regulations) took him out through the air lock in a space suit. He loved it all, but there were two things he liked in particular. 'This air you make,' he said, 'it beats the stuff we have to breathe down in New York. This is the first time my sinus trouble has gone since I went into TV.' He also relished the low gravity; at the station's rim, a man had half his normal, Earth weight – and at the axis he had no weight at all.

However, the novelty of his surroundings didn't distract Gregg from his job. He spent hours at Communications Central, polishing his script and getting his cues right, and studying the dozens of monitor screens that would be his windows on the world. I came across him once while he was running through his introduction of Queen Elizabeth, who would be speaking from Buckingham Palace at the very end of the programme. He was so intent on his rehearsal that he never even noticed I was standing beside him.

Well, that telecast is now part of history. For the first time a billion human beings watched a single programme that came 'live' from every corner of the Earth, and was a roll-call of the world's greatest citizens. Hundreds of cameras on land and sea and air looked inquiringly at the turning globe; and at the end there was that wonderful shot of the Earth through a zoom lens on the space station, making the whole planet recede until it was lost among the stars . . .

There were a few hitches, of course. One camera on the bed of the Atlantic wasn't ready on cue, and we had to spend some extra time looking at the Taj Mahal. And owing to a switching error Russian subtitles were superimposed on the South American transmission, while half the USSR found itself trying to read Spanish. But this was nothing to what might have happened.

Through the entire three hours, introducing the famous and the unknown with equal ease, came the mellow yet never orotund flow of Gregg's voice. He did a magnificent job; the congratulations came pouring up the beam the moment the broadcast finished. But he didn't hear them; he made one short, private call to his agent, and then went to bed.

Next morning, the Earth-bound ferry was waiting to take him back to any job he cared to accept. But it left without Gregg Wendell, now junior station announcer of Relay Two.

'They'll think I'm crazy,' he said, beaming happily, 'but why should I go back to that rat race down there? I've all the universe to look at, I can breathe smog-free air, the low gravity makes me feel a Hercules, and my three darling ex-wives can't get at me.' He kissed his hand to the departing rocket. 'So long, Earth,' he called. 'I'll be back when I start pining for Broadway traffic jams and bleary penthouse dawns. And if I get homesick, I can look at anywhere on the planet just by turning a switch. Why, I'm more in the middle of things here than I could ever be on Earth, yet I can cut myself off from the human race whenever I want to.'

He was still smiling as he watched the ferry begin the long fall back to Earth, toward the fame and the fortune that could have been his. And then, whistling cheerfully, he left the observation lounge in eight-foot strides to read the weather forecast for Lower Patagonia.

27

THE MAKING OF A MOON

So much for fiction (or propaganda). I certainly never dreamed, when I wrote 'Freedom of Space' in January 1957, that one day I should be taking part in just such global satellite broadcasts – for example Worldnet's celebration of COMSAT's twentieth anniversary in 1985.

Now it is time to get back to the real world, and see what actually happened. During the early 1950s, the idea of artificial satellites for ionospheric and meteorological research became widely accepted by the scientific community. One landmark event in the educational process was the International Astronautical Federation's Second Congress, held in London during September 1951 under the auspices of the British Interplanetary Society.

The theme of the congress was 'The Artificial Satellite', and on re-reading the papers almost forty years later I am amused to see how ambitious most of us were. The main emphasis was on building manned space stations, and refuelling in orbit for flights to the planets   probably with nuclear-powered rockets! There was only the briefest mention of communications satellites; as I was chairman of the proceedings, this seems a surprising oversight. However, by this time I took such unexciting trinkets for granted, and was anxious to hurry on to the Moon and Mars.

Fortunately, some of my colleagues were more practically minded. A now historic paper by K. W. Gatland, A. M. Kunesch and A. E. Dixon, entitled 'Minimum Satellite Vehicles' discussed the smallest possible rocket that could get into orbit with a worthwhile payload – such as 'a metallised balloon for use as a radio reflector . . . which could be puffed up in space'. We shall see in Chapter 29 just what came of that idea, only a decade later.

Another scientist who thought on similar conservative lines (perhaps because he had worked with real rockets, not paper ones) was a young cosmic-ray researcher attached to the US Office of Naval Research in London. Dr Fred Singer made the very sensible suggestion that we should crawl before we tried to walk – still less run – and proposed building the smallest possible satellite that could do some useful science. In a brainstorming session with the late A. V. Cleaver (Chief Engineer of the Rolls-Royce Rocket Division) and myself, the acronym MOUSE was concocted, standing for Minimum Orbital

Unmanned Satellite of Earth. (Though 'Orbital' is certainly redundant, we wanted a name that could be easily pronounced – and would convey a sense of smallness.) Our ploy worked; MOUSE received wide publicity, and played a key role in subsequent events – some of which, such as Project Orbiter, were not disclosed until years later.

One weekend in June, 1954, when I was staying with my friends Fred and Pip Durant in Washington, I encountered a whole stream of distinguished but close-lipped visitors. The other house-guest was Dr Wernher von Braun, and he was quickly joined by Dr Fred Singer, Harvard Observatory's Dr Fred Whipple (famous for his 'dirty snowball' theory of comets, proved thirty years later during the missions to Halley) and a dozen other engineers and scientists, mostly from the Army Ballistic Missile Agency and the Office of Naval Research. The Air Force was conspicuous by its absence, and I suspect that this was one – if not the chief – reason for all the secrecy.

It was obvious what was afoot, but I did not pay as much attention to the Project Orbiter plotters as I might have done because I was preparing to explore a new element myself. Realising that 'weightlessness' could be enjoyed by going downwards as well as upwards, and at considerably less expense, I had taken up diving. In a few months I would be leaving for the Great Barrier Reef, and aqualungs were now more important to me than rockets.

And so while Dr von Braun was promoting Orbiter, I was busily brainwashing him, with results which became apparent a few years later (1960), when he wrote the preface to *The Challenge of the Sea*: 'You may think it strange that I, of all people, should be writing an introduction to a book on the challenge of the sea. But, in a way, I owe it to my friend Arthur Clarke. For it was he who introduced me to the sport that has rapidly become my favourite – skin-diving.'

Project Orbiter, so it was later revealed, was a plan to launch a satellite using the Army's big Redstone missile as the first stage, and clusters of solid rockets as upper stages. It was hardly elegant, but had the great advantage that most of the hardware already existed. But politics prevailed, and the United States decided to develop a virtually new launcher for its official satellite programme, Project Vanguard – as it turned out, a most unfortunate name. When the initial Vanguards failed – with a couple of sputniks sailing overhead, to make matters worse – the von Braun team was finally given a green light, and the first US satellite, Explorer 1, was launched by Orbiter *redux*.

When President Eisenhower announced, on 29 July 1955, that the United States planned to launch artificial satellites as part of its contribution to the International Geophysical Year, 1957–8,* I was about as far from Washington

*Almost exactly thirty-five years later (21 July 1990) his successor would set a manned expedition to Mars as a US goal. I wonder what Ike would have thought of that.

as it was possible to be – sixty kilometres off the coast of Australia. With my diving partner Mike Wilson, I was on the Great Barrier Reef collecting material for *The Coast of Coral* (long out of print, alas) and we heard the news on our portable radio. Suspecting, correctly, that Fred Singer would be heavily involved in the project, I went to great trouble and expense to cable him from our base on Heron Island: 'Congratulations! May the Mouse bring forth a mountain!' When this cryptic message finally arrived, weeks later, it was hopelessly garbled – and to make matters worse, Fred had to pay for it, as the charges had been mysteriously reversed. Such were global telecommunications in 1955.

On my return to civilisation, I spent several months interviewing the scientists and engineers working on Project Vanguard. The book that resulted, *The Making of a Moon*, had the subtitle 'The Story of the Earth Satellite Program'. As it turned out, this should have read 'The Story of the Other Earth Satellite Program'. My book appeared in September 1957 – just a month before Sputnik 1 opened the Space Age, and I had to do some hasty rewriting for the second printing. However, I made no changes in the chapter 'Voices from the Sky', which opened with the words: 'It may seem premature, if not ludicrous, to talk about the commercial possibilities of satellites. Yet the airplane became of commercial importance within thirty years of its birth, and there are good reasons for thinking that this time scale may be shortened in the case of the satellite, because of its immense value in the field of communications . . .'

Today, that prediction does indeed seem ludicrous – because of its timidity. Sputnik plus thirty equals 1987; by then, communication satellites had been operating for more than twenty years.

28

'I REMEMBER BABYLON'

Now that satellites were actually orbiting the Earth – though none had yet radioed back anything except scientific data from mankind's new frontier – I once again started to exploit the fictional possibilities of comsats, and in a much more serious vein.

'Special Delivery' and 'The Freedom of Space' had been light-hearted little squibs, intended to amuse as much as to inform a public still not quite accustomed to the idea that the familiar sky was no longer the limit. A few years later, in 1960 (Sputnik plus 3), I wrote a story for a much more sophisticated audience, in which I quite deliberately – indeed, almost defiantly – violated Sam Goldwyn's dictum. As if to emphasise this fact, it is the *only* story I ever wrote which featured myself (whether as hero or villain, the future has yet to decide).

I apologise for the amount of name-dropping and the number of (now dated) topical references. But remember that this was written for a 1960 audience, and I was anxious 'to add an air of verisimilitude to an otherwise bald and unconvincing narrative'. So all the contemporary references and statements are factual.

I should also explain that 'Mike' is Mike Wilson, my partner on our various underwater expeditions (see *The Coast of Coral*, *The Treasure of the Great Reef*, etc.). After a brief but spectacular movie career as writer/director/photographer, he reincarnated himself as Swami Siva Kalki and now writes profound volumes on Buddhist philosophy.

My name is Arthur C. Clarke, and I wish I had no connection with this whole sordid business. But as the moral – repeat, moral – integrity of the United States is involved, I must first establish my credentials. Only thus will you understand how, with the aid of the late Dr Alfred Kinsey, I have unwittingly triggered an avalanche that may sweep away much of Western civilisation.

Back in 1945, while a radar officer in the Royal Air Force, I had the only original idea of my life. Twelve years before the first sputnik started beeping, it occurred to me that an artificial satellite would be a wonderful place for a television transmitter, since a station several thousand miles high could broadcast to half the globe. I wrote up the idea the week after Hiroshima, proposing a network of relay satellites 22,000 miles above the Equator; at this height, they'd take exactly one day to complete a revolution, and so would remain fixed over the same spot on the Earth.

The piece appeared in the October 1945 issue of *Wireless World*; not expecting that celestial mechanics would be commercialised in my lifetime, I made no attempt to patent the idea, and doubt if I could have done so anyway. (If I'm wrong, I'd prefer not to know.) But I kept plugging it in my books, and today the idea of communications satellites is so commonplace that no one knows its origin.

I did make a plaintive attempt to put the record straight when approached by the House of Representatives Committee on Astronautics and Space Exploration; you'll find my evidence on page 32 of its report, *The Next Ten Years in Space, 1959–1969* (H.R. Document 115, 86th Congress, 1st Session). And as you'll see in a moment, my concluding words had an irony I never appreciated at the time: 'Living as I do in the Far East, I am constantly reminded of the struggle between the Western world and the USSR for the uncommitted millions of Asia . . . When line-of-sight TV transmissions become possible from satellites directly overhead, the propaganda effect may be decisive . . .'

I still stand by those words, but there were angles I hadn't thought of – and which, unfortunately, other people have.

It all began during one of those official receptions which are such a feature of social life in Eastern capitals. They're even more common in the West, of course, but in Colombo there's little competing entertainment. At least once a week, if you are anybody, you get an invitation to cocktails at an embassy or legation, the British Council, the US Operations Mission, L'Alliance Française, or one of the countless alphabetical agencies the United Nations has begotten.

At first, being more at home beneath the Indian Ocean than in diplomatic circles, my partner and I were nobodies and were left alone. But after Mike compèred Dave Brubeck's tour of Ceylon, people started to take notice of us – still more so when he married one of the island's best-known beauties.* So now our consumption of cocktails and canapés is limited chiefly by reluctance to abandon our comfortable sarongs for such Western absurdities as trousers, dinner jackets and ties.

It was the first time we'd been to the Soviet Embassy, which was throwing a party for a group of Russian oceanographers who'd just come into port. Beneath the inevitable paintings of Lenin and Marx, a couple of hundred guests of all colours, religions and languages were milling around, chatting with friends, or single-mindedly demolishing the vodka and caviar. I'd been

*Sceptics can consult the photo in the May 1960 *Playboy* for confirmation.

separated from Mike and Elizabeth, but could see them at the other side of the room. Mike was doing his 'There was I at fifty fathoms' act to a fascinated audience, while Elilzabeth watched him quizzically – and rather more people watched Elizabeth.

Ever since I lost an eardrum while pearl-diving on the Great Barrier Reef, I've been at a considerable disadvantage at functions of this kind; the surface noise is about twelve decibels too much for me to cope with. And this is no small handicap when being introduced to people with names like Dharamasiriwardene, Tissaveerasinghe, Goonetilleke, and Jayawickrema. When I'm not raiding the buffet, therefore, I usually look for a pool of relative quiet where there's a chance of following more than 50 per cent of any conversation in which I may get involved.

I was standing in the acoustic shadow of a large ornamental pillar, surveying the scene in my detached or Somerset Maugham manner, when I noticed that someone was looking at me with that 'Haven't we met before?' expression.

I'll describe him with some care, because there must be many people who can identify him. He was in the mid-thirties, and I guessed he was American; he had that well-scrubbed, crew-cut, man-about-Rockefeller-Center look that used to be a hallmark until the younger Russian diplomats and technical advisers started imitating it so successfully. He was about six feet in height, with shrewd brown eyes and black hair, prematurely grey at the sides. Though I was fairly certain we'd never met before, his face reminded me of someone. It took me a couple of days to work it out: remember the late John Garfield? That's who it was, as near as makes no difference.

When a stranger catches my eye at a party, my standard operating procedure goes into action automatically. If he seems a pleasant enough person, but I don't feel like introductions at the moment, I give him the Neutral Scan, letting my eyes sweep past him without a flicker of recognition, yet without positive unfriendliness. If he looks like a creep, he receives the *Coup d'œil*, which consists of a long, disbelieving stare followed by an unhurried view of the back of my neck. In extreme cases, an expression of revulsion may be switched on for a few milliseconds. The message usually gets across.

But this character seemed interesting, and I was getting bored, so I gave him the Affable Nod. A few minutes later he drifted through the crowd, and I aimed my good ear towards him.

'Hello,' he said (yes, he was American), 'my name's Gene Hartford. I'm sure we've met somewhere.'

'Quite likely,' I answered; 'I've spent a good deal of time in the States. I'm Arthur Clarke.'

Usually that produces a blank stare, but sometimes it doesn't. I could almost see the IBM cards flickering behind those hard brown eyes, and was flattered by the brevity of his access time.

'The science writer?'

'Correct.'

'Well, this is fantastic.' He seemed genuinely astonished. 'Now I know where I've seen you. I was in the studio once when you were on the Dave Garroway show.'

(This lead may be worth following up, though I doubt it; and I'm sure that 'Gene Hartford' was phoney – it was too smoothly synthetic.)

'So you're in TV?' I said. 'What are you doing here – collecting material, or just on vacation?'

He gave me the frank, friendly smile of a man who has plenty to hide.

'Oh, I'm keeping my eyes open. But this really is amazing; I read your *Exploration of Space* when it came out back in, ah – '

'Nineteen fifty-two; the Book-of-the-Month Club's never been quite the same since.'

All this time I had been sizing him up, and though there was something about him I didn't like, I was unable to pin it down. In any case, I was prepared to make substantial allowances for someone who had read my books and was also in TV; Mike and I are always on the look-out for markets for our underwater movies. But that, to put it mildly, was not Hartford's line of business.

'Look,' he said eagerly, 'I've a big network deal cooking that will interest you – in fact, you helped to give me the idea.'

This sounded promising, and my coefficient of cupidity jumped several points.

'I'm glad to hear it. What's the general theme?'

'I can't talk about it here, but could we meet at my hotel, around three tomorrow?'

'Let me check my diary; yes, that's OK.'

There are only two hotels in Colombo patronised by Americans, and I guessed right the first time. He was at the Mount Lavinia, and though you may not know it, you've seen the place where we had our private chat. Around the middle of *Bridge on the River Kwai*, there's a brief scene at a military hospital, where Jack Hawkins meets a nurse and asks her where he can find Bill Holden. We have a soft spot for this episode, because Mike was one of the convalescent naval officers in the background. If you look smartly you'll see him on the extreme right, beard in full profile, signing Sam Spiegel's name to his sixth round of bar chits. As the picture turned out, Sam could afford it.

It was here, on this diminutive plateau high above the miles of palm-fringed beach, that Gene Hartford started to unload, and my simple hopes of financial advantage started to evaporate. What his exact motives were, if indeed he knew them himself, I'm still uncertain. Surprise at meeting me, and twisted feelings of gratitude (which I would gladly have done without) undoubtedly played a part, and for all his air of confidence he must have been a bitter, lonely man who desperately needed approval and friendship.

He got neither from me. I have always had a sneaking sympathy for Benedict Arnold, as must anyone who knows the full facts of the case. But Arnold merely betrayed his country; no one before Hartford ever tried to seduce it.

What dissolved my dream of dollars was the news that Hartford's connection with American TV had been severed, somewhat violently, in the early fifties. It was clear that he'd been bounced out of Madison Avenue for Party-lining, and it was equally clear that his was one case where no grave injustice had been done. Though he talked with a certain controlled fury of his fight against asinine censorship, and wept for a brilliant but unnamed cultural series he'd started before being kicked off the air, by this time I was beginning to smell so many rats that my replies were distinctly guarded. Yet as my precuniary interest in Mr Hartford diminished, so my personal curiosity increased. Who was behind him? Surely not the BBC . . .

I got round to it at last, when he'd worked the self-pity out of his system.

'I've some news that will make you sit up,' he said smugly. 'The American networks are soon going to have some real competition. And it will be done just the way you predicted; the people who sent a TV transmitter to the Moon can put a much bigger one in orbit round the Earth.'

'Good for them,' I said cautiously. 'I'm all in favour of healthy competition. When's the launching date?'

'Any moment now. The first transmitter will be parked due south of New Orleans – on the Equator, of course. That puts it way out in the open Pacific; it won't be over anyone's territory, so there'll be no political complications on that score. Yet it will be sitting up there in the sky in full view of everybody from Seattle to Key West. Think of it – the only TV station the whole United States can tune in to! Yes, even Hawaii! There won't be any way of jamming it; for the first time, there'll be a clear channel into every American home. And J. Edgar's Boy Scouts can't do a thing to block it.'

So that's your little racket, I thought; at least you're being frank. Long ago I learned not to argue with Marxists and Flat-Earthers, but if Hartford was telling the truth, I wanted to pump him for all he was worth.

'Before you get too enthusiastic,' I said, 'there are a few points you may have overlooked.'

'Such as?'

'This will work both ways. Everyone knows that the Air Force, NASA, Bell Labs, IT&T, Hughes and a few dozen other agencies are working on the same project. Whatever Russia does to the States in the propaganda line, she'll get back with compound interest.'

Hartford grinned mirthlessly.

'Really, Clarke!' he said. (I was glad he hadn't first-named me.) 'I'm a little disappointed. Surely you know that the United States is years behind in payload capacity! And do you imagine that the old T3 is Russia's last word?'

It was at this moment that I began to take him very seriously. He was perfectly right. The T3 could inject at least five times the payload of any American missile into that critical 22,000-mile orbit – the only one that would allow a satellite to remain fixed above the Earth. And by the time the US could match the performance, heaven knows where the Russians would be. Yes, heaven certainly *would* know . . .

'All right,' I conceded. 'But why should fifty million American homes start switching channels just as soon as they can tune in to Moscow? I admire the Russians, but their entertainment is worse than their politics. After the Bolshoi, what have you? And for me, a little ballet goes a long, long way.'

Once again I was treated to that peculiarly humourless smile. Hartford had been saving up his Sunday punch, and now he let me have it.

'You were the one who brought in the Russians,' he said. 'They're involved, sure – but only as contractors. The independent agency I'm working for is hiring their services.'

'That,' I remarked drily, 'must be some agency.'

'It is; just about the biggest. Even though the United States tries to pretend it doesn't exist.'

'Oh,' I said, rather stupidly. 'So *that's* your sponsor.'

I'd heard those rumours that the USSR was going to launch satellites for the Chinese; now it began to look as if the rumours fell far short of the truth. But how far short, I'd still no conception.

'You are so right,' continued Hartford, obviously enjoying himself, 'about Russian entertainment. After the initial novelty, the Neilson rating would drop to zero. But not with the programme *I'm* planning. My job is to find material that will put everyone else out of business when it goes on the air. You think it can't be done? Finish that drink and come up to my room. I've a highbrow movie about ecclesiastical art that I'd like to show you.'

Well, he wasn't crazy, though for a few minutes I wondered. I could think of few titles more carefully calculated to make the viewer reach for the channel switch than the one that flashed on the screen: ASPECTS OF THIRTEENTH-CENTURY TANTRIC SCULPTURE.

'Don't be alarmed,' Hartford chuckled, above the whirr of the projector. 'That title saves me having trouble with inquisitive Customs inspectors. It's perfectly accurate, but we'll change it to something with a bigger box-office appeal when the time comes.'

A couple of hundred feet later, after some innocuous architectural long shots, I saw what he meant.

You may know that there are certain temples in India covered with superbly executed carvings of a kind that we in the West scarcely associate with religion. To say that they are frank is a laughable understatement; they leave nothing to the imagination – *any* imagination. Yet at the same time they are genuine works of art. And so was Hartford's movie.

It had been shot, in case you're interested, at the Temple of the Sun, Konarak. I've since looked it up; it's on the Orissa coast, about twenty-five miles north-east of Puri. The reference books are pretty mealy-mouthed; some apologise for the 'obvious' impossibility of providing illustrations, but Percy Brown's *Indian Architecture* minces no words. The carvings, it says primly, are of 'a shamelessly erotic character that have no parallel in any known building'. A sweeping claim, but I can believe it after seeing that movie.

Camera work and editing were brilliant, the ancient stones coming to life beneath the roving lens. There were breathtaking time-lapse shots as the rising sun chased the shadows from bodies intertwined in ecstasy; sudden startling close-ups of scenes which at first the mind refused to recognise; soft-focus studies of stone shaped by a master's hand in all the fantasies and aberrations of love; restless zooms and pans whose meaning eluded the eye until they froze into patterns of timeless desire, eternal fulfilment. The music – mostly percussion, with a thin, high thread of sound from some stringed instrument that I could not identify – perfectly fitted the tempo of the cutting. At one moment it would be languorously slow, like the opening bars of Debussy's 'L'Après-midi'; then the drums would swiftly work themselves up to a frenzied, almost unendurable climax. The art of the ancient sculptors and the skill of the modern cameraman had combined across the centuries to create a poem of rapture, an orgasm on celluloid which I would defy any man to watch unmoved.

There was a long silence when the screen flooded with light and the lascivious music ebbed into exhaustion.

'My God!' I said, when I had recovered some of my composure. 'Are you going to telecast *that*?'

Hartford laughed. 'Believe me,' he answered, 'that's nothing; it just happens to be the only reel I can carry around safely. We're prepared to defend it any day on grounds of genuine art, historic interest, religious tolerance – oh, we've thought of all the angles. But it doesn't really matter; no one can stop us. For the first time in history, any form of censorship's become utterly impossible. There's simply no way of enforcing it; the customer can get what he wants, right in his own home. Lock the door, switch on the TV set – friends and family will never know.'

'Very clever,' I said, 'but don't you think such a diet will soon pall?'

'Of course; variety is the spice of life. We'll have plenty of conventional entertainment; let me worry about that. And every so often we'll have information programmes – I hate that word "propaganda" – to tell the cloistered American public what's really happening in the world. Our special features will just be the bait.'

'Mind if I have some fresh air?' I said. 'It's getting stuffy in here.'

Hartford drew the curtains and let daylight back into the room. Below us lay that long curve of beach, with the outrigger fishing-boats drawn up beneath the palms, and the little waves falling in foam at the end of their weary march from Africa. One of the loveliest sights in the world, but I couldn't focus on it now. I was still seeing those writhing stone limbs, those faces frozen with passions which the centuries could not slake.

That lickerish voice continued behind my back.

'You'd be astonished if you knew just how much material there is. Remember, we've absolutely no taboos. If you can film it, we can telecast it.'

He walked over to his bureau and picked up a heavy, dog-eared volume.

'This has been my Bible,' he said, 'or my Sears, Roebuck if you prefer. Without it, I'd never have sold the series to my sponsors. They're great believers in science, and they swallowed the whole thing, down to the last decimal point. Recognise it?'

I nodded; whenever I enter a room, I always monitor my host's literary taste.

'Dr Kinsey, I presume.'

'I guess I'm the only man who's read it from cover to cover and not just looked up his own vital statistics. You see, it's the only piece of market research in its field. Until something better comes along, we're making the most of it. It tells us what the customer wants, and we're going to supply it.'

'*All* of it?'

'If the audience is big enough, yes. We won't bother about feeble-minded farm boys who get too attached to the stock. But the four main sexes will get the full treatment. That's the beauty of the movie you just saw – it appeals to them all.'

'You can say that again,' I muttered.

He saw that I was beginning to get bored; there are some kinds of single-mindedness that I find depressing. But I had done Hartford an injustice, as he hastened to prove.

'Please don't think,' he said anxiously, 'that sex is our only weapon. Sensation is almost as good. Ever see the job Ed Murrow did on the late sainted Joe McCarthy? That was milk and water compared with the profiles we're planning in *Washington Confidential*.

'And there's our *Can You Take It?* series, designed to separate the men from the milksops. We'll issue so many advance warnings that every red-blooded American will feel he has to watch the show. It will start innocently enough, on ground nicely prepared by Hemingway. You'll see some bull-fighting sequences that will really lift you out of your seat – or send you running to the bathroom – because they show all the little details you never get in those cleaned-up Hollywood movies.

'We'll follow that with some really unique material that cost us exactly nothing. Do you remember the photographic evidence the Nuremburg war trials turned up? You've never seen it, because it wasn't publishable. There were quite a few amateur photographers in the concentration camps, who made the most of opportunities they'd never get again. Some of them were hanged on the testimony of their own cameras, but their work wasn't wasted. It will lead nicely into our series *Torture through the Ages* – very scholarly and thorough, yet with a remarkably wide appeal . . .

'And there are dozens of other angles, but by now you'll have the general picture. The Avenue thinks it knows all about Hidden Persuasion – believe me, it doesn't. The world's best practical psychologists are in the East these days. Remember Korea, and brainwashing? We've learned a lot since then. There's no need for violence any more; people *enjoy* being brainwashed, if you set about it the right way.'

'And you,' I said, 'are you going to brainwash the United States. Quite an order.'

'Exactly – and the country will love it, despite all the screams from Congress and the churches. Not to mention the networks, of course. They'll make the biggest fuss of all, when they find they can't compete with us.'

Hartford glanced at his watch, and gave a whistle of alarm.

'Time to start packing,' he said. 'I've got to be at that unpronounceable airport of yours by six. There's no chance, I suppose, that you can fly over to Macao and see us sometime?'

'Not a hope; but I've got a pretty good idea of the picture now. And incidentally, aren't you afraid that I'll spill the beans?'

'Why should I be? The more publicity you can give us, the better. Although our advertising campaign doesn't go into top gear for a few months yet, I feel you've earned this advance notice. As I said, your books helped to give me the idea.'

His gratitude was quite genuine, by God; it left me completely speechless.

'Nothing can stop us,' he declared – and for the first time the fanaticism that lurked behind that smooth, cynical façade was not altogether under control. 'History is on our side. We'll be using America's own decadence as a weapon against her, and it's a weapon for which there's no defence. The Air Force won't attempt space piracy by shooting down a satellite nowhere near American territory. The FCC can't even protest to a country that doesn't exist in the eyes of the State Department. If you've any other suggestions, I'd be most interested to hear them.'

I had none then, and I have none now. Perhaps these words may give some brief warning before the first teasing advertisements appear in the trade papers, and may start stirrings of elephantine alarm among the networks. But will it make any difference? Hartford did not think so, and he may be right.

'History is on our side.' I cannot get those words out of my head. Land of Lincoln and Franklin and Melville, I love you and I wish you well. But into my heart blows a cold wind from the past; for I remember Babylon.

Reading this story more than thirty years later, it seems both hopelessly dated – yet more topical than ever. Two decades later, appropriately enough, the Playboy Channel was on the air – via satellite! Alas, I never had a chance of seeing if any of its programmes lived up to my advance billing.

It was *Playboy*'s editor, incidentally, who changed my rather pedestrian title 'Blue Network' to the much more evocative (and ominous) 'I Remember Babylon'. My subconscious mind must have been doing a better job than I knew, for the choice of that name was uncannily appropriate. Babylon was the 'Babel' of the Old Testament – from which our word 'babble' is derived. In my talks on comsats I was fond of quoting Genesis 11, when 'the whole world had one language and a common speech' and men decided to build a tower reaching the skies. But the Lord said: 'If as one people speaking the same language they have begun to do this, then nothing they plan to do will be impossible for them. Come, let us go down and confuse their language so that they will not understand each other.' (New International Version.) And I went on to add that eventually comsats would establish a global language, so that 'far higher than the builders of Babel ever aspired, we may undo the curse that was visited upon them'.

The tale's other prediction has already come true: at this very moment lawyers are engaged in combat with local censors over what may, and may not, be carried by comsats. Only a few weeks ago I was fascinated to read in the newsletter *Satellite Week* (18 February 1991) that Home Dish Satellite Networks had been fined $150,000 for transmitting pornographic movies to its 30,000 subscribers. Apparently there is a 1988 federal law prohibiting such activity; it would be interesting to see what the Supreme Court could do if, as I suggested, the satellite was parked over the high seas. For that matter, I am by no means sure how far its jurisdiction applies in *any* extra-terrestrial direction.

And recently there has been a new orbiting menace, which I quite failed to foresee – religious racketeering. Pornography and televangelism have much in common. They are usually harmless, and can even be beneficial – in moderate doses. Unfortunately, both are addictive.

In excess, the first can destroy the soul – the second, the mind. And which is worse, I have never quite decided.

4

STARRY MESSENGERS

29

ECHO AND TELSTAR

'When the story of our age comes to be told, we will be remembered as the first of all men to set their sign among the stars.'

These are the words with which I ended *The Making of a Moon* when it was published in 1957. On a memorable evening only three years later, I saw them come true, more spectacularly than I had ever imagined.

Colombo, my home town for more than a third of a century, is only seven degrees north of the Equator. Days and nights are therefore of almost equal length throughout the year, and sunset is never much later than 6.30 p.m. After a brief interlude of twilight, the stars appear.

I had been asked to give a lecture on space travel at one of the local colleges, and had timed my talk carefully. With a final glance at my watch, I concluded: 'Now, if you will follow me outside . . .' Fortunately, the sky was clear – and my calculations had been (for once) correct. We had waited only a few minutes when a brilliant star rose in the *west*, defying the astronomical wisdom of the ages, and climbed steadily out of the twilight glow. It moved at about the speed of a high-flying jet, and took a few minutes to reach the meridian. Then it started to descend into the east – but long before it had reached the horizon, it suddenly began to fade. Within seconds, it was gone . . .

I am sure that none of my youthful audience ever forgot their view of Echo 1, which was probably seen by more human eyes than any other artefact in the history of the world. Echo, however, was not intended to pioneer space advertising – though such ideas have been proposed, to the consternation of astronomers.* It was a serious experiment in satellite communications, to see if a simple, passive reflector could be used instead of complex electronic equipment to send messages round the curve of the Earth.

The Moon had already been tried, but it was too far away – and too bad a radio-mirror – to be of any use. A balloon coated with a thin layer of reflecting metal film, in an orbit only a few hundred kilometres up, would obviously be much more efficient.

*In my 1956 short story, 'Watch This Space' I had COCA COLA doing precisely this. I thought it wise not to mention the matter when, on its centennial some thirty years, I made a TV commercial for the same product.

In his memoir *The Beginnings of Satellite Communications*, Dr John Pierce has described how the Echo project got started. Although we had met several times since my first visit to the United States in 1952, and had often discussed astronautics (though probably not as often as we talked SF, since John was a long-time fan and occasional author) he had not seen my 1945 paper when, in 1954, the Princeton branch of the Institute of Radio Engineers asked him to give a talk on space travel. However, by that time – to use his own slightly infelicitous phrase – 'satellite communication was in the air'.

John's address, 'Orbital Radio Relays', was published in *Jet Propulsion*, the journal of the American Rocket Society, for April 1955. It considered three possibilities: (a) hundred-foot reflecting spheres at an altitude of around 2200 miles; (b) a hundred-foot orientated plane mirror in a twenty-four-hour orbit; (c) an active repeater in a twenty-four-hour orbit. He concluded that all three solutions were feasible, and each had major advantages and disadvantages.

'Passive' mirrors would be cheap and simple, but extremely inefficient, as only a minute fraction of the energy beamed up to them would be received back on Earth; very powerful transmitters, and huge antennas, would therefore be needed on the ground.

Active repeaters ('transponders') required a thousandth of the power or even less, and could therefore work with much smaller antenna systems. However, they demanded electronic equipment which could operate reliably for long periods in space, an onboard source of electrical energy, and means of controlling their position and orientation once they were in orbit – so that their signals were beamed at the right targets.

It was not obvious, in 1955, how all these problems could be solved. Within a decade, however, space technology had advanced so swiftly that passive comsats made only a brief, but spectacular, appearance in the night sky before they were succeeded by today's active repeaters, drawing their power from the sun.

Echo, however, left an unexpected legacy which was perhaps even more important than the original project. To receive the faint radio signals reflected from the balloon (one-million-million-millionth of the original transmitted power!) the Bell Laboratories built an unusual type of ground terminal on a hill near Holmdel, New Jersey. Instead of the familiar parabolic saucer, this employed a horn, and resembled a giant ear-trumpet lying on its side.

In 1965, when it was no longer needed for communications experiments, this same horn was used by Arno A. Penzias and Robert W. Wilson to detect the faint background of microwave noise which blankets, with extraordinary uniformity, the entire sky. The discovery of this 'three-degree radiation' won Penzias and Wilson the Nobel Prize for Physics in 1978: it has been interpreted as the fading residue of the initial fireball from which the universe was born, some fifteen billion years ago. Because this appeared to provide decisive evidence for the 'Big Bang' origin of the universe, the rival 'Steady State' theory, advocated in the fifties by Hoyle, Gold and Bondi, received an apparent knock-out blow. But, in revised form, it may yet rise from the floor before the count of ten.

The universe appears to be a device contrived for the perpetual astonishment of astronomers. Many years ago, annoyed by the dogmatism of certain cosmo-theologists, I proposed my own theory: the Steady Bang. I'm no longer sure that this is a joke; in fact, recent proposals from the indomitable Sir Fred and his colleagues sound suspiciously like it. I hope they bear in mind the remark that Niels Bohr once made to another physicist: 'Your theory is crazy – but not crazy enough to be true.'

Although Echo was an outstanding success, both from the technical and the public-relations points of view, it demonstrated that satellite communication would not be practicable with passive reflectors. This was especially true for TV, which was in most need of the new technology, as the only foreseeable means of spanning oceans. The next step was clearly an active transmitter which would receive signals from the ground, amplify them, and then rebroadcast them back to the hemisphere below.

John Pierce and his colleagues at Bell Labs had been thinking along these lines even before Echo was launched, and their work soon resulted in an even more famous satellite, Telstar.* One metre in diameter, and roughly spherical, Telstar operated on solar panels; it received ground signals at 6.39 GHz and relayed them back at 4.17 GHz – at the pocket-flashlight power level to two watts.

Nevertheless, this was enough to make history, in the first live transatlantic TV broadcast on 23 July 1962. The impact of this programme was enormous; it was seen, for example, by more than half the population of Great Britain, and huge audiences world-wide. Today, the TV newscasters no longer bother to superimpose 'Live by satellite', because everyone takes this for granted. But thirty years ago, it was still a miracle.

Telstar (and its successor, Telstar 2, launched 7 May 1963) showed that active satellites could do everything that had been claimed for them, and with very modest powers – as long as they were backed up by massive ground equipment. The Bell System had built an even larger horn-antenna for Telstar than for Echo; the giant ear-trumpet at Andover, Maine, weighed 370 tons yet was able to track the speeding satellite to an accuracy of better than a twentieth of a degree.

And *that* was the big problem. Because of its relatively low altitude (between 950 and 5600 kilometres) Telstar 1 circled the Earth several times per day; its orbital period was only a fraction of the magic twenty-four hours.

*Though the original Telstar has long since burned up, the name was too good to waste: AT&T has since revived it for a new series of geostationary comsats.

From any given point, therefore, it was visible only intermittently, for periods of twenty minutes at the most. Between any two stations, it could provide only brief intervals of service; then it would drop below the horizon. This was no way to run a TV network, still less a telephone system, which is what really interested Bell/AT&T. TV was exciting and got all the headlines – but the big money was in the Yellow Pages.

There were two obvious solutions to the problem: one neat and simple, the other so complicated and messy that at first sight it seemed hopelessly impracticable.

The neat and simple answer was to use the geostationary or twenty-four-hour orbit, so that the satellite would appear fixed in the sky. Then a continuous service could be provided without the need for elaborate – and expensive – tracking equipment. Unfortunately, in the early sixties, the most powerful rockets available (at least for non-military purposes) could lift only very modest payloads to the required altitude; paradoxically, it takes rather more energy to park 22,000 miles up than to land on the ten-times-more-distant Moon. It appeared that the stationary orbit would have to wait for the development of more powerful delivery systems.

This would clearly be only a matter of time, but meanwhile there was a fundamental problem, which no technical advance could ever overcome. It was one that I never considered in my 1945 paper, because it did not affect TV broadcasting, my main concern. But it was of vital importance for any telephone service, and might even make geostationary satellites useless for this purpose.

Imagine that you are on one side of the Earth, talking to a friend on the other side via a communications satellite. Because radio waves (like all electromagnetic radiation) travel at 300,000 kilometres a second, it takes almost a third of a second for your voice to reach her. If she replies instantly, that's another third – making a total delay of two-thirds of a second before her answer reaches you. Now that may not seem very much; nor is it, to phlegmatic Anglo-Saxons. But it's enough to demoralise a substantial proportion of, to give but one example, the Latinate world – as anyone who's ever watched Italian movies will readily agree. Both parties would have grown tired of waiting for an answer and would already have interrupted each other. Result – utter chaos.

For a while, it seemed that telephony via comsats might require subscribers to learn RT procedure and talk like airline pilots: 'Over to you . . .' etc. Fortunately, this problem turned out to be much less serious than feared; it took very little experience for subscribers to adapt, and insert a courteous pause between sentences.*

*Another problem that sometimes plagues *all* long-distance circuits – satellite and terrestrial – is that of 'echo'. Few things are more inhibiting to the free flow of conversation than hearing your

One way of dealing with the worrisome time-delay problem, and the difficulty of getting worthwhile payloads up to the stationary orbit, was to continue on the Telstar route. If enough low-altitude satellites were launched, there would always be at least one in the sky at any given time. Earth stations would need two separate tracking antennas, as it would be necessary to receive signals from one satellite and relay them up to another. And to be on the safe side, a third antenna would be needed as a standby to cope with breakdowns, regular maintenance and the retrofits which are inevitable with any advanced electronic equipment.

This would have been a costly and complicated way to go. Fortunately, it proved unnecessary – at least for the global TV networks. But it may yet turn out to be just the answer for the long-awaited 'wrist-watch telephone'. The Motorola company is planning to take the cellular telephone into the sky, using a constellation of seventy-seven low-altitude satellites, weaving an orbital basket round the Earth. (My friend Dr Yash Pal has coined the phrase 'anti-Clarke orbits' for such systems.) It will be interesting to see how this project – christened 'Iridium', after Element 77 – fares in competition with geostationary satellites. It will certainly be unpopular with the radio astronomers, who are already complaining bitterly about the interference from satellites of *all* kinds. But at least most of them are in the equatorial belt. Iridium will be *everywhere*.

I'm afraid that the Earth is no longer a good place for astronomers, optical or radio. Fortunately, the ideal site for both varieties is quite close at hand, as I pointed out in 'The Uses of the Moon' (*Harper's Magazine*, December 1961; reprinted in *Voices from the Sky*, 1965):

> The far side of the Moon is a quiet place – probably the quietest that now exists within millions of miles of Earth. I am speaking, of course, in the radio sense; for the last sixty years,* our planet has been pouring an ever-increasing racket into space. This has already seriously inconvenienced the radio astronomers, whose observations can be ruined by an electric shaver a hundred miles away.
>
> But the land first glimpsed by Lunik 3 is beyond the reach of this electronic tumult; it is shielded from the din of Earth by 2000 miles of solid rock – a far better protection than millions of miles of empty space. Here, where the earthlight never shines, will be the communications centres of the future, linking together with radio and light beams all the inhabited planets. And one day, perhaps, reaching out beyond the solar system to make contact with those other intelligences for whom the

___

own words a fraction of a second later, as they bounce back from the other end of the line. (As insurance companies have discovered, this is a good test for people feigning deafness.) Fortunately, this annoyance can be completely eliminated by 'echo-cancelling' circuits; though as anyone who makes many international calls will agree, they don't always seem to be working very well.

*Now ninety!

first search has already begun. That search can hardly hope for success until we have escaped from the braying of all the radio and TV stations of our own planet.

I am happy to say that the protection of Farside from interference has now been legislated by the ITU (International Telecommunication Union), but I am not optimistic about the long-term prospects. From the earliest days of colonisation, lunar networking will be vital, so before long the Moon will have its own chattering subsatellites.

The radio astronomers will have to move again. Saturn, anyone?*

*Not an entirely facetious suggestion. In *Imperial Earth* (1976) I pointed out that ultra-long radio waves are blocked from the inner solar system by the sun's own 'ionosphere' (using that word very loosely). The moons of Saturn may be the most convenient place to study them.

30

SYNCOM

In 1961 the American Rocket Society (now the American Institute of Aeronautics and Astronautics) arranged an historic symposium at the New York Colosseum entitled 'Space Flight Report to the Nation'. One of the participants was the chairman of the Space Council, soon to become, in tragic circumstances, President of the United States: Lyndon B. Johnson.

I had to moderate a panel discussion on the US and USSR space programmes, which I did with a dictatorial hand. Bitter experience had convinced me that when experts were assembled to discuss any subject, without firm guidance the result would be more smoke than light. I had therefore concocted a series of leading questions, which, I hoped, would provoke useful responses from my victims. These included NASA Deputy Administrator Hugh Dryden, Dr Wernher von Braun, and General Bernard Schriever, Director of the Air Force's ballistic missile (ICBM) programme. I recall asking the general, with as straight a face as I could manage, how soon he thought the US and USSR space programmes could be combined – a question no more than thirty years premature.

Unsurprisingly, we could not persuade any of the Soviet delegates to join the panel. But I have vivid memories of the veteran astronomer Dr Mikhailovich reporting that he'd just seen *From Russia with Love* at a local cinema. 'What did you think of it?' we asked. 'Not as good as the book,' he answered instantly.

At some time during the panel's discussion I acted as a transponder, amplifying and relaying a suggestion that I'd overheard a few hours earlier: 'Wouldn't it be a wonderful boost for communications satellites, if one could be launched in time for the 1964 Tokyo Olympics? Just three years from now – think about it!'

This challenge was met by three young engineers at Hughes, Harold A. Rosen, Don Williams and Tom Hudspeth, who believed – in the face of much scepticism – that a 'minimum synchronous communications satellite' could be orbited, even by the relatively feeble existing launch vehicles. They designed a bare-bones model, carrying no batteries so that it could operate only in sunlight. As it would spin like a gyroscope, its axis would be fixed in space and it would require only occasional puffs of gas to keep its transmissions aimed at the Earth.

The first Syncom was launched on 14 February 1963. It reached the twenty-four-hour orbit successfully – and the rest was silence; it suddenly vanished from the radio spectrum. Months later, a powerful telescope located the tiny corpse drifting high above the Equator; apparently, a pressure vessel had exploded. One day, I am sure, it will be on display in the Smithsonian's Air and Space Museum, as the first pioneer of a vital new frontier.

Rosen et al. went back to the drawing board, and Syncom 2 was launched on 26 July 1963. It was completely successful, and so was Syncom 3 on 19 August 1964. The Syncoms were of historic importance as giving 'proof of principle'; it was no longer possible to doubt the value of the twenty-four orbit. Even the time-delay problem proved to be much less serious than feared.

While the engineers were experimenting, Congress was legislating. In 1962 an act was passed creating the Communications Satellite Corporation (COMSAT), which would be solely responsible for the new medium – and would rule out the type of uninhibited free enterprise which had created the American telephone system. As John Pierce, speaking as a loyal member of Mother Bell's extended family, wrote in his 1968 memoir: 'The Communications Satellite Act discouraged me profoundly. At that time it seemed to end any direct personal interest or participation in satellite communications. I foresaw that the Act would, as it did, considerably delay the realisation of a commercial satellite system.'

My friends at COMSAT would certainly disagree with that last sentence, and almost twenty years later John wryly pointed out how risky it is to make any forecasts in this explosive field:

> When, in connection with the production of 2001, Arthur Clarke asked for help in outfitting the Orbiter Hilton with Bell logos and equipment, I called the Public Relations Department of AT&T, thinking they would jump at this opportunity. They didn't. They said, maybe when 2001 finally rolls around things won't turn out just as Clarke and Kubrick predicted. Won't that make the Bell System look foolish?*

Well, the PR boys were perfectly correct – but not in the way they imagined. The Bell System won't be around in 2001. It was abolished, in a famous divestiture ruling, on 1 January 1984. So the Bell logo which appears when Dr Heywood Floyd makes his $1.70 call to his little daughter (Vivian Kubrick, incidentally) is what might be described as a premature anachronism.

My hope that the 1964 Tokyo Olympics would be relayed by satellite was fulfilled by Syncom 3, which could just accommodate one black-and-white

*'Space Enough for All': lecture given on receiving the Second Arthur C. Clarke Award, Colombo, 16 December 1987.

channel. However, because of the time differential between Japan and the United States, few networks showed the event 'live', on the assumption that most of their audience would be in bed. They had yet to learn that satellites would teach whole nations how to do without sleep.

The time had clearly come to put this new technology on a commercial basis. More than a quarter of a century later, it is a curious and nostalgic experience to leaf through a slim brochure which announces on its front page:

PRELIMINARY PROSPECTUS DATED MAY 27, 1964
10,000,000 SHARES
COMMUNICATIONS SATELLITE CORPORATION

This historic document announced that five million shares at $20 each had been taken up by communications companies – almost three million by AT&T, a million by IT&T, the rest by GTE, RCA and others. The remaining five million were available to the general public through a long list of underwriters, headed by the inevitable Merrill Lynch.

I doubt if even in our wildest moments we pre-World War II interplanetary enthusiasts ever dreamed that $200,000,000 would one day be invested in space – by *commercial* organisations, and only as a first instalment! I still recall with some embarrassment the claim that the British Interplanetary Society made, *circa* 1938, that a three-man lunar ship could be built for, ahem, a quarter of a million dollars. Even allowing for inflation, that was a slight underestimate.

The opening paragraph of the prospectus clearly sets out the aims and, equally important, the status of the one-year-old organisation:

> Communications Satellite Corporation was incorporated under District of Columbia law on February 1, 1963, as authorised by the Communications Satellite Act of 1962. The Act states that it is the policy of the United States to establish, in cooperation with other companies, as expeditiously as practicable, a commercial communications satellite system, as part of an improved communications network, and that the United States participation in the system shall be in the form of a private corporation, subject to appropriate Government regulation. The Corporation has been created in pursuance of such national policy, but the Corporation is not an agency or establishment of the United States Government.

In a section headed 'The Venture and its Risks', the prospectus points out that investors would be heading into unknown territory, and states cautiously: 'Satellite systems of several different types are believed to be practicable for commercial purposes. To provide further information relevant to the selection of a type of system, the Corporation plans to conduct further information and limited operations by means of a satellite to be launched by mid-1965.'

When the prospectus was issued, it was still uncertain if geostationary satellites would be practicable, so an alternative Medium Altitude System was also considered. This would have required up to eighteen satellites at an altitude of about 10,000 kilometres. Three proposals had been received for such orbital necklaces (one from AT&T, hoping for a follow-up to Telstar) and the matter could be settled only by practical experience.

The prospectus also had a section entitled 'Competition' – meaning cables and radio. Although the existing submarine telephone cables still employed vacuum tubes, the transistor revolution was now under way and it was obvious that the number of voice or telegraph channels would soon be multiplied by a factor of at least ten. On high-density routes like the North Atlantic, cables might well be able to offer a better – and cheaper – service. As we shall see, the contest between satellites and cables is still a major factor – to the great benefit of the customers. Curiously enough, this section fails to mention that *only* satellites would be able to provide intercontinental TV. It seems that back in 1964 no one realised just how important this would become; yet within a single generation, more than half the human race would sometimes be watching the same event, 'Live by satellite'.

The COMSAT prospectus was issued almost exactly one hundred years after Cyrus Field's exhausting battle to raise capital for his new cable. This time, the story was different; everyone knew that communications satellites worked. Less than seven years after Sputnik, Wall Street entered the Space Age.

No, I didn't buy any stock: I was currently exasperated by the amount of valuable time Stanley Kubrick wasted phoning his broker, when we should have been using it creatively to talk about our little movie. In any event, my attitude to discretionary funds is exactly the same as that of my good friend Isaac Asimov, who once confided to me: 'I come from generations of paupers, so I don't know what to do with money. When I have any, I leave it in the bank to rot.'

Same here; and very sensible too, considering what's happened in the Wall Street area during the last few years. But I'm glad to have five shares of COMSAT stock, presented to me in the sixties, because (a) the certificate looks handsome on my office wall and (b) I like to receive the Annual Reports. However, even at the risk of giving COMSAT's computer a nervous breakdown, I always tear up the minuscule dividend cheques. Postage and bank charges would leave me out of pocket if I paid them in.

31

EARLY BIRD

Given the responsibility of establishing the first regular, non-experimental service, COMSAT contracted with Harold Rosen's team at Hughes to design higher-powered successors to the Syncoms. The first was Early Bird (later renamed Intelsat 1); it was launched from Cape Kennedy on 6 April 1965, and I was invited to watch the countdown through a TV link to COMSAT headquarters – then a handsome private house in a Washington suburb.

Early Bird took off on time, and we watched it climb up into the sky. Then the TV was switched off, and Vice-President Hubert Humphrey started to make a speech. It was an eloquent and informative speech, but after several minutes I began to wonder what was happening to the rocket. If it had blown up, we at COMSAT HQ would be the last to know. Later, when Vice-President and rocket had both reached a successful cut-off, I told Mr Humphrey that I was writing a movie in which one of the characters would be chairman of the Space Council – thirty years hence. 'Oh', said HHHHH somewhat wistfully, 'I still intend to be chairman then.' Presumably, wilting in the massive shadow of LBJ, he had already abandoned any higher ambitions.

It is interesting to compare the capabilities of Early Bird with its successors over the next twenty years, as an indication of the astonishing progress both in comsat design and the payloads that can be placed in geostationary orbit.

	1965 Intelsat 1	1975 4A	1985 6
Voice circuits	240	6500	35000
TV channels	(1)	+2	+2

Note that Intelsat 1 could handle only a single black-and-white TV channel *or* 240 phone circuits – not both at the same time. Its successors can carry two *colour* TV channels – plus thousands of voice circuits. And by the use of clever digital multiplication techniques, this can be greatly increased (to an amazing 120,000 for Intelsat 6). However, Intelsat 7 – due to be launched in 1992 – has only (!) about half this phone capacity, though it can carry three TV channels. The gestation period of a new comsat is about five years, and after the launch failures of the 1980s Intelsat decided not to put quite so many eggs in very expensive baskets, which cost millions of dollars to insure.*

*Department of Unfortunate Coincidences. The loss of the latest Japanese DBS (Direct Broadcast) satellite was shown on local TV just an hour before I typed these words (20 April 1991). The insurance rates will be going up again.

32

THE UNITED STATES OF EARTH

On 20 August 1971, after several years of Byzantine negotiations, the final agreements setting up the world satellite communications system (IN-TELSAT) were signed at the State Department. At the invitation of Secretary William Rogers and Ambassador Abbott Washburn, the United States' representative to INTELSAT, I was asked to speak at the ceremony, immediately following Apollo 8 astronaut William Anders, then executive secretary of the National Aeronautics and Space Council.*

Mr Secretary, your excellencies, distinguished guests . . . Whenever I peer into my cloudy crystal ball and try to visualise the future of communications satellites, I remember an incident that occurred in England almost a hundred years ago.

The very alarming news had just been received from the United States that a certain Mr Bell had invented something called a telephone. So, as we British do in an emergency, we set up a parliamentary commission. It listened to the evidence of expert witnesses, who gave the reassuring news that nothing further would be heard of this impractical Yankee invention.

Among the witnesses called was the Chief Engineer of the British Post Office. Someone on the commission said to him: 'We understand that the Americans have invented a machine that can transmit human speech. Do you think that this – telephone – will be of any use in Great Britain?' The chief engineer thereupon replied: 'No, sir. The Americans have need of the telephone, but we do not. We have plenty of messenger boys.'

This very able† man totally failed to see the possibilities of the telephone, and who can blame him? Could anyone, back in 1880, have imagined that the time would come when every home would have a telephone, and business and social life would depend upon it almost completely.

*I have never forgiven Bill Anders for his failure of nerve on Christmas Day, 1968. He had been tempted, he later told me, to radio back that the Apollo 8 crew had spotted a large black monolith on the far side of the Moon.
†But also very pig-headed: see Chapter 15. You will also meet him once again in this book, I'm afraid.

I submit, gentlemen, that the eventual impact of the communications satellite upon the whole human race will be at least as great as that of the telephone upon the so-called developed societies. In fact, as far as real communications are concerned, there are as yet no developed societies: we are all in the semaphore and smoke-signal stage. And we are now about to witness an interesting situation in which many countries – particularly in Asia and Africa – are going to leapfrog a whole era of communications technology and go straight into the Space Age. They will never know the vast networks of cables and microwave links that this continent has built up at such enormous cost. Satellites can do far more, at far less expense.

INTELSAT, of course, is concerned primarily with point-to-point communications involving large ground stations, often only one per country. It provides the first reliable, high-quality, wide band with links between all nations that wish to join, and the importance of this cannot be overestimated. Yet it is only a beginning, and I would like to look a little further into the future . . .

Two years from now, NASA will launch the first satellite – ATS-6 – which will have sufficient power for its signals to be picked up by an ordinary domestic TV set, plus about 200 dollars' worth of additional equipment. In 1974 this satellite will be stationed over India and, if all goes well, the first experiment in the use of space communications for mass education will begin.

I have just come from India, where I have been making a TV film, *The Promise of Space*.* We erected, in a village outside Delhi, the prototype antenna: a simple umbrella-shaped wire-mesh affair, three metres across. Anyone can put it together in a few hours; it needs only one per village to start a social and economic revolution.

The engineering problems of bringing education, literacy, and improved hygiene to every human being on this planet have now been solved. The cost would be of the order of a dollar per person – per year. The benefits in health, happiness, and wealth would be immeasurable.

But, of course, the technical problem is the easy one. Do we have the imagination – and the statesmanship – to use this new tool for the benefit of all mankind? Or will it be used merely to peddle detergents and propaganda?

I am an optimist; anyone interested in the future has to be, otherwise he would simply shoot himself. I believe that communications satellites can unite mankind. Let me remind you that this great country was virtually created a hundred years ago by two inventions. Without them, the United States was impossible; with them, it was inevitable. Those inventions were, of course, the railroad and the electric telegraph.

Today we are seeing, on a global scale, an almost exact parallel to that

*Directed and produced by my late friend Thomas Craven, founder of Craven Film Corporation, New York.

situation. What the railroads and the telegraph did here a century ago, the jets and the communication satellites are doing now to all the world.

I hope you will remember this analogy in the years ahead. For today, gentlemen, whether you intend it or not – whether you wish it or not – you have signed far more than yet another intergovernmental agreement.

You have just signed the first draft of the Articles of Federation of the United States of Earth.

33

SATELLITES AND SARIS

In my State Department address, I referred to the forthcoming Indian educational satellite experiment, then still almost four years in the future. I also wrote an article, originally entitled 'Schoolmaster Satellite', to explain the purpose – and the high hopes – of this great experiment, in many ways the most promising of all the applications of space technology. It was later read into the *Congressional Record* (27 January 1972) by Representative William Anderson – famous for his exploration of 'Inner Space' when, in 1958, he commanded the atomic submarine *Nautilus* on its historic voyage under the North Pole.

For thousands of years, men have sought their future in the starry sky. Now this old superstition has at last come true, for our destinies do indeed depend on celestial bodies – those that we have created ourselves.

Since the mid-sixties, the highly unadvertised reconnaissance satellites have been quietly preserving the peace of the world, the weather satellites have guarded millions against the furies of Nature, and the communications satellites have acted as message-carriers for half the human race. Yet these are merely the first modest applications of space technology to human affairs; its real impact is still to come. And, ironically, the first country to receive the benefits of space directly at the home and village level will be India, where, as recently as February 1962, millions were terrified by an unusual conjunction of the sun, Moon and five planets.

In 1975 there will be a new Star of India; though it will not be visible to the naked eye, its influence will be greater than that of any zodiacal signs. It will be the satellite ATS-6 (Applications Technology Satellite 6), the latest in a very successful series launched by the National Aeronautics and Space Administration. For one year, under an agreement signed on 18 September 1969, ATS-6 will be loaned to the Indian Government by the United States, and will be 'parked' 36,000 kilometres above the Equator. At this altitude it will make one revolution every twenty-four hours and will therefore remain poised over the same spot on the turning Earth; in effect, India will have a TV tower 36,000 kilometres high, from which programmes can be received with almost equal strength over the entire country.

Since the launch of the historic Telstar in 1962, there have been several generations of communications satellites. The latest, Intelsat 4, can carry a dozen TV programmes or up to 9000 telephone conversations across the oceans of the world. But all these satellites have one thing in common; their signals are so feeble that they can be received only by large Earth stations, equipped with antennas twenty or more metres across, and costing several million dollars. Most countries can afford only one such station, and indeed that is all that they need to connect their television, telephone or other services – where these exist – to the outside world.

ATS-6, built by the Fairchild Corporation, represents the next step in the evolution of communications satellites. Its signals will be powerful enough to be picked up, not merely by multimillion-dollar Earth Stations, but by simple receivers, costing two or three hundred dollars, which all but the poorest communities can afford. This level of cost would open up the entire developing world to every type of electronic communication, not only TV. The emerging societies of Africa, Asia and South America could thus bypass much of today's ground-based technology and leap straight into the Space Age. Many of them have already done something similar in the field of transportation, going from ox-cart to aeroplane with only a passing nod at cars and trains.

It can be difficult for those from nations that have taken a century and a half to slog from semaphore to satellite to appreciate that a few hundred kilograms in orbit can now replace the continent-wide networks of microwave towers, coaxial cables and ground transmitters that have been constructed during the last generation. And it is perhaps even more difficult, to those who think of TV exclusively in terms of old Hollywood movies, giveaway contests and soap commercials, to see any sense in spreading these boons to places which do not yet enjoy them. Almost any other use of money, it might be argued, would be more beneficial.

Such a reaction is typical of those who come from developed (or overdeveloped) countries, and who accept libraries, telephones, cinemas, radio, TV, as part of their daily lives. Because they frequently suffer from the modern scourge of information pollution, they cannot imagine its deadly opposite: information starvation. For any Westerner, however well-meaning, to tell an Indian villager that he would be better off without access to the world's news, knowledge and entertainment is an impertinence. A fat man preaching the virtues of abstemiousness to the hungry would deserve an equally sympathetic hearing.

Those who actually live in the East, and know its problems, are in the best position to appreciate what cheap and high-quality communications could do to improve standards of living and reduce social inequalities. Illiteracy, ignorance and superstition are not merely the results of poverty, they are part of its cause, forming a self-perpetuating system which has lasted for centuries, and which cannot be changed without fundamental advances in education. India is now beginning a Satellite Instructional Television Experiment (SITE) as a bold attempt to harness the technology of space for this task; if it succeeds, the implications for all developing nations will be enormous.

SITE's first order of business will be instruction in family planning, upon which the future of India (and all other countries) now depends. Puppet shows are already being produced to put across the basic concepts; those of us who remember the traditional activities of Punch and Judy may find this idea faintly hilarious. However, there is probably no better way of reaching audiences who are unable to read, but who are familiar with the travelling puppeteers who for generations have brought the sagas of Rama and Sita and Hanuman into the villages.

Some officials have stated, perhaps optimistically, that the only way in which India can check its population explosion is by mass propaganda from satellite – which alone can project the unique authority and impact of the TV set into every village in the land. If this is true, we have a situation which should indeed give pause to those who have criticised the billions spent on space.

The emerging countries of what is called the Third World may need rockets and satellites much more desperately than the advanced nations which built them. Swords into ploughshares is an obsolete metaphor; we can now turn missiles into blackboards.

Next to family planning, India's greatest need is increased agricultural productivity. This involves spreading information about animal husbandry, new seeds, fertilisers, pesticides and so forth; the ubiquitous transistor radio has already played an important role here. In certain parts of the country, the famous 'miracle rice' strains, which have unexpectedly given the whole of Asia a few priceless years in which to avert famine, are known as 'radio paddy', because of the medium through which farmers were introduced to the new crops. But although radio can do a great deal, it cannot match the effectiveness of television; and of course there are many types of information that can be fully conveyed only by images. Merely telling a farmer how to improve his herds or harvest is seldom effective. But seeing is believing, if he can compare the pictures on the screen with the scrawny cattle and the dispirited crops around him.

Although the SITE project sounds very well on paper, only experience will show if it works. The 'hardware' is straightforward and even conventional in terms of today's satellite technology; it is the 'software' – the actual programme – that will determine the success or failure of the experiment. In

1967 a pilot project was started in eighty villages round New Delhi, which were equipped with television receivers tuned to the local station. (In striking contrast to a satellite transmitter, this has a range of only twenty-five miles.) It was found that an average of 400 villagers gathered at each of the evening 'tele-clubs', to watch programmes on weed control, fertilisers, packaging, high-yield seeds – plus five minutes of song and dance to sweeten the educational pill.

We who are accustomed to individual or family viewing tend to forget that even a twelve-inch set can be seen by several hundred people. Moreover, as it is always dark in India by 7 p.m., for much of the year the receiver can be set up in the open air; only during the monsoon would it be necessary to retreat into a village hall.

Surveys have been carried out to assess the effectiveness of these programmes. In the area of agricultural knowledge. TV viewers have shown substantial gains over non-viewers. To quote from the report of Dr Prasad Vepa of the Indian National Committee for Space Research: 'They expressed their opinion that the information given through these programmes was more comprehensive and clearer compared to that of the other mass media. Yet another reason cited for the utility of TV was its appeal to the illiterate and small farmers to whom information somehow just does not trickle.'

In February 1971, while filming *The Promise of Space*, I visited one of these TV-equipped villages: Sultanpur, a prosperous and progressive community just outside Delhi, only a few miles from the soaring sandstone tower of the Kutb Minar. Dr Vikram Sarabhai, chairman of the Atomic Energy Commission, had kindly lent us a prototype of the three-metre-wide, chicken-wire receiving dish which will collect signals from ATS-6 as it hovers above the Equator. While the village children watched, the pie-shaped pieces of the reflector were assembled: a job that can be performed by unskilled labour in a couple of hours. When it was finished, we had something that looked like a large aluminium sunshade or umbrella, with a collecting antenna in place of the handle. As the whole assembly was tilted up at the sky and lifted on to the roof of the highest building, it looked as if a small flying saucer had swooped down upon Sultanpur.

With the Delhi transmitter standing in for the still-unlaunched satellite, we were able to show a preview of – one hopes – almost any Indian village of the 1980s. The programme we actually had on the screen at Sultanpur was a lecture-demonstration in elementary mechanics, which could not have been of overwhelming interest to most of the audience; nevertheless, it seemed to absorb viewers whose ages ranged from under ten to over seventy. Yet it was not at Sultanpur, but over 600 kilometres away at Ahmedabad, that I really began to appreciate what could be done through even the most elementary education at the village level.

Near Ahmedabad is the big parabolic dish, sixteen metres in diameter, of the experimental satellite communications ground station, through which the programmes will be beamed up to the hovering satellite. Also in this area is AMUL, the largest dairy co-operative in the world, to which more than quarter of a million farms belong. After we had finished filming at the big dish, our camera team drove out to the AMUL headquarters, and we accompanied the chief veterinary officer on his rounds.

At our first stop, we ran into a moving little drama that we could never have contrived deliberately, and which summed up half the problems of India in a single episode. A buffalo calf was dying, watched over by a tearful old lady who now saw most of her worldly wealth about to disappear. If she had called the vet a few days before – there was a telephone in the village for this very purpose – he could easily have saved the calf. But she had tried charms and magic first; they are not always ineffective, but antibiotics are rather more reliable . . .

I will not quickly forget the haggard, tear-streaked face of that old lady in Gujarat; yet her example could be multiplied a million times. The loss of real wealth throughout India because of ignorance and superstition must be staggering. If it saved only a few calves per year, or increased productivity only a few percentage points, the TV set in the village square would quickly pay for itself. The very capable men who run AMUL realise this; they are so impressed by the possibilities of TV education that they plan to build their own station to broadcast to their quarter of a million farmers. They have the money, and they cannot wait for the satellite, though it will reach an audience 2000 times larger, for over 500 million people will lie within range of ATS-6.

There is a less obvious, yet perhaps even more important, way in which the prosperity and sometimes very existence of the Indian villagers will one day depend upon space technology. The life of the subcontinent is dominated by the monsoon, which brings 80 per cent of the annual rainfall between June and September. The date of onset of the monsoon, however, can vary by several weeks, with disastrous results to the farmer if he mistimes the planting of his crops.

Now, for the first time, the all-seeing eye of the meteorological satellites, feeding information to giant computers, gives real hope of dramatic improvements in weather forecasting. But forecasts will be no use unless they get to the farmers in their half a million scattered villages, and to quote from a recent Indian report:

This cannot be achieved by conventional methods of telegrams and wireless broadcasts. Only a space communications system employing TV will be . . . able to provide the farmer with something like personal briefing . . . Such a nationwide rural TV broadcasting system can be expected to effect an increased agricultural production of at least 10 per cent through the prevention of losses – a saving of $1600 million per annum.

A replica of Alexander Graham Bell's first membrane diaphragm telephone, 1875. An iron diaphragm placed within the field of a horseshoe magnet vibrated from the pressure waves of speech, generating current which was passed along the line (*Telefocus*)

'What do you mean I've got a wrong number?!' Alexander Bell phones Boston in 1877 (*Hulton-Deutsch Collection*)

An operator answers a call at Croydon's first telephone exchange (1880s) (*BT Museum*)

An eye to the future? This experimental videophone was trialled in Britain in the late 1960s (*BT Museum*)

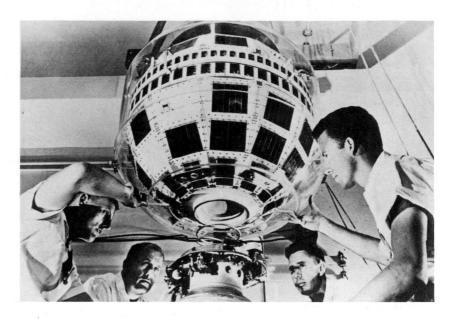

The soon-to-be-famous Telstar communications satellite being prepared for launching at Cape Canaveral in July 1962 (*Hulton-Deutsch Collection*)

President Kennedy, 1962: one of the first television pictures received at Goonhilly Earth Station from the USA via Telstar (*BT Museum*)

Global links by satellite: Intelsats III, IV, IVA and V (1968–80) (*R Matthews/BT Museum*)

Space engineers putting Early Bird (later renamed Intelsat I) through a high-speed spin test in 1965 (*Hulton-Deutsch Collection*)

An artist's impression of Intelsat VII. Up to five are due to be launched between 1992 and 1994 into geostationary orbits above the Pacific Basin. Each satellite can carry up to 90,000 voice channels and three TV channels over their planned fifteen-year lifetime (*David Ducros/Jerrican/Science Photo Library*)

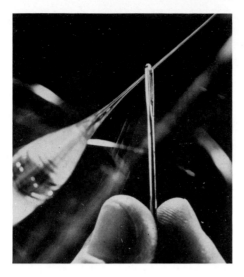

The revolution of fibre optics: a hair-thin glass fibre passes easily through the eye of a needle (*BT Museum*)

The old and the new: optical fibre in comparison with copper co-axial cable (*BT Museum*)

Laying fibre-optic cable for TAT-8 off the coast of Cornwall: modern day communications technology has returned to the sea (*Telefocus*)

Even if this figure is wildly optimistic, it appears that the costs of such a system would be negligible compared to its benefits.

And those who are unimpressed by mere dollars should also consider the human aspect – as demonstrated by the great Bangladesh cyclone of 1971. That was tracked by the weather satellites, but the warning network that might have saved several hundred thousand lives did not exist. Such tragedies will be impossible in a world of efficient space communications.

Yet it is the quality, not the quantity, of life that really matters. Men need information, news, mental stimulus, entertainment. For the first time in 5000 years, a technology now exists that can halt and perhaps even reverse the flow from the country to the city. The social implications of this are profound; already, the Canadian Government has discovered that it has to launch a satellite so that it can develop the Arctic. Men accustomed to the amenities of civilisation simply will not live in places where they cannot phone their families or watch their favourite TV show. The communications satellite can put an end to cultural deprivation caused by geography. It is strange to think that, in the long run, the cure for Calcutta (not to mention London, New York, Tokyo) may lie 36,000 kilometres out in space.

The SITE project will run for one year, and will broadcast to about 5000 TV sets in carefully selected areas. This figure may not seem impressive when one considers the size of India, but it requires only one receiver to a village to start a social, economic and educational revolution. If the experiment is as great a success as Dr Sarabhai and his colleagues hope (and deserve), then the next step would be for India to have her own full-time communications satellite. This is, in any case, essential for the country's internal radio, telegraph, telephone and telex services.

It may well be that, until it has established such a nationwide system, India will be unable to achieve a real cultural identity, but will remain merely a collection of states. And one may wonder how much bloodshed and misery might have been avoided had the two severed wings of Pakistan been able to talk to each other face to face, through the facilities which only a communications satellite can provide.

Kipling, who wrote a story about 'wireless' and a poem to the deep-sea cables, would have been delighted by the electronics dawn that is about to break upon the subcontinent. Gandhi, on the other hand, would probably have been less enthusiastic; for much of the India that he knew will not survive the changes that are now coming.

One of the most magical moments of Satyajit Ray's masterpiece *Pather Panchali* is when the little boy Apu hears for the first time the Aeolian music of the telegraph wires on the windy plain. Soon those singing wires will have gone for ever; but a new generation of Apus will be watching, wild-eyed, when the science of a later age draws down pictures

from the sky – and opens up for all the children of India a window on the
world.

Early in 1977, a team of Indian engineers flew into Colombo and installed a
massive five-metre dish – the generous gift of ISRO, the Indian Space
Research Organisation – on my roof. When SITE came in loud and clear, TV
had arrived for the first time in Sri Lanka, and everyone from the President
down came to watch the programmes. My liquor bill was enormous.

Thousands of words have been written about the successes, and occasional
failures, of the SITE experiment. The man best qualified to sum them up is Dr
Yash Pal, who took charge of the project after the untimely death of its
initiator, Dr Vikram Sarabhai:

> For 1500 people directly engaged in the experiment, SITE was a deep human
> experience. It generated new capabilities, demystified space technology, and
> helped to nucleate a large island of self-confidence. But of far greater significance
> was the generation of a new kinship between technologists and the grass-roots
> problems of the country, a common concern for the ultimate social and human goals.
>   (Vatican Study Week, October 1984: see Chapter 36)

The ATS-6 satellite through which the SITE programmes were transmitted
was loaned to India for one year only; then it was 'walked' round the Equator
so that it could broadcast to Alaska – a region which needed high-quality
communications even more desperately than India. (ATS-6 saved more than a
few lives by providing information during medical emergencies.)

During its twelve crowded months of operation, the SITE experiment
proved beyond doubt that only comsats could provide India with all the
varieties of telecommunications required to administer such a huge and
diversified country. A replacement – Insat 1 – was therefore planned, though
owing to a series of misfortunes the first Indian-designed comsat did not start
to operate until almost six years after SITE's conclusion.

And, as recounted in Chapter 35, I had to wait even longer before I would
receive satellite TV again. But by that time, programmes were pouring down
from all over the sky.

34

AT THE UN

Although I had visited United Nations Headquarters many times since the 1950s, never in my wildest moments did I imagine that one day I should be delivering a speech from the famous podium in the General Assembly Building. But this is exactly what happened on World Telecommunications Day, 17 May 1983.

Although 'Beyond the Global Village' repeats *verbatim* many of the points already made in this book, I would like to give it in its entirety, adding only a few footnotes to update or amplify my statements.

There is always something new to be learned from the past, and I would like to open with two anecdotes from the early days of the telephone. They illustrate perfectly how difficult – if not impossible – it is to anticipate the social impact of a truly revolutionary invention. Though the first story is now rather famous – and I must apologise to those who've heard it before – I hope it's unfamiliar to most of you.*

When news of Alexander Graham Bell's invention reached the United Kingdom, the Chief Engineer of the British Post Office failed to be impressed. 'The Americans,' he said loftily, 'have need of the telephone – but we do not. We have plenty of messenger boys . . .'

The second story I heard only quite recently, and in some ways it's even more instructive. In contrast to the British engineer, the mayor of a certain American city was wildly enthusiastic. He thought that the telephone was a marvellous device and ventured this stunning prediction: 'I can see the time,' he said solemnly, *'when every city will have one.'*

If, during the course of this talk, you think that I am getting a little too fanciful, please remember that mayor . . .

We have now reached the stage when virtually anything we want to do in the field of communications is possible: the constraints are no longer technical, but economic, legal or political. Thus if you want to transmit the

*This, I promise you, is Mr Preece's last appearance.

Encyclopaedia Britannica around the world in one second,* you can do so. But it may be a lot cheaper if you're prepared to wait a whole minute – and you must check with the *Britannica's* lawyers first.

Yet while recognising and applauding all these marvels, I am only too well aware of present realities. In Sri Lanka, for example, a major problem is that the village postmaster may not even have the stamps he needs – to put on the telegrams that must be mailed, because copper thieves have stolen the overhead wires. And Sri Lanka, compared to some countries, is rich. It has already imported over 100,000 TV sets and thousands of videotape recorders. That would have been unthinkable only a few years ago – but human beings need information and entertainment almost as much as they need food, and when an invention arrives which can provide both in unprecedented quantities, sooner or later everyone manages to find the money for it.

This is particularly true when the cost of the hardware drops tenfold every decade – look at the example of pocket calculators! So please don't dismiss my future because no one can afford it. The human race can afford anything it really needs – and improvements in communications often pay for themselves more swiftly than improvements in transportation. A developing country may sometimes be better advised to build telephone links than roads to its outlying provinces, if it has to make the choice.

Let me now focus on the only aspect of the communications revolution which I am at all competent to discuss, and which has profoundly affected my own life-style – not to mention that of millions of other people.

Until 1976, making an international telephone call from my home in Sri Lanka was an exercise in frustration that might last several days. Now, thanks to the Indian Ocean satellite, I can get through to London or New York in slightly less time than it takes to dial the thirteen-digit number. As a result, I can now live exactly where I please, and have cut my travelling to a fraction of its former value.

Comsats have created a world without distance and have already had a profound effect on international business, news-gathering and tourism – one of the most important industries of many developing countries. Yet their real impact has scarcely begun: before the end of this century – only seventeen years ahead! – they will have transformed the planet, sweeping away much that is evil, and, unfortunately, not a few things that are good.

The slogan 'A telephone in every village' should remind you of that American mayor, so don't laugh. I believe it is a realistic and (equally important!) desirable goal by the year 2000. It can be achieved now that millions of kilometres of increasingly scarce copper wire can be replaced by a handful of satellites in stationary orbit. And on the ground we need a simple,

*I pulled this example out of the hat – yet it is now the proud boast of the latest fibre-optics system (Chapter 42).

rugged handset and solar-powered transceiver plus antenna, which could be mass-produced for tens rather than hundreds of dollars.

At this point I would like to borrow an expression from the military – 'force multipliers'. A force multiplier is anything that increases the effectiveness of an existing system. For example, it may take fifty old-fashioned bombs to knock out a bridge. But if you give them TV guidance, you will need only a couple, though the explosive power per bomb remains exactly the same.

I suggest that the 'Telephone in the Village' would be one of the most effective force multipliers in history, because of its implications for health, animal husbandry, weather forecasts, market advice, social integration and human welfare. Each installation would probably pay for itself, in hard cash, within a few months. I would like to see a cost-effectiveness study of rural satellite telephone systems for Africa, Asia and South America. But the financial benefits, important though they undoubtedly would be, might yet be insignificant compared with the social ones. Unlike its military equivalent, this force multiplier would increase the health, wealth and happiness of mankind.

However, long before the global network of fixed telephones is established, there will be a parallel development which will eventually bypass it completely – though perhaps not until well into the next century. It is starting now, with cellular network, portable radiophones, and paging devices, and will lead ultimately to our old science-fiction friend, the wristwatch telephone.

Before we reach that, there will be an intermediate stage. During the coming decade, more and more business men, well-heeled tourists and virtually all newspersons will be carrying attaché-case-sized units that will permit direct two-way communication with their homes or offices, via the most convenient satellite. These will provide voice, telex and video facilities (still photos and, if needed, live TV coverage). As these units become cheaper, smaller and more universal, they will make travellers totally independent of national communications systems.

The implications of this are profound – and not only to media newsgatherers who will no longer be at the mercy of censors or inefficient (sometimes non-existent) postal and telegraph services. It means the end of closed societies and will lead ultimately – to repeat a phrase I heard Arnold Toynbee use forty years ago – to the unification of the world.

You may think this is a naïve prediction, because many countries wouldn't let such subversive machines across their borders. But they would have no choice; the alternative would be economic suicide, because very soon they would get no tourists and no business men offering foreign currency. They'd get only spies, who would have no trouble at all concealing the powerful new tools of their ancient trade.

What I am saying, in fact, is that the debate about the free flow of information which has been going on for so many years will soon be settled – by engineers, not politicians. (Just as physicists, not generals, have now determined the nature of war.)

Consider what this means. No government will be able to conceal, at least for very long, evidence of crimes or atrocities – even from its own people. The very existence of the myriads of new information channels, operating in real time and across all frontiers, will be a powerful influence for civilised behaviour. If you are arranging a massacre, it will be useless to shoot the cameraman who has so inconveniently appeared on the scene. His pictures will already be safe in the studio 5000 kilometres away; and his final image may hang you.

Many governments will not be at all happy about this, but in the long run everyone will benefit. Exposures of scandals or political abuses – especially by visiting TV teams who go home and make rude documentaries – can be painful but also very valuable. Many a ruler might still be in power today, or even alive, had he known what was really happening in his own country. A wise statesman once said: 'A free press can give you hell; but it can save your skin.' That is even more true of TV reporting – which, thanks to satellites, will soon be instantaneous and ubiquitous. Let us hope that it will also be responsible. Considering what has often happened in the past, optimism here may well be tempered with concern.

A quarter of a century ago, the transistor radio began to sweep across the world, starting a communications revolution in all countries, developed and undeveloped. It is a continuing revolution – a steady explosion, if I may be permitted the paradox – and it is nowhere completed. Indeed, it will accelerate when the cheap solar-powered radio eliminates dependence on batteries, so expensive and difficult to obtain in remote places.

The transistor radio has already brought news, information and entertainment to millions who would otherwise have been almost totally deprived of so much that we take for granted. But TV is a far more powerful medium, and thanks to the new generation of satellites, its time has now arrived.

I hesitate to add to the megawords – if not gigawords – written about educational TV and direct-broadcast satellites. But despite all this verbiage, there still seem to be a number of points that are not generally understood, perhaps because of the human dislike for facing awkward truths.

Attempts have been made, in some quarters, to regulate or even prohibit direct broadcasting from space. But radio waves do not recognise frontiers, and it is totally impossible to prevent spill-over. Even if country A did its best to keep its programmes from reaching its neighbour B, it could not always succeed. During the 1976 Satellite Instructional Television Experiment (SITE) the beam from the ATS-6 satellite was deliberately slanted toward

India to give maximum signal strength there. Yet good images were still received in England, a quarter of the way around the globe!

Those who would promulgate what might be called 'permission to receive' laws remind me of the fabled American state legislature, which, back in the last century, ruled that the value of pi is exactly 3, as given in the Old Testament. (Alas, this delightful story isn't true: but it can be matched by similar absurdities at this very moment.)

In any event, technology has once again superseded politics. All over the United States, the Caribbean and South America, small 'receive only' dishes are sprouting like mushrooms, tuning in to the hundreds of satellite channels now available – and there's little that anyone can do about it, without spending a lot of money on scramblers and encrypting devices which may sometimes defeat their own purpose.

In Sri Lanka, radio amateurs with quite simple equipment have been receiving excellent pictures from the Soviet Union's powerful EKRAN satellites; thanks to these, we were able to enjoy the Moscow Olympics. I would like to express my gratitude to the Russian engineers for their continuing large-scale demonstration, over the whole of Asia, that the politicians are not only talking technical nonsense, but are ignoring their own proclamations.

They are not the only ones guilty of hypocrisy, as my good friend Dr Yash Pal pointed out in these words several years ago:

> In the drawing rooms of the large cities you meet many people who are concerned with the damage that one is going to cause to the integrity of rural India by exposing her to the world outside. After they have lectured you about the dangers of corrupting this innocent, beautiful mass of humanity, they usually turn around and add: 'Well, now that we have a satellite, when are we going to see some American programmes?' Of course, they themselves are immune to cultural domination or foreign influences.

When I quoted this at the 1981 UNESCO IPDC meeting in Paris, I added these words:

> I am afraid that cocktail-party intellectuals are the same everywhere. Because we frequently suffer from the scourge of information pollution, we find it hard to imagine its even deadlier opposite – information starvation. I get very annoyed when I hear arguments, usually from those who have been educated beyond their intelligence, about the virtues of keeping happy, backward peoples in ignorance. Such an attitude seems like that of a fat man preaching the benefits of fasting to a starving beggar.
>
> And I am not impressed by the attacks on television because of the truly dreadful programmes it often carries. Every TV programme has some educational content; the cathode tube is a window on the world – indeed, on many worlds. Often it is a

very murky window, but I have slowly come to the conclusion that, on balance, even bad TV is better than no TV at all.

Many will disagree with this – and I sympathise with them. Electronic cultural imperialism will sweep away much that is good, as well as much that is bad. Yet it will only accelerate changes which were in any case inevitable; and on the credit side, the new media will preserve for future generations the customs, performing arts and ceremonies of our time, in a way that was never possible in any earlier age.

Of course, there are a great many present-day customs which should *not* be preserved, except as warning to future generations. Slavery, torture, racial and religious persecution, treatment of women as chattels, mutilation of children because of ancient superstitions, cruelty to animals – the list is endless, and no country can proclaim total innocence. But looming monstrously above all these evils is the ever-present threat of nuclear war.

I wish I could claim that improved communications would lead to peace, but the matter is not as simple as that. Excellent communications – even a common language! – have not brought peace to Northern Ireland, to give but one of many possible examples. Nevertheless, good communications of every type, and at all levels, are essential if we are ever to establish peace on this planet. As the mathematicians would say: they are necessary, but not sufficient.

I would like to end this survey of our telecommunications future with one of the most remarkable predictions ever made. In the closing decade of the nineteenth century an electrical engineer, W. E. Ayrton, was lecturing at London's Imperial Institute about the most modern of communications devices, the submarine telegraph cable. He ended with what must, to all his listeners, have seemed the wildest fantasy:

> There is no doubt that the day will come, maybe when you and I are forgotten, when copper wires, gutta-percha coverings and iron sheathings will be relegated to the Museum of Antiquities. Then, when a person wants to telegraph to a friend, he knows not where, he will call an electromagnetic voice, which will be heard loud by him who has the electromagnetic ear, but will be silent to everyone else. He will call 'Where are you?' and the reply will come 'I am at the bottom of the coal-mine' or 'Crossing the Andes' or 'In the middle of the Pacific'; or perhaps no reply will come at all, and he may then conclude that his friend is dead.

This truly astonishing prophecy was made in 1897, long before anyone could imagine how it might be fulfilled. A century later, by 1997,* it will be on the verge of achievement, because the wristwatch telephone will be coming into general use. And if you still believe that such a device is unlikely, ask yourself

*Not a bad guess. Motorola hopes to have its Iridium system operating by 1996 . . .

this question: Who could have imagined the personal watch, back in the Middle Ages – when the only clocks were clanking, room-sized mechanisms, the pride and joy of a few cathedrals?

For that matter, many of you carry on your wrists miracles of electronics that would have been beyond belief even twenty years ago. The symbols that flicker across those digital displays now merely give time and date. When the zeros flash up at the end of the century, they will do far more than that. They will give you direct access to most of the human race, through the invisible networks girdling our planet.

The long-heralded global village is almost upon us, but it will last for only a flickering moment in the history of mankind. Before we even realise that it has come, it will be superseded – by the global family.

35

COOP'S TROOP

Although in my 1945 paper I had suggested that reception from satellites would be possible with parabolic dishes as small as a foot in diameter, the first ground stations were a hundred times that size, and cost millions of dollars. But as the power of satellites steadily increased, and detectors grew ever more sensitive, so ground equipment became smaller and cheaper. By the mid-seventies it could be afforded by many US households – and a new industry was born.

At first, only a few enthusiastic amateurs – the lineal descendants of the 1920–30 radio 'hams' – got into the act, building chicken-wire dishes in their back yards and bread-boarding their own circuits. Soon, however, complete Home TVRO (TV Receive Only) systems were on the market for a thousand dollars and upwards. The luxury models had quasi-equatorial mountings, like telescopes, and could be motor-driven from horizon to horizon to point automatically to any satellite hovering in the geostationary orbit. By the early eighties there were dozens of programmes – news, entertainment, sport, and even a little culture – falling from the air for anyone to enjoy.

One of the chief promoters – indeed, pioneers – of Home TVRO was an energetic journalist/electronics buff named Robert Cooper, who began publishing a monthly magazine in 1979 full of gossip, technical news and advertisements. *Coop's Satellite Digest* was essential reading for anyone in the field, and in its brief but hectic lifetime it chronicled the rise and (temporary) fall of a multi-million dollar industry.

In 1983, Home TVRO was still booming, and Bob Cooper organised an amazing feat of logistics for which I shall always be grateful. He persuaded three of the principal manufacturers to donate their *complete TVRO units* to me, and to come to Sri Lanka to install them. Here and now I would like to record the names and affiliations of the generous donors: Bob Behar (twenty-five-foot antenna from Hero Communications, Hialeah, Florida); James Gowen (twenty-foot antenna from ADM, Poplar Bluff, Missouri); Dave Johnson (sixteen-foot Paraclipse antenna from Paradigm Manufacturing, Redding, California). In addition, valuable electronics were supplied by Avcom (Richmond, Virginia) and California Amplifier (Newbury Park,

California). I apologise to other generous donors whose names I have forgotten, or never knew . . .

Getting all this equipment round the world and safely into Sri Lanka was a nightmare, but by what now seems not one but a whole series of miracles everything arrived at the right place at the right time. The sixteen-foot Paraclipse (only the second ever made – the first had gone to the Kennedy Space Center) was erected on the balcony of my house in Colombo. The twenty-foot ADM dish was somehow levitated three storeys to the roof of the University of Moratuwa's Electronics Department. And the massive twenty-five-foot Hero antenna, with the help of a large crane, was erected outside the Arthur Clarke Centre for Modern Technologies (see Chapter 38), next door to the university.

All this could never have been done without the skill and energy of the twenty-nine Americans, Canadians and Japanese whom Coop had marshalled for the operation. In particular I would like to give credit to John Zalenka and to Fr Lee Lubbers, SJ, who has since built up a satellite educational network (SCOLA) at Creighton University, Omaha, Nebraska.*

Seven years later, virtually all this equipment is still in use, despite monsoon storms and occasional lightning-strikes. The twenty-five-foot dish was particularly valuable during the Gulf crisis, relaying CNN reports to the national TV network. And thanks to the sixteen-footer on my roof, I had access to Russian, Indonesian and Chinese programmes – as well as much of the traffic through the Indian Ocean INTELSAT birds.

By the end of the eighties, however, the uninhibited, Wild West days of the geostationary orbit were over; the big corporations had called in their lawyers to clean up the frontier, and to jail any outlaws they could catch. And, despite the screams of anguish from the TVRO pioneers, they had a good case. It cost millions to build and launch communications satellites, and millions more to feed their voracious appetites. Those who benefited from them could hardly expect to have a free joy-ride for ever.

So began a hi-tech battle of wits far above the Earth – a bloodless (usually) analogue of the electronic warfare which was to break out in the Gulf a few years later. 'Scrambling' systems were devised so that unauthorised viewers would see only a meaningless jumble on their TV; if they wanted to get a picture, they had to rent a special black box (decoder) to turn chaos into video sense. Even anyone totally ignorant of the technology involved may gather how one of the many systems worked from this quotation:

*This now transmits TV news from forty countries, twenty-four hours a day, over all the Americas – and is now negotiating with the USSR's Intersputnik to cover Eurasia. Father Lubbers assures those worried by his file-extension that the service is completely non-denominational – and has certainly proved it. I'm amused to note that the last programme listing he's sent me opens with – a reading from the Koran.

> Scrambling . . . can be done by delaying or advancing the start of picture information on one line relative to the previous line, by cutting each line's picture information into two parts and transmitting the second part before the first, with a different cut point on successive lines, or by changing the order in which lines are transmitted. Or by a combination of these.

Merely reading this description (from the chapter 'Satellite Channel Encryption in Europe' by Steven Birkill, *World Satellite Annual*, 1991) should be enough to give eyestrain to anybody.*

Needless to say, the introduction of scrambling greatly reduced sales of TVRO equipment, and put many suppliers out of business. But it was also an irresistible temptation to the electronic underground; in dozens of backrooms and garages, the successors of those who had started the personal computer revolution gleefully accepted this new challenge. Many of them did so for pure fun, but there were also fortunes involved. Before long, pirate decoders were being manufactured in Taiwan and Hong Kong, and smuggled across the Canadian border. The US Coastguard had a new headache; when Coop arranged a conference to discuss scrambling on his (British) Caribbean islands of Turks and Caicos, some of the participants had a hard time when they got back to the mainland. The authorities were not merely on the look-out for the clandestine chemicals very popular in that part of the world, but for suspicious microchips – considerably more difficult to identify.

Today, millions of law-abiding citizens in the United States, Europe and Asia pay their decoder fees and are presented with such a choice of news and entertainment as no other age has ever imagined. And they are doing it with smaller and smaller dishes – in some areas of high signal strength, as little as thirty centimetres (one foot) in diameter. Even the traditional (!) parabolic dish may soon be replaced by flat plates full of electronics that can fool the incoming signals into thinking that they are focused on one spot. These also have aesthetic advantages; when their beams can be redirected electronically without any physical movement of the antenna itself, they may be built unobtrusively into roofs and walls.

So, early in the next century, the parabolic dishes which sprouted mushroom-like over much of Europe and America during the 1980s will have gone the way of the horizontal aerial wires that swayed between the chimneys of the 1930s.

*During the SITE experiment (Chapter 33) Steve Birkill astonished everyone by receiving, in the heart of England, the programmes intended for the Indian villages.

36

APPOINTMENT IN THE VATICAN

I was still scanning the skies above Colombo with the sixteen-foot Paraclipse dish that Coop's Troop had installed on my roof when I received an unexpected and challenging invitation – to participate in a study week on 'The Impact of Space Exploration on Mankind' arranged by the Pontifical Academy of Science. As I had never been to Rome, still less to the Vatican, this was an offer I couldn't refuse. I took with me, as *consigliere* and guide into this unfamiliar territory, a long-time Sri Lankan friend, Director of the Institute of Integral Education and keen amateur astronomer, Father Mervyn Fernando.

The conference was limited to thirty-six participants from a wide selection of countries: the United States, France, Italy, Chile, Australia, Nigeria, Cuba, India, Switzerland, Indonesia – though not the United Kingdom (unless I could be regarded as a substitute). It took place during the week of 1–5 October 1984 in a beautiful villa not far from the Sistine Chapel; we had a chance of viewing Michelangelo's masterpiece, then during the controversial process of cleaning.

The proceedings were moderated by Professor Carlos Chagas, President of the Academy, and among the participants were Professor Yash Pal and Dr Cyril Ponnamperuma, famous for his detection of organic – and possibly pre-biotic – material in meteorites. On the second day we had an audience with Pope John Paul II, and I presented him with a copy of my 'Scientific Autobiography', *Ascent to Orbit*, to add to his already rather well-stocked library.

Another highlight of the visit was a trip to Castel Gandolfo, the Pope's summer residence and the location of the Vatican Observatory, whose director, Dr George Coyne, SJ, conducted us around what must be one of the most beautifully sited astronomical facilities in the world. I have since had the pleasure of showing George some of my favourite parts of Sri Lanka, which he has now visited several times. But at our initial meeting I couldn't resist telling him: 'You know, when I was invited to speak in the Vatican, my first choice of subject was 'After Giordano Bruno – who?' There was about a millisecond's delay before

George answered, 'If you had used that title, the answer would have been
– *you*.'*

Duly warned, I chose as my subject 'Space Communications and the Global
Family'. As my audience included the Director-General of INTELSAT, and
the Secretary-Generals of both the International Telecommunications Union
(ITU) and EUTELSAT, I decided that this was a good opportunity to
summarise my current thinking on comsats. So here it is, exactly as printed in
Pontificiae Academiae Scientiarum Scripta Varia, 58 (1986), under the title
'Space Communications and the Global Family'.

The late Herman Kahn used to be fond of the phrase 'surprise-free futures'.
But for better or worse, the future is seldom surprise-free. In the realms of
scientific discovery, politics and human affairs, the prophets are almost always
wrong.

One might expect them to do a better job in the limited and more
manageable field of technology; I attempted it myself, a quarter of a century
ago, in *Profiles of the Future*. Nevertheless, the record of technological
prediction is dismal, even for experts – I am tempted to say, *especially* for
experts. There seems no way of inoculating society against Future Shock: the
best vaccine yet discovered is science fiction – and even that is highly
unreliable . . .

So I am courageously attempting the impossible by trying to predict the
future of satellite communications, despite its record of continual surprises. In
1945, I certainly never dreamed that the global COMSAT and INTELSAT
organisations would be only twenty years ahead. In 1965, who could have
imagined that there would be a million Earth stations by 1985 – some with
dishes *less than a metre across*? So, what about 2005?

As a preliminary exercise in mind-stretching, let me tell you a story from
the dawn of the Telephone Age – still little more than a century ago. When he
heard about this wonderful new invention, one far-sighted American mayor
was wildly enthusiastic. Despite the hysterical laughter of his friends, he
made this brave prediction: 'I can foresee the time when *every city* will have
one.'

Remember that mayor, before you start laughing at me. I'm trying to
reverse Diaghilev's famous order to Jean Cocteau. I want to *prevent* you from
being 'astonished'.

So first, let's look at a few recent technological astonishments and see what
we can learn from them. They all stem from what is probably the most

*Bruno's belief in the plurality of worlds was not the only – or even the main – reason why he was
burned at the stake in 1600; amongst other heresies, he was interested in the occult. Considering
the garbage now littering our bookstores, I'm all in favour of reinstating this penalty.

important invention since the wheel – one, indeed, that will do a good deal to uninvent the wheel, and none too soon. I refer of course to the microchip – using that term in the very widest sense to cover the whole range of solid-state electronics.

No one would ever have dreamed that one day there would be more radios than people on the planet Earth. (If we've not already reached that stage, we soon will.) Yet the transistor revolution is still just beginning, for one key element was missing until recently. In remote parts of the world, radios can be out of commission for weeks, because batteries aren't available – or are too expensive. The advent of cheap solar cells is about to change that situation, as has already happened with pocket calculators.

Before long the world will be flooded with inexpensive radios – and other low-powered electronic devices – that will cost nothing to run and will last virtually for ever. They will be scrapped only because of technological obsolescence, not because they wear out.

The economic and socio-political consequences of this will be profound. Even an expensive piece of equipment, if it costs little to run, lasts many years, and fills some overwhelming demand, will eventually reach the average man and woman, in every country. The bicycle and the sewing machine are classic examples from the Pre-electronic Age. The transistor radio, the Sony Walkman, and now the video-cassette recorder are their successors. And please understand that I'm not talking merely about 'developing' countries. In this context, there's no other kind.

Now I want to consider a very simple little 4 × 4 matrix which, it seems to me, maps out virtually the entire universe of communications, not only for the man in the street, but also for the man in the jungle.

STATION	SERVICE
1. Person (1)*	1. Text messages (300 Hz)†
2. Vehicle (10)	2. Data (300–3000 Hz)
3. Home (100)	3. Speech, music (3–15 Khz)
4. Village (1000)	4. Video (5–10 Mhz)

*Cost (arbitrary units – say a week's wages?)
†Bandwidth, hertz (cycles/second)

I have ignored towns and cities on this listing, for two reasons. Obviously, anything that a village can afford will be available many times over in larger human settlements. They will have access to cables and Earth stations of enormous capacity; I am focusing here on the requirements of the smallest possible groups, down to individual human beings, and asking this question: 'What are the services which *only* communications satellites can provide?'

The simplest and most basic service – though far from the cheapest in terms of power and bandwidth – is of course telephony. So let us start with our old science-fiction friend, the wrist-watch telephone.

Frankly, I don't believe in it. I'm not going to stand like an idiot holding my arm in front of my face. The telephone of the future will be a waistbelt box – just like the Walkman and its successors – with a very light earpiece and throat microphone, working through an optical or electromagnetic link so that one doesn't get continually entangled in tiny wires.

The main unit can hardly be smaller than today's pocket calculators, because it will require at least a one-line visual display *and* a full alphanumeric keyboard. People who talk about wrist-watch telephones seldom mention that small but essential extra – the wrist-watch telephone *directory* – in this case, a global one, with several billion entries. Although the most used numbers would have to be loaded into memory, keyboarding would often be necessary to access Directory Inquiries.

Something like this facility will soon be available in many areas, through the ground-based 'cellular' networks now being established. But I am talking about the whole planet – three-quarters of which, please remember, is ocean. Only satellites can provide universal, global coverage. And it doesn't really matter whether those satellites are in the high stationary orbit or, as Dr Yash Pal has advocated, in low orbits with periods of an exact number of hours. I'm sure we'll need both.

The fact that close satellites will be moving swiftly across the sky is no longer a handicap, at least in this application. The personal telephone – shall I call it a Talkman? – need have no more directionality than the ordinary transistor radio or cordless telephone. As long as there is an appropriate satellite above the horizon, that will be sufficient.

At some cost in complexity, however, the system *could* be made directional, thus reducing satellite power levels by factors of tens or even hundreds. Antennas have already been installed in the roofs of cars which automatically lock on to the source, despite any movement of the vehicle – or, for that matter, the satellite. The Rutherford Appleton Laboratory in the UK is working on such a system, using satellites in the high-inclination, twelve-hour orbit suggested many years ago by Dr William Hilton and pioneered by the Soviet 'Molynias'. It is not difficult to imagine a simpler man-rated version for personal use.

If you don't believe this, would you accept the attaché-case or executive model? The flat antenna is built into the lid, which has merely to be tilted in the approximately correct direction, and the phasing elements automatically take care of the rest. Its facilities would, of course, include printer and full visual display. In fact it would be very much like the portable word-processors which are now changing journalists' lives, as they sit in front of the TV and gather the news. But instead of a modem connected to the local phone system, there would be a microwave beam pointing up at the sky.

For the first time in the history, business men, reporters, tourists, travellers on the high seas, would have full, real-time communications with anyone they wished, wherever they might be. The tedious polemics about the free flow of information and cross-border data transfer are going to be decided by the engineers, not the politicians. The implications of this for human affairs will be at least as great as that of the telephone itself; I will address only a few particular issues.

The most obvious one is this: how will today's sovereign states view this instrumentality, which so blithely ignores all national frontiers? Even countries which consider themselves open will be concerned by possible loss of telecommunications revenue, as well as such problems as security and copyright. But once a technology arrives which fills an irresistible need, there is no way of holding it back – though it can be delayed.

I have two cautionary stories to demonstrate this point. When I first described the 'attaché-case' Earth station, in my address at the United Nations on World Telecommunications Day (17 May 1983), I used these words:

> You may think this a naïve prediction, because many countries wouldn't let such subversive machines across their borders. But they would have no choice; the alternative would be economic suicide, because very soon they would get no tourists and no business men offering foreign currency. They'd get only spies, who would have no trouble at all concealing the powerful new tools of their ancient trade.

Well, just a few months later, a gentleman from a country I won't mention was found in another which I shall likewise refrain from naming, carrying exactly this kind of equipment. (For a small consideration, I'll give you the address of the manufacturer.) The transmit-receive unit looked like a pocket calculator, the antenna like an ordinary umbrella. For all I know they were just that; but they were also a good deal more . . .

My second tale is even more instructive, and begins almost two centuries ago. It shows how a nation of notoriously intelligent people can bring ruin upon itself by trying to restrict – censor, if you like – a new communications technology.

France was the first nation in the world to have a telegraph system – installed, *mirabile dictu*, in 1793. Of course it was not electric, but purely optical, depending on chains of semaphores observed through telescopes. In this way, the central government was able to communicate with the provinces – *and control them*. No one else was allowed to use the system; indeed, a law was passed imposing jail sentences of up to a year on anyone – I quote –

'transmitting unauthorised signals from one place to another by the telegraph machine or any other means'.

When Samuel Morse's invention threatened this system – as satellites now threaten the monopoly of terrestrial systems – the visual telegraph had its fanatical defenders. Significantly, they argued that 'supervision would be impossible' with wired networks. Listen to this *cri de cœur* from one of the bureaucrats who knew what was best for the people:

> No, the electric telegraph is not a sound invention. It will always be at the mercy of the slightest disruption, wild youths, drunkards, etc. . . . . The visual telegraph on the contrary has its towers, its high walls, its gates well guarded from the inside by strong armed men . . . substitution of the electric telegraph for the visual one is a dreadful measure, a truly idiotic act . . .

So much for the free flow of information in mid-nineteenth-century France. Yet ten years later, despite violent opposition, this 'idiotic act' had been carried out, and the electric telegraph began to spread across the country. Nevertheless, the legacy of state control over internal communications lingered on for another century, with the disastrous result that until very recently the French telephone system was the laughing-stock of the world. Though this story has now had a happy ending, who can estimate the trillions of francs that the Republic lost through decades of state mismanagement? Those who are now considering their countries' involvement in the next generation of comsats would do well to compare the fortunes of the French and American telephone systems between 1880 and 1970.

Returning to my little 4 × 4 matrix, after 'person' the next entry is 'vehicle'. Although these divisions are arbitrary – and indeed overlapping – I am thinking specifically of bicycles, cars and boats, which might justify more expensive installations. And in this context I was delighted to see a photograph in a recent issue of *Time* magazine showing a gentleman sitting beside his bicycle somewhere in the wilderness, typing away on a solar-powered Hewlett-Packard portable. This is exactly the sort of thing I had in mind; and I'm not ruling out bullock carts, either.

Item 3 – the home – is included for completeness, but I will bypass it because it will be a very long time before most of the world's homes contain any form of permanently installed telecommunications device. Let us go straight to Item 4 – the village – because that is still the basic unit in society for most of the planet, as it has been ever since the invention of agriculture.

The importance of providing good communications to *all* human settlements for economic and cultural reasons, as well as for dealing with medical and natural emergencies, is so overwhelming that there should be no need to stress it. Unfortunately, it is not yet obvious to everyone; telephones are not as glamorous as factories or steelmills, and don't provide as much political mileage.

For the majority of the human race that is not yet urbanised – and with any luck never will be – only satellite technology can provide good, real-time communications. And when the economy-sized solar-powered Earth station comes to the village in the jungle, history, you may be surprised to learn, will be repeating itself. Something very similar happened in Europe and America a century and a half ago. The telegraph sounder in the local railway station or post office brought, for the first time, instant news of the outside world to communities whose isolation we can no longer easily imagine.

And I can see the rise of a new profession, as universal and as essential as that of the village blacksmith in earlier times. Someone will have to learn the modest skills needed to run the community's ground station, and to access the global data banks and information networks. Not everyone need acquire electronic literacy – but any intelligent and properly motivated person can do so in a surprisingly short time. Within another generation, every community of more than a few hundred people will need a member of this newest trade.

I will do no more than glance at the other four elements of the little matrix – text, data, speech, video – arranged in increasing (but often overlapping) bandwidth. A great deal can be done with very narrow bandwidths, and hence low powers; the so-called 'electronic blackboard' is an obvious example. But for all except very specialised applications a speech capability is essential; for people who cannot read or write there is no substitute for the human voice, at least where two-way communication is required.

At this point I can't resist the temptation of passing on a hundred-year-old piece of Bell System folklore. After the linesman had installed the first telephone seen in the New Jersey countryside, the farmer came up to him and said anxiously, 'I forgot to ask – can I talk Italian over it?'

The engineer shook his head. 'You should have told me that before,' he remonstrated. 'Now I'll have to put in an extra wire – and it will cost you another fifty dollars.'

That's more than just a joke. It probably sums up rather well the reactions *we* would have, to the communications systems that will exist when the telephone celebrates its second centennial, in 2076 . . .

I concluded my address in the Vatican with a plea not only for communications but also for reconnaissance satellites – watchdogs in the sky which could monitor the political (and military) state of the world. Less than a decade later, the brief but deadly Gulf War demonstrated the importance of this idea: Chapter 40 – Peacesat – will go into it in more detail.

37

Happy Birthday, COMSAT!

On 18 February 1988 COMSAT's president Irv Goldstein threw a little party in Washington for a few hundred intimate friends to celebrate the organisation's twenty-fifth birthday. I was invited to join the festivities, which I did in the most appropriate way:

This is Arthur Clarke, sending greetings to you from practically on the Equator. It gives me a nice feeling to know that the Indian Ocean satellite that keeps me in touch with the world is right overhead . . .

And so, by an interesting coincidence, is the most stable point in the Earth's gravitational field. Exhausted geostationary satellites also end up there, milling round and round above Sri Lanka in a celestial Sargasso Sea when they've run out of gas.

Well, I guess there must be at least twenty old friends here at COMSAT today, so I can't say 'Hello' to them all – but *they* know who they are . . .

Now I'm going to say something that may upset quite a few people, especially the bean-counters who calculate our phone bills. I can see someone yelling, 'Cut him off!' about a minute from now.

For I want to remind you of something that happened in England just 150 years ago. In those days, sending a letter from one part of the country to another was enormously complicated and expensive. Why? Because an army of clarkes – sorry, clerks – calculated the exact amount you had to pay on every piece of mail, *according to the distance it travelled!* Just think of the manpower and paperwork that must have been involved!

Then along came a genius named Rowland Hill, who did what we'd now call 'a systems analysis'. He discovered (surprise! surprise!!) that the cost of sending a letter was almost independent of distance – virtually all the labour went into the handling at the beginning and the end of the journey. So Mr Hill made a revolutionary suggestion. He said, 'Let's have a flat rate, irrespective of distance. People can pay for letters in advance, simply by purchasing a stamp. I calculate that it need cost only one penny, and even if we don't break even at first, the explosion in correspondence will soon give us a profit. And the benefits to commerce and society will be immeasurable.'

Rowland Hill was one of the creators of the world we know, and, needless to say, he was shouted down at first. But he persisted, and the Penny Post started in 1840. Incidentally, one of those first penny stamps wouldn't leave much change now from a million dollars, but that's another story . . .

Surprisingly, it only took five years for Mr Hill to win his battle with the bureaucrats. They did things a lot faster in those days. Not so many committees to deal with.

I'm sure you'll see what I'm driving at, and because I can never resist an opportunity for a commercial, I'd like to end by reading to you a paragraph from my *latest* last book:

> For in the beginning, the Earth had possessed the single super-continent of Pangaea, which over the aeons had split asunder. So had the human species, into innumerable tribes and nations; now it was merging together, as the old linguistic and cultural divisions began to blur . . . With the historic abolition of long-distance charges on 31 December 2000, every telephone call became a local one, and the human race greeted the new millennium by transforming itself into one huge, gossiping family.
>
> (*2061: Odyssey 3*, Chapter 3)

38

The Clarke Awards

I never imagined (as Clifton Fadiman once remarked in an attempt to reassure the members of the Book of the Month Club, 'Mr Clarke does not appear to be a very imaginative person') that I should ever be responsible for an Act of Parliament. But on 6 July 1984 the Government Publications Bureau in Colombo issued a thirteen-page leaflet (price: Rupees 1.20) which bore on the cover, under the presidential seal:

PARLIAMENT OF THE DEMOCRATIC
SOCIALIST REPUBLIC OF
SRI LANKA

ARTHUR C. CLARKE CENTRE
FOR MODERN
TECHNOLOGIES
Act No. 30 of 1984

***

The Act established a centre whose aims and objects would be 'the acceleration of the process of introduction and development of modern technologies in the fields of communications, computers, space technologies, energy and robotics'. The whole operation had been planned – without my knowledge, much less participation – by my friends in government, industry and academia, with the active assistance of UNESCO. By great good fortune everything came together at just the right time. The $35,000 of the Marconi Award allowed construction of the initial building to begin immediately, without having to wait for Treasury approval. (Most of the Centre's income – about $100,000 a year – comes from the State.) Almost simultaneously, Bob Cooper and his merry men (and women) arrived with equipment and, equally important, inspiration.

The Centre was formally opened by President J. R. Jayawardene on 30 November 1983 and its first director was the distinguished scientist Dr Cyril Ponnamperuma, long-time chief of NASA's Laboratory of Chemical

Evolution and one of the principal experimenters on the Viking-Mars programme. In his inaugural address he pointed out how essential it was for the so-called developing nations to bypass the intermediate stages in technology that more advanced societies had been forced to go through; after all, it was no longer necessary to reinvent the automobile, the aeroplane – or the transistor. He expressed the hope that the Arthur Clarke Centre would be Sri Lanka's secret weapon in this 'leapfrogging' process, and gave the startling – but encouraging – example of a developing country which had managed to award only twenty-two Ph.Ds in seventeen years. This state of affairs, one of its few intellectuals lamented, 'makes us view the past with humility and the future with despair'. Believe it or not, that country was the United States – little more than a century ago!

Despite problems caused by Sri Lanka's tragic political and racial conflicts during the 1980s, the Centre has made considerable progress, and our hope is that one day it may trigger the development of an indigenous 'Silicon Valley'. Numerous foreign – and local – investors have shown interest in the Centre, and UNESCO recently funded a report on its progress. In addition, the 'Arthur Clarke Foundation of the United States' (Executive Secretary Frederick C. Durant III) has been set up in Washington to help raise funds.

One of the Centre's first actions was to initiate an annual award for distinguished services to satellite communication. This takes the shape of a handsome brass replica of the *2001* monolith, in which is set a hollow crystal sphere. And floating inside the sphere, three equidistant satellites orbit an Earth which, for artistic reasons, is not exactly to scale . . .

The first Award went to Dr John McLucas, who has played almost as many roles as Alec Guinness. He has been at various times Secretary of the US Air Force, Administrator of the Federal Aviation Administration, NATO Assistant Secretary-General – and President of COMSAT World Systems. It was for this last incarnation that he received the Arthur Clarke Award; but lest you should imagine his interests are purely technical, he has also been chairman of the picturesquely named Wolf Trap Foundation. (I have often wondered how Wolf Trap's famous open-air concerts compete with the jets operating from nearby Dulles; perhaps John simply used his clout with the FAA to ground them.) In 1991 he published a book entitled *Space Commerce* (Harvard University Press). Few people are better qualified to write on this subject.

The 1987 winner was Dr John Pierce, whom you have already met many times in this book. In his address, 'Space Enough for All' (given on my seventieth birthday!) he explained how his work on communications at the Bell Labs had led to his present position as Professor of Music at Stanford's Center for Computer Research in Music and Acoustics, CCRMA (felicitously pronounced *karma*). More than thirty years ago John and his colleagues made a recording to demonstrate the current state of the art of sound synthesis. The highlight was a computer singing 'Daisy, Daisy': Stanley Kubrick and I are very grateful to him for the inspiration.

In 1988, the third Award went to Dr Harold Rosen. Unfortunately, owing to the disturbed situation then prevailing in Sri Lanka, the presentation ceremony could not take place until 16 December 1990 – which also happened to be the centennial of the Japanese telephone system! As a result, I spent part of a rather hectic seventy-third birthday on a satellite link to Tokyo with two other old friends, Carl Sagan and Marvin Minsky.

Hal Rosen's address started with Hertz's pioneering experiments in 1887 (using microwaves!) and ended on the far side of the Moon – the only place, he suggested, quiet enough to receive signals from civilisations in our next-door neighbour, the Andromeda galaxy. I could not help thinking that Hal (no relation to any computer of the same name) had expanded his horizons a long way from the stationary orbit – which had once seemed barely accessible to our technology.

The winner of the Fourth Arthur Clarke Award has now (August 1991) been announced, and because my birthday is inconveniently close to Christmas, the date of the presentation has been changed to the Spring. So around May 1992 – just about the time this book appears – my old friend Dr Joseph Charyk will be travelling to Sri Lanka. After distinguished academic careers at Cal Tech, the Jet Propulsion Lab and Princeton University, Joe was appointed Under-Secretary of the US Air Force in 1960. In 1963 he became the first President of COMSAT, and in 1983 its Chairman. He played a crucial role, therefore, in the first twenty years of the communications satellite revolution.

Incidentally, there are now at least *three* different Clarke Awards, of which the best known is probably that for science fiction, first won by Margaret Atwood in 1987 for *The Handmaid's Tale*. Although I much appreciate the motives of the organisers – no more, please! I can't keep track of them; and they are beginning to make me feel distinctly posthumous.

39

CNN LIVE

On 3 December 1984, during the première of *2010: Odyssey Two*, I was staying at Los Angeles' famous Beverly Wilshire when I heard through the grapevine that a birthday party was being thrown for another guest – Jacques Cousteau. I'd not seen Jacques for years – indeed, since he had been kind enough to write the Introduction for my young person's guide to skin-diving, *The First Five Fathoms* (1960). So I promptly invited myself to the party, and was happy to resume contact with Jacques and his son Michel, who told me that they were about to launch a TV special in honour of Jacques's seventy-fifth birthday ('The first of a short series . . .').

Presently, as something of an afterthought, I asked, 'Who's the host?' – and was promptly introduced to Ted Turner. This was an opportunity too good to miss.

'Delighted to meet you, Ted. By the way, you owe me 10 per cent of your income.'

At the time, I now realise, this was not a very tactful thing to say, and (for once) Ted was speechless. He should have answered, 'You mean my losses.' His cable-and-satellite empire was then haemorrhaging at the rate of megabucks a month, and CNN was not yet the household name that it was to become to the whole world after January 1991.

This book was conceived, and most of it written, before the outbreak of the Gulf War. I then put it aside, realising that the ending had to wait until the events of the next few months had unfolded. I might add that I had a particular interest in the outcome – even more so than most people. My next-door neighbour, sharing our eight-foot-high party wall, happens to be His Excellency the Iraqi Ambassador. I have not seen him for some considerable time, and am not even sure if he is still at home.

Like much of the world, I lost a great deal of sleep between January and March 1991. At first, the two local TV channels carried only brief reports of the war, but every day the Arthur Clarke Centre – which was acting as a 'node' for CNN in the region – sent me the material it had videotaped overnight. Later, the national network (Rupavahini) replayed an hour of the day's CNN after the main programme had ended around 11 p.m. All the major – and not a few minor – hotels also advertised CNN coverage for their customers, though how many actually paid for the service is another matter. (From mid-1991 transmissions will be scrambled, so it will no longer be possible to receive them without paying a fee.)

During the Gulf crisis, I was frequently asked for my views on the world's first satellite war, and I repeated many of the points I had made over the last decades. Then I added two more topical comments – the first tongue-in-cheek, the second deadly serious.

Watching CNN's coverage, I told Reuter's correspondent (who duly spread it all over the globe) I'd been struck by a sudden vision of the future, just a few years ahead. I imagined that Ted Turner had been offered the post of World President – but had rejected it, because he didn't want to give up power.

Soon after hostilities commenced, I suggested another and slightly more probable scenario. For the first time in human history, millions of people were seeing the true horors of modern mechanised war *while they were actually happening*. I expressed the hope that the impact would cause such a wave of revulsion that, ultimately, the leaders of our various national tribes would stop paying lip-service to the virtues of peace and actually do something to ensure it. If this seems unrealistic to the naïve pessimists who so often pose as 'practical men', I would answer that the world is now much too dangerous for anything short of Utopia. And by Utopia, I mean a world in which *all* weapons of mass destruction have been eliminated.* (After Iraq and Kuwait, who needs nukes?)

Many years ago, I called comsats 'weapons of peace' – necessary, but not in themselves sufficient, tools for the prevention of war. Although, like any medium of communication, they can transmit lies as easily as truth, the diversity of channels created by direct broadcasting makes it impossible even for closed societies to insulate their people from the real world.

The Gulf War has accelerated this process more than any other event in recent times. A perfect example was given in a recent (8 March) issue of *Le Monde*, describing the situation in Algiers. The ruling party there had 'so often celebrated Baghdad's victory in advance' that it had to announce that Iraq's withdrawal from Kuwait was the result of President Bush's threat to use nuclear weapons, *because the coalition he was leading had already lost 170,000 dead or missing*.

Dr Goebbels, it would seem, is alive and well in Algeria. But *Le Monde* goes on to report that the authorities cannot prevent the truth reaching millions of

---

*I am making a short list of weapons that should be permitted in a civilised world. They include quarter-staffs; aerosol sprays; 'peace gas' (see *Things to Come*); acoustic, actinic and smoke bombs; and – only when authorised at the highest level – single-shot telescopic rifles, preferably firing tranquillisers. I am open to further suggestions, but will not consider any delivery systems more sophisticated than bicycles.

families 'via the satellite dishes that are everywhere to be seen on the roofs of buildings in big cities'. And I am delighted to read that the enemies of this free flow of information rather wittily denounce such antennas as '*paradiabolique*'.

Paradiabolical – I like that! And in this context, speaking of the Devil reminds me of the famous tirade Shaw gave him in Act 3 of *Man and Superman*. Written almost a century ago, it has, alas, become dated only by the details of its technology:

> In the arts of life Man invents nothing; but in the art of death he outdoes Nature herself, and produces by chemistry and machinery all the slaughter of plague, pestilence and famine . . . In the arts of peace, Man is a bungler . . . I know his clumsy typewriters and bungling locomotives and tedious bicycles; they are toys compared to the Maxim gun, the submarine torpedo boat. There is nothing in Man's industrial machinery but his greed and sloth; his heart is in his weapons.

His heart is in his weapons. That is indeed a chilling indictment. It cannot be denied that satellite technology was born and nurtured in war.

Yet out of it may yet come a tool that may save our civilisation, and make this indeed One World – the Peacesat.

POSTSCRIPT – THE SECOND RUSSIAN REVOLUTION

The seismic events of the August revolution, which appear to be rapidly reversing those of the October one, are unfolding even as I write these words. I could hardly have expected so swift an endorsement of the thesis advanced in the above chapter, which indeed forms the basis of this entire book.

And I was delighted to hear Alistair Cooke make exactly the same point in his regular 'Letter from America' (BBC World Service, 24 August 1991). Contrasting the 1917 'Ten days that shook the world' with this year's sixty hours, he stated: 'The coup failed because of something new – satellite broadcasting'. He then went on to pay a tribute to CNN, which, as in the Gulf War, once again served as a two-way, interactive medium, creating history even as it reported it.

40

PEACESAT

For many years I have been interested in the peace-keeping potential of satellites, having been first alerted to this possibility by Howard Kurtz, founder and President of War Control Planners (PO Box 19127, Washington, 20036).* Although I frequently mentioned the idea in lectures and essays, it took the Strategic Defense Initiative (a.k.a., to George Lucas's annoyance, as 'Star Wars') to start me promoting it seriously.

This is not the place to discuss the pros and cons of SDI; I will merely comment that it comes in at least as many varieties as a well-known condiment. Some make a good deal of sense, but others – especially the much ballyhooed but now discreetly buried vision of an 'umbrella over the United States' – were pure fantasy. (Not, as some critics said, science fiction. In that case they would have been worth taking seriously.)

In 1986 I was given a superb platform for airing my views on the subject, when invited to give the annual Nehru Memorial Address in New Delhi. I called it 'Star Wars and Star Peace'. The first part was depressing; it described the consequences of an all-out nuclear war and the impossibility of countering it by technology. This scenario, I trust, has now been bypassed by history; so I will quote only the second part of my address.

The real problem is not military hardware, but human software – though the right kind of hardware can certainly help. A stable peace will never be possible without mutual trust; without that, all agreements and treaties are worse than useless, because they obscure the real issues.

Yet trust cannot be blind; it must be based on past experience – and even then may require constant testing.† This is true of individuals, and even more so of sovereign states, whose governments and policies may change overnight.

The greatest enemy of trust is fear, and it makes little difference whether

*For more than three decades, at great personal sacrifice, Howard has been publicising the concept by means of countless letters to Congressmen, media representatives, Pentagon brass, etc. I am very grateful to him for the information he has supplied me over the years.
†As President Reagan liked to say: 'Trust – but verify.'

that fear is baseless or well founded. It is not paranoia but prudence that compels military planners to assume a 'worst-case' scenario when they are ignorant of a potential enemy's capabilities. That ignorance, and the fear it generates, can be dispelled only by accurate and timely information. It follows therefore – almost like a theorem in mathematics – that the only road to lasting peace is through truth.

A classic example of this is the infamous 'missile gap' debate which dominated the Kennedy–Nixon campaign of 1960. After the initial shock of Sputnik, which opened the Space Age in October 1957, there was a tendency in the United States to exaggerate all Russian accomplishments in this area. Propagandists, ably assisted by the US military-industrial complex, claimed that the USSR was far in advance in the development of ICBMs – so the United States must start a crash programme to overcome this 'enormous' lead.

Well, the missile gap was a total illusion, destroyed when the new American reconnaissance satellites revealed the truth about Soviet rocket deployment. President Johnson later remarked that its reconnaissance satellites had saved the United States *many times* the entire cost of the space programme, by making it unnecessary to build the counterforce originally planned. I would like to quote his exact words (with my emphasis), which should be inscribed in letters of gold above the doors of the Pentagon:

We were doing things we didn't need to do; we were building things we didn't need to build; *we were harbouring fears we didn't need to harbour*.

You will not be surprised to learn that the USSR reacted with great indignation to the existence of American 'spy satellites' probing into its secrets. Indeed, in 1962 it proposed to the United Nations that they be banned. These protests suddenly stopped when its own reconnaissance satellites started orbiting that very same year, and both sides recognized their great value as stabilising agents. They make possible such arms control agreements as we do have, as is disclosed by the formula always used when referring to them: 'National technical means of verification' (NTM).

Although none of the high-quality images made by these NTMs has ever been released,* you can't classify the laws of optics, and photography is now a rather well-established art; so we know exactly what reconnaissance satellites can do. In daylight, under good conditions, they can show individual soldiers and the weapons they are carrying. Although they can be frustrated by cloud and darkness, radar-equipped satellites now exist that can overcome even these limitations.

*Interesting (but probably not 'state of the art') examples appeared in the January 1991 *Scientific American* (see 'The Future of Space Reconnaissance' by Jeffrey T. Richelson).

So it is probably true to say that no large-scale military preparations or activities can ever again escape surveillance – at least by nations with NTMs. At present this means the United States and the Soviet Union, who sometimes dole out snippets of orbital information to help their friends at moments of crisis. And on at least one occasion they have co-operated. A few years ago the USSR informed the US that it had detected preparations for a nuclear test in South Africa. Washington took the necessary steps, and no more was heard of the matter – at least, for the time being . . .

In 1978 the Government of France, in a rather untypical fit of global responsibility, made a dramatic proposal. It might be a good idea, President Giscard d'Estaing suggested, if there was an *international* body doing for the whole world what the Americans and Russians were selfishly doing for themselves. Such an International Monitoring Satellite Agency could verify arms control agreements, check border violations and defuse crisis situations, by acting as a watchdog for the world.

Establishing what I like to call 'Peacesats' would present major political, administrative and financial challenges – but the reward might be nothing less than the salvation of mankind.*

While I was preparing this address, there was dramatic proof of a 'public access' satellite's ability to provide information of vital importance to the whole world. After the accident to the nuclear reactor at Chernobyl, the American Eosat and French SPOT Earth-resources satellites were able to monitor the damage, and provide reassurance while official information was still lacking. Some of the TV coverage was not very accurate; one US commentator displayed an infra-red image of the site and then solemnly pointed out a 'hot-spot' that happened to be the black asphalt of a sun-warmed car park. As World War II amply proved, reconnaissance material is only as good as its interpreters; but the experts are getting very good indeed at interpreting images from space after they have been skilfully massaged in their computers.

I would like you to consider the following scenario, which has the great advantage that it could be realised not only without the co-operation of the nuclear powers, but even in the teeth of their opposition.

An advanced SPOT with a resolution of say one metre (compared to SPOT's present ten metres – and the *tenth* of a metre of a reconnaissance satellite under favourable conditions) is launched by a consortium of non-aligned countries, which makes its results available to everyone (probably, but not necessarily, through the UN). Most forms of military secrecy would then become impossible, and charges of fraud and cheating could be

*See UN Report A/AC 206/14, 6 August 1981: 'Study on the Implications of Establishing an International Satellite Monitoring Agency'. Also 'War and Peace in the Space Age' in *1984: Spring*.

scrutinised by the whole world. And although there would be many clandestine activities that the Peacesat could not detect, its psychological impact would be enormous. As California's Representative George Brown has put it in the *Congressional Record* (23 October 1979), 'A shared intelligence system would . . . not make pacifists out of rogues but it would pin down the rogues in the international forums with hard evidence.'

The countries sponsoring and building Peacesat might be Japan; Canada (already planning a very advanced survey satellite); Sweden, with its high technology and interest in peace. They could go it alone if they wished, but moral and financial support should be forthcoming from many non-aligned nations. Even the fanatically neutral Swiss might be induced to join such a project.

We would enter what has been aptly called an 'Age of Transparency'. Like most people, many nations would not like to live in glass houses. They may not realise the extent to which they are already doing this. Quite apart from the US, USSR – and Chinese – satellite operators with their rather restricted clientele, SPOT is up there right now, churning out beautiful images of all terrestrial activities for anyone who will pay a dollar a square kilometre for them. As the Age of Transparency dawns, political *and* military wisdom will lie in co-operating with the inevitable.

I would like to end with some words I was privileged to deliver in October 1984, at the space symposium arranged by the Pontifical Academy of Science. The meeting brought together experts on science, communications and weaponry. A few hundred metres from Michelangelo's *Creation of Adam*, we were discussing how his descendants might save – or destroy – themselves:

> During the last decade, something new has come into the world. Two-dimensional communications networks are replacing vertical chains of command, in which orders moved downwards and only acknowledgements went upwards. We are witnessing the rise of the Global Family – or Tribe, if you like. Its electronically linked members will be scattered across the face of the planet, and its loyalties and interests will transcend all the ancient frontiers. Those frontiers which are so conspicuously absent in the photographs from space: those frontiers which to call 'sacred' in the age of thermonuclear weapons is no longer patriotism – but blasphemy.
>
> It has been wisely said that the State has now become too big for men – but too small for Mankind. Is the present proliferation of nations – over 150 at the moment – a planetary cancer, or an evolution towards a healthier world, in which political structures will be built on a more human scale?
>
> And to continue the analogy from evolution, let us remember something that happened on this planet once before. There was a time when it was dominated by monsters who tried to protect themselves by ever more cumbersome armour, until they were walking fortresses. They never noticed, as they blundered through forest

and swamp, the little creatures that skipped out of their way: the first mammals – our ancestors.

Intelligence, not armour, was to inherit the Earth. May it do so once again.*

The above chapter was written several months before Prime Minister Gandhi's tragic assassination, so I think it now appropriate to give the whole text of the speech of thanks he gave at the conclusion of my address, despite my embarrassment at his excessively complimentary remarks.

The following words – which were entirely impromptu – have been transcribed directly from the video tape of the proceedings. Their wit, grace and conciseness gives some indication of what India – and the world – has lost through the speaker's untimely death.

'Professor Clarke, Yashpaljee, Shri B. K. Nehru, Ladies and Gentlemen – Professor Clarke has given us a tremendously enlightening talk. His intellectual sweep, his brilliance, but perhaps even more the deep humanity that he has shown, will remain with us for a long time. He is a seer of modern science.

'Forty years ago he has said, and he reminded us today, that the only defence against the weapons of the future is to prevent them being used. Perhaps we could add to that, we should prevent them being built.

'Today there is still no change in this very basic prescription. "Star Wars" or SDI – which we have ourselves been opposing, because we have felt that it is not feasible, it is not practical, and that it could not be built. Today, Professor Clarke has given us many more reasons why it is not a peace weapon or peace shield, but perhaps a new "Project Damocles" as he has called it. India and the Six Nation Initiative have worked with the Non-Aligned Movement and many other nations against increases in the arms race, against this delusion of a shield and this delusion of the defensive nature of the SDI. As Professor Clarke has said, lasers which can destroy very rapidly-moving missiles in fractions of a second can be used very effectively against stationary or very slow-moving targets. In fact the SDI could well turn into a new, very high-technology weapon.

'He has also added to our fears of a Nuclear Winter with that of the Plutonium fallout. It's time that we all heed his warning. The vulnerability of the hardware, *and* the software, of "Star Wars" has been brought home to us. I just hope people in other World Capitals also are listening.

'Lastly, let me assure him that if there *are* any restrictions on our allowing

*(I gave a later version of this address, 'Star Peace', at the Lindbergh Award ceremony in Paris, on the sixtieth anniversary of the *Spirit of St Louis*'s historic flight, 20 May 1987.)

Playboy into this country, it is not because of anything that he might have written in that magazine! Thank you very much, Professor Clarke . . .'

The next morning, hearing that I wished to see the Taj Mahal but could not face the long and dusty round trip in the short time I had left, Sri Gandhi very kindly detailed two senior Air India pilots to fly me to Agra in his personal aeroplane. The long walk through the magnificent gardens was tiring but exhilarating; the Taj is one of those wonders, like the Grand Canyon, which fully lives up to its advance billing.

As it turned out, owing to medical problems my slow amble through the Taj gardens was the last walk of any distance I ever expect to make. I can imagine no better finale to my career as a pedestrian, and I shall always be grateful to Rajiv Gandhi for his kind gesture, when he had the cares of a continent upon his shoulders.

5

LET THERE BE LIGHT!

41

CABLE COMEBACK

After adventuring in space, it may seem something of an anticlimax to return to the depths of the ocean, and the now well-established – if indeed not quaintly old-fashioned – technology of submarine cables. However, far from being made instantly obsolete, the cables showed an amazing capacity for growth. And, to the astonishment of practically everyone, only twenty years after the launch of Early Bird they began to challenge comsats in their own territory.

The immediate success of TAT-1, the first reliable, high-quality transatlantic telephone service, started a new explosion of cable-laying across the oceans of the world. Although the transistor was already nine years old in 1956, it was not until 1970 that AT&T's understandably cautious engineers went 'solid state' with TAT-5 (see table on p. 249).

An important *mechanical* development also entered the picture. In 1957, the British Post Office carried out pioneering experiments with a submarine cable in which the armouring which had been a standard feature for more than a hundred years was abandoned, and all the strength was provided by a steel wire at the *centre* of the cable. The only external protection was a tube of tough plastic, which is all that was needed in the calm of the ocean depths.

This new, lightweight cable put much less strain on the laying machinery, and was thus far easier to handle and pay out than the armoured variety it replaced. Most important of all, it had no tendency to twist and kink; because of the spiral armouring, the older cables often rotated hundreds of times on their way to the sea-bed, with the unfortunate results mentioned in Chapter 8. Plastic-covered cable, on the other hand, is wholly free from torsion and uncoils almost as easily as a length of string. With such a cable, there is no danger of disastrous kinks developing if bad weather holds up laying. The cable need no longer be paid out in one continuous operation, so the ship can be stopped in deep water to splice and lower the bulky, rigid repeaters which – despite the allure of their great capacity – could not be used in the deep-ocean segment of TAT-1. And so a purely *mechanical* development – ridiculed by the brilliant Professor Thomson a century earlier – had far-reaching communications consequences.

Mention must also be made of a very ingenious electronic device which more than doubled the capacity of TAT-1 soon after it went into service, and has since been applied to all cables. This is 'Time-Assignment Speech Interpolation' – shortened, needless to say, to TASI.

TASI depends upon the fact that a great deal (surprisingly, over 60 per cent) of ordinary conversation actually consists of silences. A sufficiently swift-acting device could listen out for these pauses, and take advantage of them by instantly switching over to another conversation.

An analogy from ordinary life may be helpful here. A telephone cable is rather like a multi-laned highway, the separate syllables of speech being dotted along it like individual automobiles. Seen from the air, at least 50 per cent of even the most crowded highway is empty space; its capacity could be doubled or tripled if vehicles could instantly 'lane-hop' to plug any gaps as soon as they appeared. Unfortunately the laws of inertia, not to mention a few other difficulties, rule out such a happy solution to the traffic problem. But electric impulses, which have no inertia, and, equally important, all travel at exactly the same speed, can perform this useful trick.

As a result, the first thirty-six-channel TAT-1 had its capacity increased almost at once to about a hundred channels. Later, ninety-six-channel cables were able to carry no less than 235 simultaneous conversations, which jumped from circuit to circuit in fractions of a second. The mind boggles at all this multiple channel-hopping; presumably if, by bad luck, all 235 subscribers spoke at *precisely* the same moment, TASI would blow its fuses. However, the laws of probability indicate that such a catastrophe would not happen even once in a universe as short-lived as ours.

By the end of the first year's operation of TAT-1 (1957), telephone traffic between the United States and England had doubled. A second cable, TAT-2, of identical design, went into service in 1959; however, it followed a different route, linking not Newfoundland and Scotland but Newfoundland and France.

A cable from Scotland to Canada, CANTAT-1, started operating in 1961 and was based on the new, non-twisting cable. It was now possible to have eighty circuits in a single cable, instead of only thirty-six in *two* cables. This immediately halved both the cost of laying, and the risk of damage.

TAT-3, in 1963, was the first cable direct from England to the United States: despite the greater distance involved, it was able to carry 138 circuits. TAT-4 (1965) provided a similar service between France and the United States.

In 1970 the all-transistor TAT-5 represented a real quantum jump in performance – 845 channels compared with the original thirty-six of TAT-1, only fourteen years earlier. It used a new, southern route, from Spain to the United States; and four years later, it in turn was eclipsed by CANTAT-2 – an amazing (for those days) 1840 channels!

The Atlantic was not, of course, the only ocean where the cable-ships were plying – notably AT&T's *Long Lines*, the queen of this highly specialised fleet. A few months after the opening of TAT-1, a project of almost comparable magnitude was completed on the other side of the United States, when the Washington–Alaska cable went into operation. This 2000-kilometre link from Seattle to Skagway could have been established entirely overland, but the reliability of the submerged repeaters was considered so good that the sea route was preferred. The circuits had to pass through territory where underwater conditions were frequently much less unpleasant – and more equable – than those on land.

Principal Atlantic and Pacific Telephone Cables

NAME	YEAR	TERMINALS	CIRCUITS
TAT-1	1956	Scotland–Canada	36
TAT-2	1959	France–Canada	48
CANTAT-1	1961	Scotland–Canada	80
COMPAC	1963	Canada–Australia	80
TAT-3	1963	England–US	138
TRANSPAC	1964	Hawaii–Japan	138
TAT-4	1965	France–US	128
SEACOM	1965	Australia–Singapore	160
TAT-5	1970	Spain–US	845
CANTAT-2	1974	England–Canada	1840
TAT-6	1976	France–US	4000
TAT-7	1983	UK–US	4200

No sooner had the Alaska service been opened than work started on a project even more ambitious than the original Atlantic cable – the 3800-kilometre 'Pacific Voiceway' between California and Hawaii. Once again, *Monarch* played the leading role in the operation, but this time she was supported by another British cable-ship, Submarine Cables Limited's *Ocean Layer*. Between them they laid 114 submerged repeaters in waters up to five kilometres deep, and the survey carried out to find the best route for the twin cables helped to fill in some of the blanks in the world's greatest ocean. An uncharted peak towering three kilometres above the sea-bed was discovered at one stage of the survey, and the cables were laid through the picturesquely named 'Moonless Mountains', a range that runs from north to south for 1500 kilometres between California and Hawaii. When this second ocean cable was opened on 8 October 1957, it became possible to speak by cable from one side of the earth to the other.

Four days earlier, Sputnik 1 had started the 'space race'. But already, another race was quietly under way in laboratories all over the world. Its objective, to achieve 'light amplification by stimulated emission of radiation', seemed unlikely to inspire the same headlines as Russian satellites; yet within the next decade the acronym LASER would be instantly recognised by all educated persons.

In 1960 the first laser, developed by Theodore Maiman in the Hughes Research Laboratories, began to generate a 'light that never was on land or sea'. Although a remarkable scientific achievement, for several years any important practical applications seemed remote; the laser was often referred to as 'a solution looking for a problem'.

No longer. By the mid-seventies the laser had become mature enough to challenge the whole basis of telecommunications. After almost two centuries, the apparently impregnable monopoly of copper and electricity was about to end.

42

TALKING WITH LIGHT

Fifty-five years later, I cannot remember what impulse prompted me to send speech along a beam of light; certainly I had no idea that Alexander Graham Bell had performed this feat long before I was born. The previous high-point of my experimenting had been running telephone circuits round our Somerset farm, using its galvanised-iron wire fences as conductors.

The most sophisticated part of my new hardware was the detector – a photoelectric cell from a movie projector (yes, sound had reached our village, about ten years earlier . . .). It was, of course, a vacuum tube, and had been presented to me by my uncle George Grimstone, the engineer of the local institution for the mentally unbalanced, whose inmates were entertained (or pacified) by suitable movies every Saturday night. I draw no conclusions from the curious coincidence that there were *two* such establishments within four kilometres of our home; but as Mother frequently pointed out, sooner or later all our neighbours went crazy.

I have fond memories of George, a burly, good-natured man who undoubtedly did much to encourage my interest in technology. The PE cell he gave me had an easily curable defect; the anode cap on the top of the envelope had been knocked off. I simply packed it with tinfoil to make a connection, and glued it on again. Thereafter the cell worked fine – or not at all, until I gave it a smart tap. You can't make repairs like that with microchips. (I've just inadvertently typed 'microchops'; we all know restaurants where these are served.)

Uncle George drew a circuit diagram of a single-stage amplifier, and I assembled the components – PE cell, triode valve, sundry resistors and capacitors – inside a cigar-box, with a little window closed by a convex lens to focus the incoming beam. After testing that the device made satisfactory clicking noises in a pair of earphones when a light shone into it, I tackled the more difficult problem of the transmitter.

My first concept was elegant but impracticable; it would have used pure sun-power – *if* it had worked. The principle was that of the heliograph; it was obvious that a mirror with so little mass that it could be set vibrating by sound waves would modulate a beam of reflected sunlight. (This principle is now used in laser eavesdropping systems.) However, the manufacture of so delicate a piece of optics was quite beyond my skills, and I quickly adopted an alternative approach.

This involved two transparent sheets in close contact, engraved with identical sets of parallel black lines, separated by clear spaces of the same width. Normally, opaque and clear areas would coincide, so no light could be transmitted. However, the slightest movement – for example, that produced by the vibrations of the human voice – would open the optical gate; the louder the sound, the brighter the light . . .

Once again, my mechanical skills weren't up to the job; so I quickly abandoned elegance and went for a brute-force approach. (Computer programmers will recognise the syndrome.) My solution was, in fact, so crude that I'm almost embarrassed to describe it.

The ingredients could hardly be more low-tech; one bicycle lamp (electric);* one carbon microphone; one six-volt car battery; one rheostat. I put them in series – and the monstrosity worked! When I spoke into the microphone, the light fluctuated in accordance with my voice. There were some minor problems: I had to pack extra carbon granules into the mike to pass sufficient amperage for the lamp bulb, and there were ominous frying noises from the interior when power was switched ·on. But the device transmitted perfectly intelligible speech from one room to another through a glass window in the Taunton Technical Institute, where the young gentlemen of Huish's Grammar School emulated the late Dr Frankenstein several times a week under the watchful eye of physics master Mr W. G. Pleass. (That was in 1935; and I'm happy to say that 'Bobby' Pleass is still interested in science.)

When I was setting the equipment up, I used a metronome as a source of sound – and I can still recall the almost hypnotic 'flash – flash – flash' of the abused bike lamp as the current pulsed through it. A decade later, on RAF radar stations, I would be responsible for pumping out similarly shaped waves at a much lower carrier frequency – but with a million times the power.

I suppose the maximum distance I sent messages was ten metres, but that was limited by room-space; I am sure that much greater ranges could have been achieved even with this simple equipment, especially at night. In any event, I was only interested in demonstrating the principle of the 'photophone' (as Bell had christened it), and abandoned all further experiments once I had succeeded.

However, the idea continued to fascinate me, and I returned to it a dozen years later when I delivered a paper to the British Interplanetary Society, 'Electronics and Space Flight'.† While discussing the problem of interplanet-

---

*Would you believe I can still remember the acrid smell of acetylene and calcium carbide?

†*Journal of the British Interplanetary Society*, vol. 7, no. 2, March 1948. Reprinted in *Ascent to Orbit: A Scientific Autobiography* (John Wiley, 1984).

ary communication I concluded that, although radio was perfectly adequate for most purposes, 'for very long-distance circuits optical waves may be more suitable, and may require much lower powers, than radio'.

By 'very long distances' I was thinking of *millions* of kilometres, not the mere hundreds of thousands involved in talking to the Moon. So I was slightly embarrassed when electronics engineer George O. Smith casually shot me down, in the 1952 Space Flight Symposium, at the New York Hayden Planetarium.

After calculating that it would require about the power level of a three-cell flashlight to talk *by radio* between Earth and Moon, George added: 'At this point I would like to lay a ghost. Time and again someone has suggested the use of blinker lamps or heliograph for interplanetary communications. I would like to see how far anyone can get with a three-cell flashlight, winking the thing at the Earth from the crater Plato.'* Now, George could not be accused of lacking imagination; as I remarked in Chapter 25, his *Venus Equilateral* stories, featuring a relay station equidistant from Earth and Venus, may well have contributed to my own ideas on geostationary satellites.

I am glad to say that George lived to see the feat which he said was impossible performed with much less than the power of a *one*-cell flashlight. He failed to anticipate the laser, which has revolutionised optical communications, and much else. Indeed, who could?

Well, one man who could – and did – happened to be our mutual friend John Pierce. In a less reputable phase of his career, long before he got involved with Echo and Telstar, John wrote occasional pieces for *Astounding Stories*, under the pseudonym 'J. J. Coupling'. When scanning the May 1945 issue of that estimable journal, in the course of writing my own 'Science Fictional Autobiography' *Astounding Days*, I was astonished – sorry, astounded – to come across an article that John had written on 'heat rays'. He pointed out that it was impossible to make a *really* tightly focused beam of thermal radiation, because 'it was disorganised energy – that is, energy of many wavelengths'. He then went on to make this truly remarkable prediction: 'If heat rays are to be effective, they must presumably be single-wavelength beams.' Decades before laser weapons became practicable, John Pierce realised that they must depend on coherent (i.e. laser) radiation. Needless to say, when I pointed it out to him decades later, he had completely forgotten this piece of technological forecasting.

So George Smith – whose engineering background was much sounder than mine – was wrong for the right reasons, and I was right for the wrong ones. Neither of us conceived of the breakthrough in light amplification which

*'Radio Communications across Space', (*Journal of the British Interplanetary Society*, vol. 12, no. 1, January 1953).

would make optical communications theoretically possible over not merely interplanetary, but *interstellar* distances.

And not even John Pierce, I suspect, imagined the still more amazing advance which brought this technology right down to earth, and revolutionised terrestrial communications. If anyone had ever told me that it would one day be possible to shine light through a piece of glass a hundred – even a thousand! – kilometres thick, I should have laughed at them. To borrow a phrase which one unfortunate Astronomer Royal was never able to live down, when reporters asked him for his views of space exploration, I might even have said that they were talking Utter Bilge.

That light waves, because their frequency was hundreds of thousands of times greater than even the shortest radio waves, could in theory carry a correspondingly greater amount of information had been obvious for years. Any practical application of this, however, seemed very short-range, and severely limited by weather. The most sophisticated open-air *optical* communication system could be immobilised by a heavy rainstorm. To be of any use, the light waves would have to be protected from the environment.

One suggestion was the use of hollow pipes with internal mirror-surfaces – 'optical waveguides' – which would give ranges of a few hundred metres and, equally important, carry the light-beams round corners. However, such systems presented no advantage over conventional modes of transmission, and certainly could not challenge submarine cables.

There was, however, another well-known way of confining and directing light, by shining it into plastic rods or hair-thin fibres of glass. (I once possessed a beautiful 'light fountain' ornament based on this principle: alas, the fibres were brittle and kept ending up in the carpet. So I had to get rid of it.)

Physicians were also very familiar with devices (endoscopes) based on this principle; they could be made flexible enough to explore the body and reveal details which had never before been seen by the naked eye – much less filmed. The awe-inspiring movies of human embryos in the womb were made possible by such techniques. For these applications, it did not matter if most of the light was lost in transmission; there was still plenty available, when distances of only a few metres were involved. Beyond that, fade-out was swift and total.

How total can be suggested by looking again at the super-astronomical number given in Chapter 18 for the theoretical energy loss along the 3000 kilometres of the transatlantic telephone cable; it was a number with more than 300 zeros. But a beam of light attempting to travel through the glass generally available in the 1960s would have experienced that much attenuation *after a single kilometre*.

In 1966 two scientists (K. C. Kao and G. A. Hockham) at the UK's

Standard Telecommunications Laboratories suggested that enormous, and previously unimagined, improvements in 'transparency' could be achieved with carefully purified glass. Within a few years, the target they mentioned (a loss of 20 dB per kilometre) had not only been achieved – but far surpassed. The combination of the laser and the barely visible threads of fibre that could carry its light for incredible distances gave birth to a new industry and a new science. Electronics was about to be matched by 'optronics', in some ways its mirror image. Almost every task that the electron could perform could also be done by the photon, often more cheaply and efficiently.

In 1975, AT&T made the first public demonstration of the new technology in Atlanta, Georgia, laying a fibre-optics cable which could carry up to 50,000 telephone calls. That was the starting shot in the race to rewire (*sic*) the United States – and the world. By 1983, AT&T had linked Washington and New York with a system carrying not only thousands of voice circuits but also video-conferencing – a facility which, it was believed, only fibre optics could provide economically. (The Bell System was still smarting over the failure of its much-heralded but low-quality 'Picturephone' a generation earlier, and was determined not to make the same mistake again.)

Pressure from competitors – especially GTE and MCI in the United States, and of course the major European and Japanese corporations – forced rapid advances in the technology. The 1975 Atlanta demonstration had employed repeaters up to eleven kilometres apart, but in 1983 the Bell System showed that it could now increase that distance to more than a hundred kilometres – while carrying not a 'mere' 50,000 telephone calls, but *half a million*. Such a dazzling achievement was utterly beyond anything possible with copper circuits.

The time was clearly ripe for fibre to move undersea, with the Atlantic as the first challenge. TAT-7, carrying 4200 circuits, would be the last cable based on the old electronic technology of copper and transistors. The glass fibres of TAT-8, which began operating in 1988, would carry 40,000 conversations on pulses of light between the United States and Europe, giving it just 1000 times the capacity of that ancient artefact, TAT-1. And barely two years later its successor, TAT-9, would provide double that capacity between Canada, the US, France and the United Kingdom.

Perhaps the most dramatic – maybe the only! – way of appreciating the information-carrying power of such a cable is to realise that it could transmit the contents of the entire *Encyclopaedia Britannica* across the Atlantic in a single second. For once, the cliché 'mind-boggling' is fully justified; one cannot help wondering what the old-time telegraph operators would have thought of this feat, as they struggled to send their handfuls of words per minute.

As fibre-based telephone cables started to snake beneath all oceans of the world, the two-decades-long near-monopoly of the communications satellites was threatened. TAT-8 was predicted to cost INTELSAT half a billion dollars in lost business, and COMSAT fought a bitter delaying (pun quite unintentional) action against it. The winner in this battle of megacorporations was, of course, the customer, and eventually a truce was declared on the sound principle of 'If you can't lick them, join them'. When TAT-9 was planned, COMSAT was one of the partners in the enterprise, and President Irv Goldstein declared gracefully that 'communications satellites are more compatible with fibre optics than they ever were with copper . . .'

There are, in fact, times when both kinds of cables need satellites – desperately. Although the deep ocean is a relatively benign and stable environment, this is not always the case. In 1929 an earthquake off the Grand Banks sent an avalanche of mud racing out into the Atlantic at fifty kilometres an hour, snapping the cables one after the other. Such events are rare and unpredictable; much more frequent are breaks caused in shallow water by trawlers and ships' anchors. When such interruptions occur, traffic is immediately switched to satellite, and the cable companies' misfortunes have long been a major source of revenue to COMSAT – whose first president once confided to me, 'Of course, you know who those trawlers *really* belong to . . .'*

Even if, as seems certain to be the case, cables will dominate the heavy-traffic routes (e.g. New York–London, Los Angeles–Hawaii, Tokyo–Hong Kong) there is not the slightest danger that satellites will be forced into a minor ecological niche. They alone can provide economical coverage of huge regions – up to 30 per cent of planet Earth from a single satellite – which will never be 'wired' like the densely populated areas of the world.

Only VSATs (Very Small Aperture Terminals), with dishes no more than a metre in diameter, will make it possible for business men, news-gatherers, conference organisers, scientific expeditions, relief agencies – the list is endless – to start operating, anywhere on Earth, at a moment's notice.

It is in the enormous and still almost untapped field of *mobile* communications, however, that comsats have perhaps their greatest potential. When the massive thirty-metre-diameter, million-dollar antennas of the 1970s were being built, it would have seemed inconceivable to most people that the time would come when trucks, automobiles and even back-packers and Arctic sledgers would carry satellite receivers. INMARSAT, though its original concern was with the vitally important field of maritime commerce, pioneered this field with the development of transportable, low-cost terminals for use on land as well as on sea: millions saw these in operation during the Gulf War.

*In defiance of statistics, five cable breaks occurred simultaneously in 1990. I immediately faxed INTELSAT Director-General Dean Burch: 'Once is an accident – twice a coincidence – three times a conspiracy. But *five* times??'

There is enough business here to fill the geostationary orbit several times over, leaving the cables to handle the fixed, high-density routes for which they are ideally suited. Some years ago I suggested that INMARSAT adopt as its slogan: 'Who's Afraid of Fibre Optics?' I'm happy to see that, after the initial shock, COMSAT and INTELSAT seem to be adopting the same point of view.*

A more benign – and sophisticated – use of fibre optics with mobile terminals is to control the ROVs (Remotely Operated Vehicles) now employed extensively in underwater exploration (see Robert Ballard's filming of the *Titanic*) and offshore oil operations. Appropriately, ROVs also play an important role in laying submarine cables – often burying them in the sea-bed out of harm's way.

*Surprisingly, fibre optics can be used, very effectively indeed, with a rather restricted class of mobile 'customers' – enemy tanks and helicopters. The FOG-M (Fibre-Optic Guided Missile) carries a spool from which it spins out fifteen kilometres of gossamer-like thread. Through this (unjammable) link, the controller can observe his target and home on to it with deadly accuracy. For further information, consult the Pentagon.

43

As Far As Eye Can See

As the century which saw the birth of both electronics and optronics draws to a close, it would seem that virtually everything we would wish to do in the field of telecommunications is now *technically* possible. The only limitations are financial, legal and political.

But have we indeed reached the limits of communications technology? Time and again in the past men – even able men – have proclaimed that there is nothing more to invent, and they have always been proved wrong.

Electricity has been our most valuable and versatile tool for only about 1 per cent of human history – yet see what it has done in that brief time! Now we are uniting electron and photon to develop the new science of optronics, which will create devices whose names will be as familiar to our children as TV, videotape, CD, comsat, laser, floppy disc are today – and as meaningless to us as these would have been to our great-grandparents.

Since radio waves would have been so inconceivable even a few lifetimes ago, one cannot help wondering what other useful surprises Nature has up her sleeve. The electromagnetic spectrum has been thoroughly explored – contrary to Edgar Rice Burroughs' hero John Carter, who discovered two new 'colours' on Mars. But are there any other radiations, fields, or whatever, still to be found, perhaps with properties which might make them even more valuable than radio waves?

It must be sixty years since I encountered a story in *Boy's Own Paper* – almost the only source of science fiction in my youth – about a 'telescope' which allowed one to see *through the solid Earth*, and observe events on the other side. (How the CIA would have loved that; however, reconnaissance satellites are a very good substitute.) I doubt if the author went into technical details about his planet-piercing radiation; he probably talked glibly about X-rays – after all, *they* go through solid matter, don't they? – and left it at that.

Amazingly enough, there are indeed rays – or rather particles, which in modern physics comes to the same thing – which can travel right through the Earth as if it wasn't there. The ghostly neutrino interacts so rarely with what we are pleased to call solid matter that it could pass through a sheet of lead millions of millions of miles thick with no inconvenience.

Our nuclear reactors generate neutrinos in enormous quantities. If a neutrino source could be modulated to carry a signal, that signal could be beamed straight through the Earth, travelling from pole to pole in a seventh of a second. There would be none of the annoying time delays unavoidable with satellites in the 36,000-kilometre-high stationary orbit . . .

Unfortunately, there are some practical difficulties. The only way to modulate a neutrino source is to switch a nuclear reactor on and off. Nuclear reactors do not appreciate such treatment (*vide* Chernobyl) and even if one was specially designed for this purpose, the rate of data transmission would be about the same as the first Atlantic cable – a few words an hour.

And that is the least of the problems. To receive a message, you have to collect *something* – and because matter is so transparent to them, neutrinos are almost impossible to detect. If you want to catch a neutrino, you must fill a tank with several hundred of tons of liquid, in the hope that one or two particles a day of the quadrillions passing through may be unlucky enough to make a direct hit on a nucleus, and produce a signal indicating their demise.

At the risk of having Clarke's First Law ('When a distinguished but elderly scientist says that something is impossible, he is very probably wrong') thrown at me once again, I will venture a daring prediction: no one will ever put a wrist-watch neutrinophone on the market.

If you think that neutrino communications is a hopeless prospect, here is an even more unlikely one. According to Einstein's General Theory, the universe is permeated by 'gravitational waves' which travel at the speed of light. Heroic attempts have been made during the last quarter of a century to detect them, so far without success, but few scientists doubt their existence. The problem is that they are incredibly feeble, but ever more sensitive instruments are now searching for them, and it seems unlikely that they will elude us for very much longer.

The difficulty of detecting gravitational waves, however, is nothing compared with the problem of generating them. To get a power equivalent to that of a medium-sized radio station, you need to take a couple of neutron stars (only a few kilometres across, but weighing several thousand million tons per *spoonful*) and shake well.

Alternatively, trigger a supernova explosion, collapsing a star to a neutron core that vibrates briskly for a few seconds. That will signal to the universe a message saying, if not 'I'm here', then at least 'I *was* here.'

Even if neutrino beams and gravitational waves could be used for telecommunications, they would still be limited by the speed of light. As we move out into the solar system, what would be *really* useful would be something that moves a lot faster than a miserable 300,000 kilometres a second. Because of this speed limit, a real-time conversation with anyone beyond the Moon is impossible. You can easily fax your Mars office – but not telephone it.

Contrary to popular opinion, there are many things which move faster than light; it depends on what you mean by 'things'. Let me give an example familiar to most air travellers. Many airports have a line of strobe lights down the centre of the runway in use, which can be triggered one after the other to give a visual aid to a pilot making a night landing. The impression from the air is as if a bolt of lightning is hurtling along the runway at an enormous speed. Obviously, the interval between flashes can be adjusted to any value desired; the shorter it is, the quicker the – shall we call it a visual phantom? – will appear to move along the runway. It would be an easy trick to make it move faster than light; in fact, if the flashes were simultaneous, its speed would be infinite.

A little thought will show, however, that nothing is *really* moving; no message – no *information* – is being transmitted. There are many similar examples in physics, and even in everyday life. One of the most dramatic may be seen at coast defence works during a storm. When a line of waves is moving towards a breakwater, the explosion of spray can race along the wall at an enormous speed; the smaller the angle of approach, the greater its velocity. When the approaching wave-front is *exactly* parallel to the breakwater, spray erupts along its whole length simultaneously – i.e., the apparent speed is infinite! But nothing material is moving at more than a few score miles an hour.

Is there no way, therefore, in which we can ever break the light barrier? Probably not; but there are a few far-out possibilities.

Some physicists have pointed out that although Einstein's equations state that no object can travel at exactly the speed of light (because its mass would then be infinite) they do not rule out the existence of particles which *can never travel more slowly than light*. It is true that such particles (christened 'tachyons', meaning 'swift ones') would have some very odd properties; but who would have believed neutrinos a few decades ago?

In any event, no one has been able to prove that tachyons are impossible – and we can thus conjure them into existence by applying Feynman's Totalitarian Principle, useful in so many branches of physics and astronomy: 'Anything that is not forbidden is compulsory.' Whether we will be able to detect them – still less use them – is another matter. Meanwhile they have been a godsend to science-fiction writers.

And so – to those who understand it, which does not include this writer – has been the notorious Einstein–Podolsky–Rosen Paradox. According to this, under certain conditions one particle can have an *instantaneous* influence on another, even if the two are light-years apart! (I am aware that 'instantaneous' is a dirty word in Relativity Theory, but cannot think of a better one.) Although the E–R–P Paradox appears to have been confirmed in exquisitely sophisticated laboratory tests, debate continues as to what it really means –

and the majority opinion is that, even in theory, it will not permit supra-light-velocity transmission of signals. Too bad.

Some unorthodox scientists have invoked E–P–R and similar weird quantum effects to explain a type of communication which probably does not exist – telepathy, or direct contact between two human minds without any physical connexion. There are so many apparently well-authenticated examples of this phenomenon that I hesitate to dismiss it completely; in my *World of Strange Powers* book and TV series I gave it a rating of +2 – 'Barely possible: worth investigating'.

However, even if *natural* telepathy does not occur, I have no doubt that future science will be able to provide an artificial variety. As we understand more and more of the functioning of the brain and the central nervous system, we may learn to – literally – read thoughts. To a limited extent this is done already, with the bionic limbs now available to amputees. A person wearing such a prosthesis simply *wills* a movement – and the electronics does the rest. I am not sure if I would altogether welcome a plug-in microchip to replace the telephone, but it's an interesting possibility – especially to the various military labs which are working on it at this very moment. ('See – no hands!')

But enough of these humdrum, down-to-earth concepts. Let us end with the most speculative of all. In *Profiles of the Future: An Enquiry into the Limits of the Possible* (1962) I devoted a chapter to 'teleportation' – the long-distance transmission of material objects, including persons. Although seemingly fantastic, and certainly unlikely, this does not appear to be completely forbidden by the laws of physics. The required technology, however, is as far beyond us today as TV would have been beyond Leonardo, the most brilliant mind of the Renaissance.

Scanning and then reconstructing a human being – or even an inanimate solid object – would be orders of magnitude more difficult than creating a system that merely carried images. The amount of information involved would be so enormous that its transmission might take astronomical periods of time. In *Profiles of the Future* I calculated that a circuit with the same capacity (bandwidth) as one of today's TV channels would take about twenty million *million* years to transmit a human being's physical pattern, and concluded very reasonably, 'It would be quicker to walk.' Even fibre optics would only knock off one of those millions, so I fear it will be a long time before anyone says the equivalent of 'Beam me up, Scotty'.

Perhaps the feat could be accomplished, under certain circumstances, not by a 'scanning' technique but by taking a short cut through the 'wormholes in space' postulated by some physicists. Unfortunately, only very small worms could make it through these holes: they appear to be not merely submicroscopic, but subnucleonic in size. Stephen Hawking summed it up very well when he said, in a TV discussion with Carl Sagan and myself* that a traveller would end up looking like spaghetti or 'a passenger in some airlines my lawyer won't let me mention'.

*'God, the Universe, and Everything Else'.

Epilogue

Fin de siècle – or Dawn of a New Millennium?

The answer, of course, is both. As we enter the final decade of the most brilliant yet barbarous century that mankind has ever known, we should feel a kinship with the Roman god Janus, who looked forward and backwards simultaneously. But Janus was also the god of new beginnings (hence 'January'): if we can learn from the past, there is hope for the future.

That future, as H. G. Wells warned us long ago, will be a race between education and catastrophe. Television is the most potent educational medium ever devised, and programmes deliberately intended to instruct are only the tip of an enormous iceberg. Every time the camera looks at a political demonstration, a parliamentary debate, a UN relief operation – even a sporting event – it serves the cause of education, in the widest sense of that word.

This was proved most convincingly in the spring of 1991, when for the first time in history the world saw what war – and, even more important – its aftermath – was really like. This had not happened in Vietnam, or even in the Falklands conflict, simply because the images were already history when they reached the viewer. There is an immense psychological gulf between Real Time and Replay.

During the Gulf War, comsats became the conscience of the world – a role already rehearsed in such global telecasts as the concerts in aid of Bangladesh and Ethiopia. There is a danger, of course, that over-exposure to disaster and tragedy will induce 'compassion fatigue', but the alternative – the indifference of ignorance – is surely worse.

Another danger, and perhaps a more serious one, is that all these wonderful new services will overload our capacity to absorb them. For there is still more – much more – to come. Already there have been spectacular demonstrations of High-Definition TV (HDTV), and now there is the equally exciting promise of CD (digital) quality sound to cheap radio receivers – both via direct-broadcast satellites. DB 'radiosats' may make the old short-wave services instantly obsolete, and give rise to new global networks of major importance.

Yet, bombarded with megabytes, we may simply switch off, or not bother to use these wonderful new toys when their initial novelty has been exhausted.

Satellite empires have already risen and fallen, and the money lost in the early Atlantic cables has been far eclipsed by the fortunes that have evaporated in mergers and launch-pad explosions.

But these, I am sure, are temporary setbacks. The sky will continue to fill with new stars whose names would puzzle the old-time astronomers – Anik, Palapa, Statsionar, Arabsat, Asiasat . . . Let us use them well – always remembering that information is not knowledge, and knowledge is not wisdom.

This book opened with Toynbee's 'Unification of the World'; let me close by recalling once again one of the most powerful myths of the Old Testament, already referred to in the chapter 'I Remember Babylon'.

It may be more than a myth; a recent article in *Scientific American** traces the 'homeland' of half today's languages to an area only 500 kilometres north of Babylon! Be that as it may, there is an eerie symbolism in the fact that today's comsat makers are now busily *unbuilding* the Tower of Babel – 36,000 kilometres above the Equator.

To quote Genesis 11 again, this time from the King James Version: 'And the Lord said: Behold they are one people, and they have all one language, and this is only the beginning of what they will do, and nothing that they propose to do now will be impossible for them.'

On that first occasion, those words were a warning of disaster. Today, they should be a message of hope – a description of the future that lies within our grasp.

*'The Early History of Indo-European Languages', by Thomas V. Gamkrelidze and V. V. Ivanov, March 1990.

REFERENCES AND ACKNOWLEDGEMENTS

The bibliography of modern telecommunications is now so enormous – and expanding so rapidly – that most references are out of date before they have left the printing press (or even the modem). The only way to keep in sight of the frontier is to subscribe to the many trade and professional newsletters, and popular science journals like *New Scientist, Scientific American, Discover*.

The 1958 and 1974 editions of *Voice across the Sea* made acknowledgement to many organisations and individuals who assisted me; I would like to repeat my thanks here.

Books which have proved particularly valuable in the preparation of that work's successor are:

From Semaphore to Satellite, Anthony R. Michaelis (ITU, Geneva, 1965)

Never Beyond Reach, Brendan Gallagher (INMARSAT, 1989)

The Rewiring of America, C. David Chaffee (Academic Press, 1988)

Three Degrees Above Zero, Jeremy Bernstein (Charles Scribner's Sons, 1984)

Oliver Heaviside: Sage in Solitude, Paul J. Nahin (IEEE Press, 1988)

The 1991 World Satellite Annual and *World Satellite Update* (Monthly), Mark Long (PO Box 159, Winter Beach, Fla. 32971)

Space Commerce, John L. McLucas (Harvard, 1991)

Satellite Week, Warren Publishing, Inc.

Appendix 1

THE SPACE-STATION: ITS RADIO APPLICATIONS

The following is the text of the Memorandum prepared for the Council of the British Interplanetary Society by Arthur C. Clarke in May 1945. The original of this document is now in the archives of the Smithsonian Institution in Washington.

1.   The space-station was originally conceived as a refuelling depot for ships leaving the Earth. As such it may fill an important though transient role in the conquest of space, during the period when chemical fuels are employed. Other uses, some of them rather fantastic, have been suggested for the space station, notably by Hermann Noordung.[1] However, there is at least one purpose for which the station is ideally suited and indeed has no practical alternative. This is the provision of world-wide ultra-high-frequency radio services, including television.

2.   In the following discussion the word 'television' will be used exclusively but it must be understood to cover all services using the u.h.f. spectrum and higher. It is probable that television may be among the least important of these as technical developments occur. Other examples are frequency modulation, facsimile (capable of transmitting 100,000 pages an hour[2]), specialised scientific and business services, and navigational aids.

3.   Owing to bandwidth considerations television is restricted to the frequency range above 50 Mc/sec and there is no doubt that very much higher frequencies will be used in the immediate future. The American Telephone and Telegraph Company are already building an experimental network using frequencies up to 12 000 megacycles.[3] Waves of such frequencies transmitted along quasi-optical paths and accordingly receiver and transmitter must lie not far from the line of sight. Although refraction increases the range, it is fair to say that the service radius for a television station is under 50 miles. (The range of the London service was rather less than this.) As long as radio continues to be used for communication, this limitation will remain, as it is a fundamental and not a technical restriction.

4.   Wide-band frequency-modulation, one of the most important of radio developments, comes in the same category. FM can give much better quality and freedom from interference than normal amplitude-modulation, and many hundreds of stations are being planned for the post-war years in America alone. The technical requirements of FM make it essential that only the direct signal be used, and ionospheric reflexions

cannot be employed. The range of the service is thus limited by the curvature of the Earth, precisely as for television.

5.   To provide services over a large area it is necessary to build numerous stations on high ground or with radiators on towers several hundred feet high. These stations have to be linked by landline or subsidiary radio circuits. Such a system is practicable in a small country such as Britain, but even here the expense will be enormous. It is quite prohibitive in the case of a large continent and it therefore seems likely that only highly populated communities will be able to have television services.

6.   An even more serious problem arises when an attempt is made to link television systems in different parts of the globe. Theoretical studies[2] indicate that using a radio relay system, repeater stations will be necessary at intervals of less than 50 miles. These will take the form of towers several hundred feet high, carrying receivers, amplifiers and transmitters. To link regions several thousand miles apart will thus cost many millions of pounds, and the problem of trans-oceanic services remains insoluble.

7.   In the near future, the large airliners which will fly great circle routes over oceans and uninhabited regions of the world will require television and allied services and there is no known manner in which these can be provided.

8.   All these problems can be solved by the use of a chain of space-stations with an orbital period of 24 hours, which would require them to be at a distance of 42,000 km from the centre of the Earth (Fig. 1). There are a number of possible arrangements for such a chain but that shown is the simplest. The stations would lie in the Earth's equatorial plane and would thus always remain fixed in the same spots in the sky, from the point of view of terrestrial observers. Unlike all other heavenly bodies they would

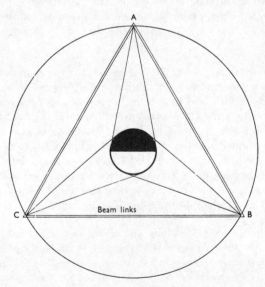

Fig. 1.

never rise nor set. This would greatly simplify the use of directive receivers installed on the Earth.

9.   The following longitudes are provisionally suggested for the stations to provide the best service to the inhabited portions of the globe, though all parts of the planet will be covered.

30 E – Africa and Europe.
150 E – China and Oceana.
90 W – The Americas.

10.   Each station would broadcast programmes over about a third of the planet. Assuming the use of a frequency of 3000 megacycles, a reflector only a few feet across would give a beam so directive that almost all the power would be concentrated on the Earth. Arrays a metre or so in diameter could be used to illuminate single countries if a more restricted service was required.

11.   The stations would be connected with each other by very-narrow-beam low-power links, probably working in the optical spectrum or near it, so that beams less than a degree wide could be produced.

12.   The system would provide the following services which cannot be realised in any other manner:

(a) Simultaneous television broadcasts to the entire globe, including services to aircraft.
(b) Relaying of programmes between distant parts of the planet.

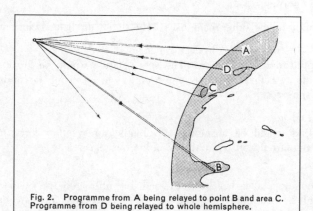

Fig. 2.   Programme from A being relayed to point B and area C.
Programme from D being relayed to whole hemisphere.

13.   In addition the stations would make redundant the network of relay towers covering the main areas of civilization and representing investments of hundreds of millions of pounds. (Work on the first of these networks has already started.)

14.   Fig. 2 shows diagrammatically some of the specialised services that could be provided by the use of differing radiator systems.

15.   The numerous technical problems involved in this communication system cannot be discussed here but it can be stated that none of them present any difficulties even at the present time, thanks to the development of hyperfrequency engineering. It is hoped to discuss them in a later paper when security conditions permit.

16.   The receiving equipment at the Earth end would consist of small parabolas perhaps a foot in diameter with dipole pickup. These would be sufficiently directive to prevent interference in the three doubly-illuminated zones. They would be aimed towards the station with the least zenithal distance and once adjusted need never be touched again. Mobile equipment would require automatic following which presents slight mechanical complications (a few valves and a servo motor) but no technical difficulties.

17.   The efficiency of the system would be nearly 100%, since almost all the power would fall on the service area. A preliminary investigation shows that the world broadcast would require about 10 kilowatts, while the beam relay services would require only fractions of a kilowatt. These powers are very small compared with present-day broadcasting stations, some of which radiate hundreds of kilowatts. All the power required for a large number of simultaneous services could be obtained from solar generators with mirrors about 10 metres in radius, assuming an efficiency of about 40%. In addition, the conditions of vacuum make it easy to use large and fully demountable valves.

18.   No communication development which can be imagined will render the chain of stations obsolete and since it fills what will eventually be an urgent need, its economic value will be enormous.

19.   For completeness, other major uses of the station are listed below:

(a) *Research* – Astrophysical, Physical, Electronic.
     These applications are obvious. The space-station would be justified on these grounds alone, as there are many experiments which can only be conducted above the atmosphere.

(b) *Meteorological*.
     The station would be absolutely invaluable for weather forecasting as the movement of fronts, etc., would be visible from space.

(c) *Traffic*.
     This is looking a good deal further ahead, but ultimately the chain will be used extensively for controlling and checking, possibly by radar, the movement of ships approaching or leaving the Earth. It will also play an extremely important role as the first link in the solar communication system.

REFERENCES

1. Noordung, Hermann, 'Das Problem der Befahrung des Weltraums'.
2. Hansell, C. W., 'Radio-Relay-Systems Development'. (*Proceedings of the Institute of Radio Engineers*, March 1945, pp. 156–168.)
3. Guy, Raymond F., Address to I.R.E., Philadelphia, 7 December 1944.

Appendix 2

Extra-Terrestrial Relays

The following article was first published in Wireless World *in October 1945, and subsequently republished in* Electronics World & Wireless World *in November 1991.*

Although it is possible, by a suitable choice of frequencies and routes, to provide telephony circuits between any two points or regions of the earth for a large part of the time, long-distance communication is greatly hampered by the peculiarities of the ionosphere, and there are even occasions when it may be impossible. A true broadcast service, giving constant field strength at all times over the whole globe would be invaluable, not to say indispensable, in a world society.

Unsatisfactory though the telephony and telegraph position is, that of television is far worse, since ionospheric transmission cannot be employed at all. The service area of a television station, even on a very good site, is only about a hundred miles across. To cover a small country such as Great Britain would require a network of transmitters, connected by coaxial lines, waveguides or VHF relay links. A recent theoretical study[1] has shown that such a system would require repeaters at intervals of fifty miles or less. A system of this kind could provide television coverage, at a very considerable cost, over the whole of a small country. It would be out of the question to provide a large continent with such a service, and only the main centres of population could be included in the network.

The problem is equally serious when an attempt is made to link television services in different parts of the globe. A relay chain several thousand miles long would cost millions, and transoceanic services would still be impossible. Similar considerations apply to the provision of wide-band frequency modulation and other services, such as high-speed facsimile which are by their nature restricted to the ultra-high-frequencies.

Many may consider the solution proposed in this discussion too far-fetched to be taken seriously. Such an attitude is unreasonable, as everything envisaged here is a logical extension of developments in the last ten years – in particular the perfection of the long-range rocket of which V2 was the prototype. While this article was being written, it was announced that the Germans were considering a similar project, which they believed possible within fifty to a hundred years.

Before proceeding further, it is necessary to discuss briefly certain fundamental laws of rocket propulsion and 'astronautics'. A rocket which achieved a sufficiently great speed in flight outside the earth's atmosphere would never return. This 'orbital' velocity is 8 km/s (5 miles/s), and a rocket which attained it would become an artificial satellite, circling the world for ever with no expenditure of power – a second moon, in fact. The German transatlantic rocket A10 would have reached more than half this velocity.

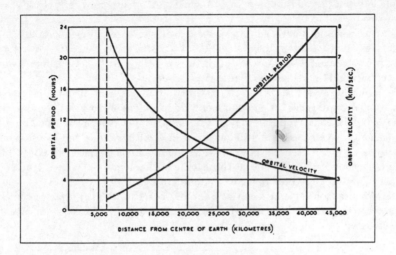

Fig. 1. Variation of orbital period and velocity with distance from the centre of the earth.

It will be possible in a few more years to build radio-controlled rockets which can be steered into such orbits beyond the limits of the atmosphere and left to broadcast scientific information back to the earth. A little later, manned rockets will be able to make similar flights with sufficient excess power to break the orbit and return to earth.

There are an infinite number of possible stable orbits, circular and elliptical, in which a rocket would remain if the initial conditions were correct. The velocity of 8 km/s applies only to the closest possible orbit, one just outside the atmosphere, and the period of revolution would be about 90 min. As the radius of the orbit increases the velocity decreases, since gravity is diminishing and less centrifugal force is needed to balance it. Fig. 1 shows this graphically. The moon, of course, is a particular case and would lie on the curves of Fig. 1 if they were produced. The proposed German space-stations would have a period of about four and a half hours.

It will be observed that one orbit, with a radius of 42,000 km, has a period of exactly 24 hours. A body in such an orbit, if its plane coincided with that of the earth's equator, would revolve with the earth and thus be stationary above the same spot on the planet. It would remain fixed in the sky of a whole hemisphere and unlike all other heavenly bodies would neither rise nor set. A body in a smaller orbit would revolve more quickly than the earth and so would rise in the west, as indeed happens with the inner moon of Mars.

Using material ferried up by rockets, it would be possible to construct a 'space-station' in such an orbit. The station could be provided with living quarters, laboratories and everything needed for the comfort of its crew, who would be relieved and provisioned by a regular rocket service. This project might be undertaken for purely scientific reasons as it would contribute enormously to our knowledge of astronomy, physics and meteorology. A good deal of literature has already been written on the subject.[2]

Although such an undertaking may seem fantastic, it requires for its fulfilment rockets only twice as fast as those already in the design stage. Since the gravitational stresses involved in the structure are negligible, only the very lightest materials would be necessary and the station could be as large as required.

Let us now suppose that such a station were built in this orbit. It could be provided with receiving and transmitting equipment (the problem of power will be discussed later) and could act as a repeater to relay transmissions between any two points on the hemisphere beneath, using any frequency which will penetrate the ionosphere. If directive arrays were used, the power requirements would be very small, as direct line of sight transmission would be used. There is the further important point that arrays on the earth, once set up, could remain fixed indefinitely.

Moreover, a transmission received from any point on the hemisphere could be broadcast to the whole of the visible face of the globe, and thus the requirements of all possible services would be met (Fig. 2).

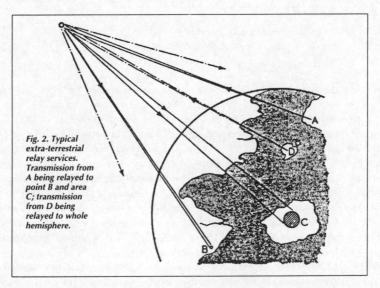

Fig. 2. Typical extra-terrestrial relay services. Transmission from A being relayed to point B and area C; transmission from D being relayed to whole hemisphere.

It may be argued that we have as yet no direct evidence of radio waves passing between the surface of the earth and outer space; all we can say with certainty is that the shorter wavelengths are not reflected back to the earth. Direct evidence of field strength above the earth's atmosphere could be obtained by V2 rocket technique, and it is to be hoped that someone will do something about this soon as there must be quite a surplus stock somewhere! Alternatively, given sufficient transmitting power, we might obtain the necessary evidence by exploring for echoes from the moon. In the meantime we have visual evidence that frequencies at the optical end of the spectrum pass through with little absorption except at certain frequencies at which resonance effects occur. Medium high frequencies go through the E layer twice to be reflected from the F layer and echoes have been received from meteors in or above the F layer. It seems fairly certain that frequencies from say, 50 Mc/s to 100,000 Mc/s could be used without undue absorption in the atmosphere or the ionosphere.

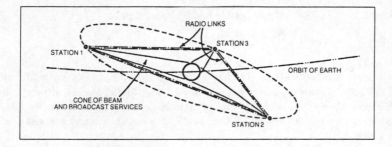

Fig. 3. Three satellite stations would ensure complete
coverage of the globe.

A single station could only provide coverage to half the globe, and for a world service three would be required, though more could be readily utilised. Fig. 3 shows the simplest arrangement. The stations would be arranged approximately equidistantly around the earth, and the following longitudes appear to be suitable:

> 30 E – Africa and Europe
> 150 E – China and Oceana
> 90 W – The Americas

The stations in the chain would be linked by radio or optical beams, and thus any conceivable beam or broadcast service could be provided.

The technical problems involved in the design of such stations are extremely interesting,[3] but only a few can be gone into here. Batteries of parabolic reflectors would be provided, of apertures depending on the frequencies employed. Assuming the use of 3000 Mc/s waves, mirrors about a metre across would beam almost all the power on to the earth. Larger reflectors could be used to illuminate single countries or regions for the more restricted services, with consequent economy of power. On the higher frequencies it is not difficult to produce beams less than a degree in width, and, as mentioned before, there would be no physical limitations on the size of the mirrors. (From the space station, the disc of the earth would be a little over 17 degrees across.) The same mirrors could be used for many different transmissions if precautions were taken to avoid cross modulation.

It is clear from the nature of the system that the power needed will be much less than that required for any other arrangement, since all the energy radiated can be uniformly distributed over the service area, and none is wasted. An approximate estimate of the power required for the broadcast service from a single station can be made as follows:

The field strength in the equatorial plane of a $\lambda/2$ dipole in free space at a distance of d metres is[4]

$$e = 6.85 \, \frac{\sqrt{P}}{d} \text{volts/metre}$$

where P is the power radiated in watts.

Taking d as 42,000 km (effectively it would be less) we have

$$P = 37.6e^2 \text{ watts}$$

(e now in μV/m).

If we assume e to be 50 mV/m, which is the FCC standard for frequency modulation, P will be 94 kW. This is the power required for a single dipole, and not an array which would concentrate all the power on the earth. Such an array would have a gain over a simple dipole of about 80. The power required for the broadcast service would thus be about 1.2 kW.

Ridiculously small though it is, this figure is probably much too generous. Small parabolas about a foot in diameter would be used for receiving at the earth end and would give a very good signal/noise ratio. There would be very little interference, partly because of the frequency used and partly because the mirrors would be pointing towards the sky which could contain no other source of signal. A field strength of 10 mV/m might well be ample, and this would require a transmitter output of only 50 W.

When it is remembered that these figures relate to the broadcast service, the efficiency of the system will be realised. The point-to-point beam transmissions might need powers of only 10 W or so. These figures, of course, would need correction for ionospheric and atmospheric absorption, but that would be quite small over most of the band. The slight falling off in field strength due to this cause towards the edge of the service area could be readily corrected by a non-uniform radiator.

The efficiency of the system is strikingly revealed when we consider that the London Television service required about 3 kW average power for an area less than fifty miles in radius.[5]

A second fundamental problem is the provision of electrical energy to run the large number of transmitters required for the different services. In space beyond the atmosphere, a square metre normal to the solar radiation intercepts 1.35 kW of energy.[6] Solar engines have already been devised for terrestrial use and are an economic proposition in tropical countries. They employ mirrors to concentrate sunlight on the boiler of a low-pressure steam engine. Although this arrangement is not very efficient it could be made much more so in space where the operating components are in a vacuum, the radiation is intense and continuous, and the low-temperature end of the cycle could not be far from absolute zero. Thermo-electric and photo-electric developments may make it possible to utilise the solar energy more directly.

Though there is no limit to the size of the mirrors that could be built, one fifty metres in radius would intercept over 10,000 kW and at least a quarter of this energy should be available for use.

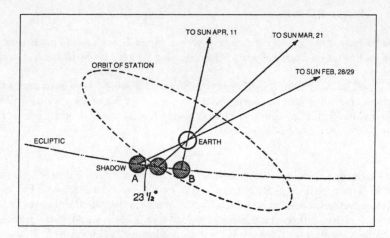

*Fig. 4. Solar radiation would be cut off for a short
period each day at the equinoxes.*

The station would be in continuous sunlight except for some weeks around the equinoxes, when it would enter the earth's shadow for a few minutes every day. Fig. 4 shows that state of affairs during the eclipse period. For this calculation, it is legitimate to consider the earth as fixed and the sun as moving round it. The station would graze the earth's shadow at A, on the last day in February. Every day, as it made its diurnal revolution, it would cut more deeply into the shadow, undergoing its period of maximum eclipse on March 21st. On that day it would only be in darkness for one hour nine minutes. From then onwards the period of eclipse would shorten, and after April 11th (B) the station would be in continuous sunlight again until the same thing happened six months later at the autumn equinox, between September 12th and October 14th. The total period of darkness would be about two days per year, and as the longest period of eclipse would be little more than an hour there should be no difficulty in storing enough power for an uninterrupted service.

Conclusion

Briefly summarised, the advantages of the space-station are as follows:

(1) It is the only way in which true world coverage can be achieved for all possible types of service.
(2) It permits unrestricted use of a band at least 100,000 Mc/s wide, and with the use of beams an almost unlimited number of channels would be available.
(3) The power requirements are extremely small since the efficiency of 'illumination' will be almost 100%. Moreover, the cost of the power would be very low.
(4) However great the initial expense, it would only be a fraction of that required for the world networks replaced, and the running costs would be incomparably less.

NOTE – ROCKET DESIGN

The development of rockets sufficiently powerful to reach 'orbital' and even 'escape' velocity is now only a matter of years. The following figures may be of interest in this connection.

The rocket has to acquire a final velocity of 8 km/s. Allowing 2 km/s for navigational corrections and air resistance loss (this is legitimate as all space-rockets will be launched from very high country) gives a total velocity needed of 10 km/s. The fundamental equation of rocket motion is

$$V = v \log_e R$$

where V is the final velocity of the rocket, v the exhaust velocity and R the ratio of initial mass to final mass (payload plus structure). So far v has been about 2–2.5 km/s for liquid fuel rockets but new designs and fuels will permit considerably higher figures. (Oxyhydrogen fuel has a theoretical exhaust velocity of 5.2 km/s and more powerful combinations are known.) If we assume v to be 3.3 km/s, R will be 20 to 1. However, owing to its finite acceleration, the rocket loses velocity as a result of gravitational retardation. If its acceleration (assumed constant) is α m/s^2, then the necessary ratio R_g is increased to

$$R_g = R \, \frac{\alpha + g}{\alpha}$$

For an automatically controlled rocket α would be about 5g and so the necessary R would be 37 to 1. Such ratios cannot be realised with a single rocket but can be attained by 'step-rockets',[2] while very much higher ratios (up to 1000 to 1) can be achieved by the principle of 'cellular construction'.[3]

EPILOGUE – ATOMIC POWER

The advent of atomic power has at one bound brought space travel half a century nearer. It seems unlikely that we will have to wait as much as twenty years before atomic-powered rockets are developed, and such rockets could reach even the remoter planets with a fantastically small fuel/mass ratio – only a few per cent. The equations developed in the appendix still hold, but v will be increased by a factor of about a thousand.

In view of these facts, it appears hardly worth while to expend much effort on the building of long distance relay chains. Even the local networks which will soon be under construction may have a working life of only 20–30 years.

REFERENCES

1.   'Radio-Relay Systems', C. W. Hansell, *Proc IRE*, Vol 33, March, 1945.
2.   *Rockets*, Willy Ley (Viking Press, N.Y.).
3.   *Das Problem der Befahrung des Weltraums*, Hermann Noordung.
4.   *Frequency Modulation*, A. Hund (McGraw-Hill).
5.   'London Television Service', MacNamara and Birkenshaw, *JIEE*, Dec. 1938.

6. *The Sun*, C. G. Abbot (Appleton-Century Co).
7. *Journal of the British Interplanetary Society*, Jan. 1939.

Index